Adventures on the
Wheels of Steel

Dave Haslam DJ-ed over four hundred times at the Haçienda through the 'Madchester' years and has since DJ-ed regularly at clubs like Home in London and 'Cream' in Liverpool, and round the world, including Ibiza, Chicago, Paris, Berlin, Zurich and Detroit. He has played gigs with dozens of bands, including the Stone Roses at Spike Island and New Order at G-Mex. Among his current residencies are 'Golden' and 'Tonto Bongo' (Manchester), and 'Strictly Handbag' (Dublin). He has written for *NME*, the *Face* and the *Observer*. His first book, *Manchester, England*, was the *Sunday Times* Pop Music Book of the Year and was short-listed for the Ericsson Prize.

Also by Dave Haslam

Manchester, England

Adventures on the Wheels of Steel

The Rise of the Superstar DJs

DAVE HASLAM

FOURTH ESTATE • *London*

This paperback edition first published in 2002
First published in Great Britain in 2001 by
Fourth Estate
A Division of HarperCollins*Publishers*
77–85 Fulham Palace Road,
London W6 8JB
www.4thestate.com

A catalogue record for this book is available from the
British Library

ISBN 978-1-84115-433-6

Designed by Geoff Green Book Design
Typeset by Rowland Phototypesetting Ltd,
Bury St Edmunds, Suffolk

Find out more about HarperCollins and the environment at
www.harpercollins.co.uk/green

Contents

Adventures on the Wheels of Steel

God is a DJ

Sasha and the Irresistible Rise of Dance Culture

On Wednesday night he was DJ-ing in Mexico City, on Friday he was in New York, last night he was in the biggest arena at the Homelands dance music festival in Wiltshire, and tonight he's about to play a set to 2,000 people in Glasgow. Since Wednesday morning when he left his home in Henley-on-Thames, Sasha has travelled 18,000 miles and DJ-ed to around 20,000 people. This has been a normal working week for Sasha.

Sasha was one of the first British DJs to command a fat fee for turning up to clubs around the country with a box or two of records, and then playing them. Putting one record on after another seems such a simple business, but dance music and club culture have grown so big that DJs are now working at the centre of something lucrative, global and powerful. Sasha is an unassuming man and generally downbeat about his achievements, but he has a reputation for being able to hold his own with club culture's most extreme party people, and a CV that includes working with Madonna (she pronounces his name Sar-sha). He's as happy as anybody should be who gets to travel the world with a couple of boxes of records and be worshipped.

Sasha has been at the top of the DJ league for over ten years. Before him there were dozens of DJs with no commercial profile but lots of credibility: American DJs playing in underground gay clubs or semi-legal parties in New York, and British DJs with a cult following on the various specialist soul and hip hop scenes. Sasha was the first to have both a commercial profile and credibility. His rise to fame wasn't manufactured. It started with tales of queues outside obscure venues, and clubbers who had travelled across Northern England to hear him play. This was in 1990, 1991. Only a few years before, nearly all club disc jockeys talked between records, told bad jokes and ran wet t-shirt competitions. In the modern era the big name DJs like Sasha make a living from just playing records; their success, or otherwise, is down to their taste, skill, ability to read a crowd, and talent, or luck, in managing their career.

When Sasha started out, dance music was buoyant after the emergence of acid house, but the guest DJ, who would travel to clubs and play a set for two or three hours, was still a rarity; most clubs employed resident DJs who played the full six or seven hours. But as DJs like Sasha began to have particular crowd-pulling power, clubs around the country wanted a piece of the action. Now that house music is a worldwide phenomenon, the circuit is international.

Sasha's room in the Devonshire Gardens Hotel in Glasgow is the size of a small club. It also has a fully stocked mini-bar and a four poster bed. Sasha has just checked in with his mate Sparrow and three girls from America called Zoe, Charity and Jennifer. He's showered, changed, and now he's sorting out his records. He goes through the two boxes meticulously, putting the right records into the right sleeves, dumping to one side a dozen or so that he definitely won't need later. He is imagining his set at the Arches tonight. He works his way through the boxes, having a quiet drink, while Sparrow bounces around, regaling me with stories of the time he and Sasha shared a flat in Salford.

At half past midnight a driver knocks on the door. Sasha tells him he'll be ready in five minutes. Twenty minutes later we're heading out of the room, down the stairs and into a Shogun parked just up the road. Charity is handing out very minty mints. I'm carrying one of Sasha's record boxes. Tonight I am Sasha's box boy.

From the front door, the club doesn't look like much, but as we're ushered along the corridors leading from the entrance to the far side, our walk takes us through crowds of excited people. Many of them call out and cheer as they spy Sasha surrounded by us, his scurrying entourage. 'Sasha, hey Sash-aah!' they shout. Their enthusiasm is infectious. The auditorium is packed and Sasha is the main attraction.

This is a new kind of pop stardom. For young dance music fans, DJ-ing is a route to *Top of the Pops* as well as a lucrative career presiding over club dancefloors, gathering air miles and emptying mini-bars. The profile of DJs has been boosted since Sasha's early days by the recent success of recording artists with their roots in DJ-ing (the Chemical Brothers, Fatboy Slim, Artful Dodger and Sonique, for example). Radio One's garage DJs, the Dreem Teem, have persuaded Premiership footballers Kieron Dyer and Emile Heskey to celebrate their goals with a DJ mime: one hand over their left ear like a headphone, the other spinning a record on the deck. Toy manufacturers Mattel have even added a new male doll to their Barbie range to compete with Barbie's ageing companion, Ken: he's DJ Guy Blaine, dressed in baggy trousers, a retro shirt and shades, with 'headphone accessories'.

What happens behind nightclub doors has come to shape culture at large. Clubland has provided a focus for ideas in music, design and fashion, and clubs have served as centres of community, capturing the imagination and drawing the crowds. The advertising industry is always keen to tune into what young people with disposable income are thinking, and there's no clearer evidence of how dance culture has shaped the entertainment industry and mainstream culture than the number of TV commercials which feature shots of DJs on the wheels of steel (including ads for Yellow Pages and Motorola mobiles). Even more spectacular is the widespread use of club hits to soundtrack commercials, from Leftfield's 'Phat Planet' on a Guinness ad, to Rhythmes Digitales helping to sell Sunny Delight. Then there are the peak-time TV trailers using tunes by Basement Jaxx or Paul van Dyk to plug holiday programmes; and sports programmes using music by the Chemical Brothers to spice up their highlights packages. The vocabulary of DJ-ing has also seeped out into the wider world. On a KFC commercial the breakdancing Colonel announces a 'hot new remix' of his Twister, whatever that is. Rave classics turn up in the most unlikely places: Jaydee's 'Plastic Dreams' was a cult club record nearly ten years ago, now it's a favoured backdrop to Channel Four's Italian football coverage.

The surge in interest in DJ-ing is a shift in music culture; more pairs of decks are now sold each year than electric guitars. At HMV you can buy a Numark Battle Pak, a big box which contains two direct drive turntables, a mixer, a pair of monitor speakers and a pair of headphones – the tools of the trade for £429.99 ('All the Cables Included To Get Started Today!'). As part of the Labour Government's New Deal of 1999, specially researched info packs were produced giving career guidance for aspiring DJs. DJ courses have now been developed which teach students to use the equipment, and, just as importantly, provide hints on handling a career. There are conferences like the annual Red Bull Music Academy, where young DJs from New Zealand, Poland, California and Austria gather to listen to established DJs lecture and to gain studio experience. These DJs are all part of a thriving club scene in their own country, but they know that it's a hugely competitive industry, and short cuts and trade secrets are invaluable. They also realise that no country has bought into the whole club culture/DJ phenomenon with as much fervour as Britain.

In Britain, the key moment of change, the birth of the rave era, is generally reckoned to have been the summer of 1988 and the arrival of acid house, yet earlier in the 1980s hip hop had emerged from America and had already rewritten the rules of DJ-ing (and musicmaking) by throwing a spotlight on the role of the DJ.

At the beginning of the twenty-first century, evidence of this cultural change, and also of the way big business has profited from it, is all around us. Back in 1988, Peter Powell, a Radio One DJ, described house music as 'mass zombiedom' and campaigned to have it taken off the airwaves. Now Radio One embraces house music and the club scene, employing DJs with dancefloor pedigrees, promoting nights in Ibiza and broadcasting live from clubs. House music is pop, and thus, in the space of just over a decade, club culture has gone from being popular but marginalised to being thoroughly mainstream. Dance music magazines are papershop best sellers; nightclubs have been key catalysts in the regeneration of British cities (the Haçienda in Manchester and 'Cream' in Liverpool being two examples). In London, Home opened in September 1999, a huge building on one corner of Leicester Square, a seven-storey, multi-million-pound superclub.

Home was ambitiously attempting to bridge the gap between the cooler clubbers and a mainstream clubbing crowd. Three floors up from the main room was a VIP bar where Puff Daddy and John Galliano partied, as well as other names more often associated with the tabloid newspapers than the history of dance music (Tamara Beckwith, Patsy Palmer, Jordan, Chris Eubank, Rod Stewart, Denise van Outen, Jay Kay, Victoria Beckham and Gazza). Costing eight million pounds to build, Home burned more money in its first few months; the spend on press advertising alone in the four weeks before it opened was £70,000. The advertising campaign highlighting the DJs involved was backed by marketing which made as much of the design and the architecture of the building as the music policy. It was announced that queuing customers would have the benefit of an LED 'multi-media interface screen' on the corner of the building. Once inside, glass lifts would transport VIPs direct to the sixth floor. Paul Oakenfold, unquestionably one of the biggest names in DJ-ing, headed the line-up of DJs and was designated Home's 'director of music'.

A PR company were on board to boost media awareness of the club; their press release declared Home to be 'a new concept in leisure, a club experience for the 21st century'. One Sunday paper ran a feature in its Business section focusing on the owner, Ron McCulloch, who had made his reputation as a club designer and owner, with a hand in Dublin club the Pod, the Tunnel in Glasgow and, with silent partner George Swanson, the Big Beat organisation. His cousin, Ken McCulloch, was the founder of the Malmaison hotel chain. Ron McCulloch was almost as active as Paul Oakenfold in doing the pre-publicity interviews, full of confidence and expertly discussing the merchandising opportunities (or the 'ancillary income streams' as he called them). With half an eye on existing clubs – especially Ministry of Sound – McCulloch and co. knew that the real riches would arrive if they could use a successful club in London as a base on which to build a worldwide brand.

Darren Hughes had been a partner in 'Cream' in Liverpool with James Barton. By the end of the 1990s 'Cream' was a huge success, based on a thriving Saturday night at Nation in Liverpool, but also embracing compilation LPs, club tours and an annual dance music festival. But after a far from amicable split from 'Cream', Hughes took up with the Big Beat organisation and became Home's promoter in chief. Promoters are the impresarios of clubland, masterminding events, hiring DJs, booking nights into venues and overseeing the publicity and marketing. In interviews given before Home opened, Darren Hughes had a stock phrase: 'Home will be the best club in the world.' Darren had great faith in this mantra, as though if he kept saying the words, it would somehow come true.

The opening party was a great night. The stunning view over London from the VIP room was all but ignored; most people weren't looking out of the windows, they were surveying the celebrities in the room. A young man in a tight t-shirt and yellow spectacles came up to me and grabbed my hand. 'You're Norman Cook,' he said, awestruck. I shook his hand without putting him right.

Within just a few weeks of opening, however, Home had a serious rival for the attentions of the music press and the dancing public: Fabric. Situated in a more congenial part of London (Farringdon), away from the commerciality of Leicester Square, Fabric joined other large, fashionable clubs – Ministry of Sound, Turnmills, the End – in providing challenging competition for Home. Darren Hughes kept chasing the perfect formula: DJ Danny Rampling soon left and Jon Carter was in and then out. I DJ-ed there most Saturdays for the first six months and was then replaced – my music wasn't deep enough (too many Jocelyn Brown records, I guess). The biggest surprise in Home's first year was Oakenfold's departure. He said he was now too busy to commit himself to the club, but the implication was that Home had promised the earth but had failed to deliver; to him it clearly hadn't proved itself to be the best club in the world. Looking back over the first eighteen months, Darren had a couple of regrets but still bags of optimism: 'If I had the chance again, I wouldn't have the club here in Leicester Square, but it's people that make places. This is a great place.'

By the beginning of 2001, Danny Tenaglia and Steve Lawler had emerged as the two DJs now most closely associated with Home. Tenaglia was an experienced, influential New York DJ, and Lawler had been a resident DJ at Home since the first weekend; it was widely acknowledged that Lawler was one of the rising stars in clubland. But then, in a move revealing a growing power struggle between the big clubs and the superstar DJs, Lawler announced he would be leaving Home at the end of March 2001 to concentrate on other gigs and his recording career. Just a few days later, an even bigger blow hit Home when the club's music and dance licence was revoked by Westminster City Council with immediate effect. The Council, taking advice after an undercover police operation, alleged unchecked drug dealing on the premises. After nineteen months of trading, the club was forced to close on 30 March 2001. In the former VIP room, Ron McCulloch held a press conference and admitted the situation was 'catastrophic'.

Nothing stays still in clubland. While the big clubs continue to invest tens of thousands of pounds in ever grander schemes, there's also constant, vibrant activity at smaller venues. One-off parties or specialist nights materialise every month, some with flair, some destined to fail. Every club night is like a business in any other industry; subject to merger, takeover or bankruptcy. In addition, clubs, historically a focus for all kinds of criminal activity, are still learning how to be legitimate businesses. Despite the problems at Home, we're still in the phase of big clubs and commercial expansion; now most cities have big clubs booking big DJs. It's a cut-throat world: good ideas get nicked and innovators battle it out against imitators.

My gigs at Home were among the highlights of my own personal adventures on the wheels of steel. They were fun, well paid and fairly high profile, but they also made me confront just how far club culture had come. I'd had some great DJ-ing years at the Haçienda in Manchester, doing gigs in places like Paris, Detroit, Berlin, as well as promoting club nights, warming up for the likes of the Stone Roses and New Order, and playing with many of the biggest DJ names of the era. My career coincided with a decade and a half of major change, an explosion in dance music; in fact, if there hadn't been a dance music boom, there probably wouldn't have been a career for me. Back in the mid-1980s, few people imagined they would have a career as a DJ.

There couldn't be a larger contrast with the massive commercial might and ambition of Home than the first club that gave me a residency: a basement club on Whitworth Street West in Manchester which is now called the Venue. In 1984 some guys from Moss Side and Wythenshawe took over the running of the club and called it The Wheel. I'm not sure why they picked that particular club; it had a terrible reputation as some kind of empty, sleazy, pick-up place. But we had loads of mates and a great passion for what we were doing. There was no marketing budget and no press release to launch The Wheel. There were no flyers, no guest DJs and no adverts in *Mixmag* (there was no *Mixmag*). On the opening night no soap star or celebrity was spotted, and no feature writer from the Sunday papers came to profile the architect or the director of music. The Budweiser was served warm, the toilets overflowed and the dancefloor buckled when the crowd jumped on it, but we opened the place without too much shame and the first night was a massive success.

Sasha now plays monthly at Fabric, at venues world-wide and at major festivals like Homelands and the big 'Gatecrasher' events, but he started out playing in pub back rooms and clubs with sticky carpets – places no better than The Wheel.

For the devotees, dance music isn't just about Saturday nights; mods had their all-dayers, soul boys had their weekenders; Sasha is in Glasgow on a Sunday. Thankfully it's a Bank Holiday weekend so no-one has any reason to get up early the next day. The stage – eight pieces of steel decking – is set up at one end of the venue. Behind the stage there's a clump of amps and wires and other equipment, and a few people with a backstage view, including the promoter, Ricky McGowan, and Erick Morillo, who is due to play a set in the other room later in the evening.

When we arrive with the boxes of records, DJs Craig Richards and Lee Burridge are on, their decks illuminated by a bright green desk light. Either side of them are two semi-spherical mirrorballs which send mini-spots of light spinning round the room. Next to the stage are two banks of speakers, on top of which giant floodlights punch beams into the crowd. Three or four yards from the decks, crash barriers have been set up, and the crowd is right up against them. The bulk of the hall is swathed in blue and purple lights.

The American girls pass Sasha their coats for safe-keeping, Sparrow disappears, and Sasha starts sorting his vinyl again, taking records from each box and putting them in a pile behind the decks. Just before 1.30 he appears at Craig Richards' shoulder, ready to take over, and a big cheer goes up. This is the sharp end of DJ-ing, when the talking and preparations are over. Now it's down to the DJ, his records and the excitement – the energy contained in the room.

The likes of Sasha, Paul van Dyk, Paul Oakenfold, Pete Tong and Danny Tenaglia are big name DJs with their own devoted following, and the music magazines are filled with heated debates on their various qualities. Clubs like 'Cream' and Fabric are only one part of a wide spectrum; every scene has its own stars and clubs: Trevor Nelson playing r&b, Top Buzz and Ratty playing hardcore anthems, Richard Searling doing his Northern Soul thing and Paul Taylor with his massive 'Retro' rave nights. Not forgetting, of course, that you can always hire a mobile DJ for your sister's 40th, your step-brother's 21st, or any family wedding. The conventional DJ who is thrown in for free when you hire a function room at a hotel or who brings along his own equipment still has trade secrets and great stories to tell.

At a big gig you're treated like royalty, like a pop star. At 'Cream' someone will pick you up from the hotel, someone will carry your records from the car to the DJ booth, and the doormen will be on hand to escort you through the club. The first time I played at 'Cream' I was desperate for a drink, so I leaned over to the lighting guy, gave him a tenner and asked him to get us both a drink. 'Is your fridge empty?' he asked, pointing to a white cupboard behind me, under the ledge I'd put my record boxes on.

You get the star treatment. You might arrive at a club and the promoter's runner is sent to see if you want any Class A drugs. You might end up at a party in some place you don't know in a town you've never visited before. You might spend one early morning walking through Detroit with two girls whose names will always escape you. You might get back to a hotel at five in the morning and feel an inexplicable urge to rearrange the potted plants in the hotel foyer. There might be a bunch of you in the same hotel; it might be you and the Dope Smugglaz and Parks & Wilson. You might be the one who gets called by reception early in the morning: 'I think your colleague Mr Wilson has lost a shoe.'

Some DJs are team players, some are egomaniacs. Some are moaners, some are geniuses. Most working DJs aren't in the big league. While Paul Oakenfold is paid anything from £5,000 upwards for an appearance, an established DJ on the circuit will be getting somewhere between £400 and £800, and your local Ritz jock will be earning around £150. Since Wednesday morning, on the other hand, Sasha has earned something in the region of £15,000. DJs like Paul Oakenfold also earn extra dollars through remix work and production or via the proceeds from record labels or sponsorship and endorsements. But most DJs don't have the luxury of making a good living purely from club work; many are students or work in record shops, and I know of other DJs who have worked as gas fitters and telephone repairmen. I know one who is Head of English at an inner city comprehensive school. Later we'll meet a DJ who trained to be a lawyer, and another who left home at sixteen to become a member of the Institute of Grocers. We'll hear tell of a policeman who played progressive house but for whom it all went horribly, horribly wrong.

Clubland is also dominated by men. In Britain there are established and successful female DJs like DJ Rap, Lisa Loud and Heaven, and they've been joined in recent years by Lottie, Lisa Lashes, Andrea Parker, Paulette Constable,

Angel and Lisa German. Then there's Sister Bliss, one of
the stars of the group Faithless, but also a distinguished DJ
in her own right. There's DJ As-If, the only female DJ to
have reached the final of the DMC Mixing Championships. These are some of the exceptions to the general rule
that DJ-ing doesn't seem to be an industry in which many
women get on, despite the fact that women are more
prone to Saturday night fever than men.

In what follows we will be drawn to many of the
big-noise, big name DJs because their story reflects the
commercial power and influence of dance music today.
But we'll also take a look elsewhere, because there's still
plenty of activity which is less about the money and more
about the love of the music. There are hundreds of DIY
nights – undercapitalised, held in a small room, with a DJ
and his or her mates. No-one's making much money out
of it, but it's still a great night. The dancefloor may buckle;
the DJ is maybe playing for a few drinks, a lift home, and
the buzz.

The power, the fame, the corporate interests – it's all a
long way from clubland before acid house. In 1982 Paul
Oakenfold was selling sweaters at Woodhouse, then got
a job in the A&R department at Champion, then moved
on to work for Profile, the New York hip hop label. In 1986
he was trying to push Profile in Britain. In 1986 Pete Tong
was a DJ on the soul boy circuit in the South-East of
England and a staff writer for *Blues & Soul*, but had
started working at London Records and had just licensed
'Love Can't Turn Around'. For others, their rise through
the ranks had barely started. In 1986 Fatboy Slim – then
known as Norman Cook – had three top twenty hits with
the jangly guitar group The Housemartins. In 1986 Sasha
was working in a fish factory; it was 1988 before he did
what he calls his 'first bit of proper DJ-ing'.

Sasha's debut on the decks was a night of Chicago

house that he hosted with his friend Piers in the back room of a student venue in Bangor; Piers had also just taught Sasha how to skin-up. They had a few Chicago house compilations, but not much else. 'I was playing some horrendous records,' he recalls. It was trips over to the Haçienda from his home in North Wales which had opened Sasha's ears and inspired him to get on the decks.

At the end of the 1980s there were few rules and no career structures for DJs. No-one knew how long the surge in interest in dance music would last or how big it would get; it was just a matter of getting out there and enjoying the weekend. Whereas music in clubs is now pigeon-holed, labelled and segregated – garage, trance, deep house, techno – in those first years of acid house, the dancefloor was open-minded and the genres were crossed. At the Haçienda, Sasha would have heard all kinds of music; at 'Spectrum' and 'Shoom' in London, and a lot of the big raves in 1988 and 1989, you'd hear house and techno, but also hip hop, indie dance, Euro disco tracks by Italian production teams, and even the odd record sequestered from a different era altogether. Some rewriting of history has gone on since, with DJs trying to convince us of their purist credentials, that they were very Detroit, or very New York, and very under-ground, but it wasn't really the case; most DJs were throwing down all kinds of vinyl. In fact, that was a great strength of the scene rather than a weakness. The audi-ences wanted to dance, and they didn't care whether the artists were black or white, American or European, on a major label or an independent. You felt you could play anything.

The thing that underpinned this open-minded attitude in the audience was, of course, the arrival of a new club drug: ecstasy. The evolution of the music is important in the story of the rise of the DJ, but ecstasy use changed clubs forever. The Haçienda opened in 1982, but it was only after 1986 that the policy of the club shifted from being primarily a gig venue to doing club nights. By 1987 we were having some great nights there, but once ecstasy arrived – in the early months of 1988 – it was as if everything moved up a level; a night at the Haçienda went from being a great night out to an emotional, life-changing experience.

Ecstasy created a loved-up vibe, loosened bodies and gave the club a carefree atmosphere. Socially, and musically, there wasn't much discrimination. Socially, this meant that the club housed students, girls, gays, lads from the terraces. Musically, this meant there were occasions when you could have put on a recording of a vacuum cleaner and the crowd would have roared with approval, which was funny, but also provided an opportunity to experiment, to play stuff a more uptight audience might have rejected. Wherever the open-mindedness came from, it was an attitude which opened up new ways of experiencing Saturday nights.

Certain kinds of records had all the right sounds to seduce a Haçienda audience. The rhythm and the spaciness of acid house, the warmth of acid house, the slightly melancholic side of acid house seemed to exaggerate and feed the effects of ecstasy. The spooky noises and the breakdowns were perfect for the Haçienda, a cavernous old warehouse. The new sounds filled the room, and it was all a long way from the structure of the conventional rock song – or, for that matter, the classic soul song: no verse chorus, verse chorus. The enormity of this change is hard to appreciate now, but it required a shift in the way most people listened to music. House music embraced a new generation of computer technology, with more and more boxes of computer trickery emitting the requisite throbbing beats and subsonic squelching basslines; literally new noises, a new palette. We had entered the digital age, and our lives were being played out to a new soundtrack.

In many cases, tracks had no lyrics, or the vocals were sidelined; in records like 'Voodoo Ray' there were voices but no lyrics, just a hook, a texture, but no message. On tracks like 'Go' there were six and a half minutes of fast beats, atonal bleeps, melodic keyboard lines echoing the theme from *Twin Peaks*; 'go' was shouted thirty-seven times, and 'yeah' twenty-three times. In 1998 Faithless had a hit record with 'God is a DJ', which, though not quite as grand as their previous single, 'Insomnia', was still a massive track, overflowing with rolling breakdowns, minor chord keyboard lines and an emotional, positive message from rapper Maxi Jazz. He addresses the all-consuming club experience: 'This is where I heal my hurt,' he tells us, lost in the pulse, the beat and power of the music. He's found what he's looking for, a world in a megabyte of sound, a world, he says, 'contained in the hum between voice and drum'.

Into the first couple of years of the twenty-first century and the instrumental tracks, subsonic basslines, bleeps and noises from the early techno pioneers are now normalised. Hard, mad sounds which might once have only been appreciated by New York art-rockers, or electronic musicmakers under the influence of LSD, are now high in the charts; 'Phat Planet', for example, or Azzido Da Bass's 'Doom's Night' would have sounded alien fifteen years ago. When instrumental dance music emerged, it was greeted in the same way as abstract art in the 1960s, with a similar grappling for points of reference, human interest, narrative. Now Mark Rothko is on your living room wall and 'Plastic Dreams' on your TV.

Sasha couldn't get a regular gig at the Haçienda, but it

was away from Manchester that he made his name and got his big break, with a little help from Gary McLarnan. Sasha had been playing at Shaboo in Blackpool, but it had closed; McLarnan was a photographer who'd been around most of the best dancefloors since the beginnings of acid house. Together they started a night called 'Delight' at Shelley's in Longton in Stoke. Sasha soon came to understand the drive and intensity of a room full of E-heads. He'd arrive at the club at eight o'clock and there would already be a thousand people in the queue. By ten the club would be full of the sounds of whistles and airhorns. At the time, Sasha was playing banging Italian-style piano anthems – Alison Limerick's 'Where Love Lives', FPI Project's 'Rich in Paradise' – stuff he admits sounds cheesy now; 'But it hadn't been done before,' he says, 'and it had a real innocent energy.'

He'd get on the decks and he could feel the surging power of the crowd, the rush building. 'The big thing for me was holding the crowd back; they'd be gagging to hear a record they knew, and as soon as they did the whole place would go mental; from that point onwards I had to completely go for it. I knew that as soon as I put that one record on, the airhorns would go off and that would be it, I'd have to completely hammer it.'

Ecstasy began to circulate in larger quantities. One of its early nicknames, 'disco biscuits', was a reflection of how sweet and safe the drug was considered, like 'Smarties' (another nickname). The pills had different imprints, came in different colours and had different effects – Doves would make your head light and warm your emotions; Dennis the Menaces would make your legs heavy and blank your brain. By the end of 1991 the overall quality was dropping and it was said that dealers based in Amsterdam were offloading all the rubbish into the UK. It was an era of indiscriminate necking of pills, some of them bad E, GHB or ketamine. Of course, the bad drugs caused bad vibes.

The acid house era had started innocently enough, but the role in the scene of a Class A illegal substance meant that criminality and gangsters got involved. Later still came the corporatisation of dance music seen today. But none of that was predictable; there was no plan, no-one had any idea where it would lead. All we knew was that the dancefloor was where it was at, and that these new records were making every old record, especially every old rock record, sound dull and old-fashioned.

The new acid house culture wasn't about DJs at first. If the DJs, even the good ones, weren't quite anonymous, they certainly weren't stars. In the spirit of the times, there weren't barriers. Even the pop stars didn't lord it; at the Haçienda you'd see Bernard Sumner from New Order dancing in the crowd, or Bez or Johnny Marr standing under the balcony. Sasha remembers going to the Haçienda unaware of who was DJ-ing; uninterested, in fact. The first time I met him I was DJ-ing and he came into the DJ box with my friend Zeeba.

I DJ-ed at the Haçienda nearly 500 times, and I have just five flyers with my name on, mainly because there was no need to advertise – the club's reputation had built through word of mouth, until there was a massive buzz and continuous queues – but also because there was nothing to advertise: there were no guest DJs, no bands or singers playing live or even miming to backing tapes, nothing. The night's entertainment consisted of a DJ – we all did four- or five-hour sets – and the most enthusiastic crowd imaginable, and nothing more. We needed nothing more.

As the scene grew, other clubs opened, more DJs started playing, and you began to realise that some nights were better than others, some DJs were more consistent, some more populist, some were great technically but couldn't work a crowd, some were great at warm up, some pure peak time. The atmosphere in a club is down to the music, the mix of people, perhaps even the drugs, but the most significant chemistry is that between the music and the crowd. The DJ is somewhere at the centre of it all, a catalyst. The significant chemistry of clubland isn't the ecstasy doing strange things inside people's brains; ecstasy without music is a worthless thing – you're just running round hugging trees and grinning at bus drivers. But a drug-free dancefloor still bounces, or buckles.

To get that right, to work those dancers, is the DJ's dream. Once you've accepted that differences exist between DJs – that some might be more populist and peak time, or some more challenging, or some just plain uncommercial – and once you've witnessed the way the right guest DJ can prompt a queue round the corner and massive press attention, then you're acknowledging that every DJ has a market value; hence the inflationary fees that DJs with the right reputations can pick up.

But the growth in the status of DJs from the early 1990s onwards was also down to the fact that the music press and the record industry needed stars of some sort, figureheads, icons; club culture is no respecter of artists, but it needed something to sell, a viable commodity. Rock music had its stars and their guitars, but the dance music-makers were often studio-based individuals without major label support churning out one-off tracks with no desire to go out and play live. Techno pioneer Derrick May lives a thousand miles away and even if you could persuade him to turn up on *This Morning* with Richard and Judy he wouldn't win over the audience sitting there hitting keys and miming the programming of a computer. This lack of faces, or heroes, among the music-makers created a vacuum, and left the best DJs, then just making a name for themselves, perfectly placed to take centre stage. As author Matthew Collin explained in an interview for Channel Four's *Chemical Generation* documentary, 'DJs have become the superstars because who else has there been to focus on? You've got anonymous producers sitting in back rooms and they're not Mr Gorgeous in any way. And then you've got the clubbers themselves; how can you turn them into a brand? You can't. The DJ is the only human figure who can be taken and marketed. There was a need for a star and the DJ happened to be it.' In December 1991 Sasha was *Mixmag* magazine's cover star, with the headline 'Sasha – the First Pin Up DJ?'.

As Sasha's career progressed, he took a residency at 'Renaissance' with John Digweed. 'Renaissance', promoted by Geoff Oakes, a Shelley's regular, started in Mansfield and then went to the Conservatory in Derby until the end of 1994. In February 1994, Sasha was on the cover of *Mixmag* again – 'Sasha – the Son of God?' was the headline this time. In the feature Dom Phillips described Sasha like this: 'Like the best DJs, he knows how to make a mediocre record sound good, how to make a great one get you screaming. How to tantalise, intrigue, and excite a crowd, kept balanced on a knife edge between the new and expected.'

What reinforced the status of DJs was their involvement in making records, aided by computers. New technology was creating new ways of communicating, buying, selling, creating and music-making. Computer technology had opened up the musicmaking process in the sense that you didn't need years of formal training, a 48-track recording studio and a £250,000 video to succeed, so long as you had access to a sampler, a computer, a pressing plant and an audience. Records were being made by production teams, remixers, techno boffins and DJs.

That DJs would have an input into the making of dance music was inevitable; they're supposed to know what makes a good dance record and what doesn't – and how to win over an audience to a record they've never heard before. The most exciting times for a DJ are when your record boxes are filled with white labels, hard to find mixes, bootlegs. When Sasha was sorting through his records at the Glasgow hotel, at least three-quarters of them were pre-release test pressings or white labels; acts like Breeder make specially recorded acetates and one-offs just for him to play.

Sasha's involvement in music-making has been fitful; early in the 1990s he released a number of singles, including 'Be As One' and 'Higher Ground', and since then has talked about getting a proper album together, but has contented himself with more one-off singles ('Xpander' and 'Scorchio'), collaborations and remixes. In 2000, with Charlie May from Spooky, he wrote the 'Wipeout 3' soundtrack.

That first bit of front cover stardom ten years or so ago could have been the peak of Sasha's career, but despite his slightly unfocused attitude to his work, he's survived, and somehow still gives the impression that his best days lie ahead. In 1991 he'd already come a long way from that student venue in Bangor, just as club culture has come a long way from dodgy rooms in damp basements, the first discotheques and sound system parties. But he'd also got a long way to go – global stardom, celebrity collaborations, more front covers. He says he never had a career plan, but here he is, so much in demand, attracting so much devotion, putting one record on after another.

Now I'm looking out to see what he can see when he stands at the turntables. Beyond the first few yards, the audience is just a tumult of raised hands, sweaty bodies, silhouettes and darkness, and at the front staring faces pale with expectation. Someone is onstage with a microphone: 'Glasgow, welcome the man called Sasha!' The lights start strobing, the cheer is massive. Sasha puts on the first record; not some big, banging tune that everyone knows, but a quiet, complicated record, just the gentle sounds of tablas. In our backstage area the American girls start to dance. Sparrow returns with armfuls of Miller Draft. Sasha's drawing out the tension, introducing layers of sound over the rhythms. The beat starts to boom, boom; twisting basslines and snatches of melody bounce around the brick arches. Sasha barely registers the crowd's presence; there are no theatrics. He caresses the records with loose, light movements, a touch on the crossfader, his hands gently flickering over the mixer. He's building, building his set. Out front it's pandemonium.

CHAPTER 1

How Much Can You Take?
In and Out of Fashion with Paul van Dyk

'Renaissance' resident Dave Seaman describes the life of a DJ as 'a bit of a plate-spinning job' – juggling demands, going on the road, doing gigs and working in the studio. Even without studio work, the schedule can already be quite full and take its toll. After a particularly good night you can feel your brain cells running away; midweek you might get a foggy head and an urge to go to sleep at 3.30 in the afternoon. It can be relentless. You need to take time off to recover.

Not all DJs are on the guest circuit, though. Most of the best clubs in the world have built their success on quality resident DJs, who are in the club week in and week out and give the night consistency. The way DJs sail into a club, play for two hours, leave, go to the next gig, play the same records in the same order, then go home, is a bit of a creative dead end. DJs who have reacted against this include Laurent Garnier, Sasha and Paul Oakenfold, none of whom plays more than one gig a night. Laurent loves to get five- or six-hour sets.

Sometimes gigs abroad are turned down for reasons other than commitment to a residency. DJ Elliot Eastwick discovered he had a fear of flying, and therefore had to refuse gigs in places like Canada, New Zealand, Australia and South Africa. He went on a course to conquer his fear but on his way to the airport for a trip to Italy his phobia returned and he pulled the gig. Eventually, after another course, he was cured. After five years of having to pass some of his most exciting gigs to other people, he was on a plane and off to America.

When travelling, you need to know the kind of club you'll be playing – or, at least, your agent has to be aware – or the consequences can be embarrassing. Gilles Peterson is head honcho at the Talkin Loud label and a DJ of great taste, with a regular Monday night at Bar Rumba and one of the best shows on Radio One. The other summer he was booked to play at 'Home' at Space in Ibiza at a gig set up by Radio One (for live broadcast). Due to follow Carl Cox, Gilles had a few reservations, but Radio One reassured him. 'So I had to go on straight afterwards to two thousand absolute ravers and live on Radio One,' he recalls. 'I killed it. It was horrendous really.'

You hope the promoter is on top of his game and hasn't booked a load of techno DJs in a soul club, or an underground house DJ in a rave club. Gilles Peterson playing his downtempo, eclectic mix of breaks, beats, soul and hip hop was never going to appeal to a crowd who had just been dancing to Carl Cox's tough, four-to-the-floor house. You have to match the right DJ to the right audience. If you're playing in a big hall you might have to accept that to reach out to everyone in there you're going to have to find some records that will mean something to a mainstream clubber; if you're playing an intimate space, with a smaller dancefloor, you can keep it more experimental.

As we shall see, the notion of a guest circuit in Britain was in full force during the Northern Soul scene in the mid-1970s, and the soul weekender scene in the late 1980s, but the current circuit has its roots in a Balearic network which developed around Boy's Own, Flying,

'Most Excellent' and 'Venus' in Nottingham in 1989 and 1990. This was less about big name guests pulling a crowd, however; more about a bunch of like-minded DJs – Terry Farley, Phil Perry, Andrew Weatherall, Justin Robertson – swapping gigs at the various clubs they were involved with. As demand for good DJs multiplied, it was actually the clubbers who did the most travelling; journeying round the M25 to raves, to Shelley's to hear Sasha, or to the Haçienda or Quadrant Park. Then, instead of clubbers spending hours on motorways in search of their favourite DJs, the DJs started taking gigs in different towns, sometimes two or three a night.

The guest DJ circuit was boosted by the arrival in Britain of a group of American DJs who dominated the circuit for three or four years from 1992 onwards, playing at clubs like Ministry of Sound and 'Hard Times'. Legendary either through their DJ-ing prowess or through their production work, DJs like Tony Humphries and David Morales would jet over from America for three or four high profile gigs and then jet home again. In 1992 Todd Terry played his first Manchester gig for £800, but he was rapidly becoming one of the star names on the circuit and just three years later charged the Haçienda £15,000 for an appearance on New Year's Eve. This marked the height of his market value, though.

Around 1995 there was a drift to a new generation of homegrown stars. British DJs were moving in various directions, some a long way away from American house towards a more Euro sound: the hard house of Tony De Vit and Tall Paul, or bubbly trance like Nick Warren and Dave Seaman, for instance. Dave Seaman had been one of the DJs at Shelley's alongside Sasha, and went on to 'Renaissance'; Dave Seaman, Sasha and Digweed all regularly featured there in its early days, playing epic house.

By the mid-1990s dance music had fragmented; the mix and range of music that filled the Haçienda dance-floor in the first flush of acid house euphoria was replaced by specialist DJs hosting specialist nights. Hardcore rave had its own scene, as did drum & bass, downbeat hip, trance, techno and retro disco. Despite this fragmenta-tion, overall the scene was getting bigger; dance music on radio began to boom, and the biggest sound commer-cially was uplifting vocal house – a more direct version of the American garage sound. Vocal house encompassed some DJs who knew their stuff and kept away from the cheesier elements – DJs like Pete Heller and Graeme Park – as well as younger DJs like Alistair Whitehead and the pop star turned DJ, Boy George. Then there was Carl Cox; with a techno tinge to much of what he plays, he's kept ahead of the mainstream, and, like Sasha, has a real big underground, uncontrived reputation.

Now the very best of the American DJs – Danny Tenaglia, David Morales and Erick Morillo – are still getting good work in Britain, but British DJs are also becoming stars in America. Mix CDs by Pete Tong, Sasha, Oakenfold and the other big British names sell well. Carl Cox and Fatboy Slim are regular guests over there. Today, dozens of international DJs criss-cross the world; check your club listings guide and you'll find DJs from Holland playing in Ireland or Yorkshire; DJs from New York in Manchester or Sheffield; DJs from Manchester in Israel or New Zealand; DJs from Glasgow in London; London DJs in Finland, Ibiza or San Francisco.

One of the most well-travelled DJs is Paul van Dyk; from his home in Berlin he jets out to play big crowds from Sydney to Helsinki, Florida to the Philippines. He has witnessed the transformation Berlin has experienced – including a role in the early days of the Love Parade – and has been playing regularly in Britain for the past three years or so, particularly at 'Gatecrasher' in Sheffield. His records get massive MTV play and usually chart high. He has a monthly residency in New York. He has had one of the most successful and intriguing DJ careers imaginable, and epitomises the DJ as a career-focused professional, a great plate spinner.

While I'm waiting in Cardiff for Paul van Dyk to arrive (he's being driven up from Heathrow Airport), I idle about in the Hilton Hotel. I have a fine time idling. One of the channels on the TV plays Radio One, so I warm up for the night ahead by messing about in the shiny bathroom, unravelling the thread in the free sewing kit so thoughtfully provided by the hotel, and listening to Pete Tong's programme. I'm obviously in the right place at the right time; Tong announces that his big new record of the week is by Paul van Dyk. A few hours later, when Paul finally arrives, he tells me that the car radio was tuned in and he cheered when Tong made the announcement.

But I'm restless, so I surf the dial and have a listen to Dragon FM. They play Chaka Khan and then Luther Vandross. I phone the promoter of Paul's gig tonight and check I'm on the guest list. It's a night called 'Time Flies' that's recently moved from the Emporium to Mine on Greyfriars Road. The promoter is Henry Blunt, and when we're introduced someone says, 'This is Henry Blunt, but no-one has ever seen him roll one,' and everyone laughs, even Henry.

By ten o'clock Paul van Dyk has arrived and I meet him in the hotel restaurant for dinner. Sitting round the table are Rob Deacon (boss of Deviant Records, Paul's UK record label), Markus Nisch (Paul's German assistant) and Richard Keen, who used to work for Slice PR but now works with Rob at Deviant. As well as Paul and his business colleagues, there's me and Henry Blunt. Henry has left his co-promoter Paul Whittaker to open up the club tonight while he socialises. Practically all the tickets have been sold in advance, and Henry is happy. He'll pay for our dinners, no problem.

Before we start, Henry phones Paul to double check my name is on the guest list (DJs have this thing: never pay into clubs). Paul Whittaker is a Scouser. He recognises my name; he booked me to play a gig in Swansea in 1991. Henry turns to me: 'Do you remember?' he asks.

'Yeah,' I say. 'There were ten, maybe twelve people there that night.' He laughs, but I don't. It was a disaster. He calls Paul again. He confirms my memory of the night.

DJs remember two things: the bad gigs and the times they didn't get paid. Most of the good gigs melt into one; when it flows, you're on auto-pilot, everything's done by instinct, you don't have to think about it. The bad gigs are a nightmare that every DJ suffers, when the technology breaks down, the decks jump, no-one turns up, or no-one likes your music. In 1994 Paul van Dyk went to Marseilles: 'It was in a club that was too extreme. I just don't have any gabba records in my box, but this was a pure hardcore gabba club. I actually played for two hours in front of an empty dancefloor.'

My Swansea night was miserable. It was cold and wet and very foggy. The club was on a hill. I like to think the ten people there had a good time. They danced most of the night; in fact, I think I got on the dancefloor too, just to make up the numbers. By the end of the night we were all best friends, and I nearly invited the entire audience back to my bed and breakfast.

During dinner at the Cardiff Hilton, Markus and Paul discuss business in their native German. Rob says that Markus and Paul always talk business and always argue in German. Although he intends to get round to it one day, Rob has never learnt the language so he's at a disadvantage at moments like this. Soon they switch to English and we talk about the menu; Henry Blunt orders some wine.

Paul has sole with mussels, but it isn't much of a portion compared to everyone else's, and even with a large side order of new potatoes Paul isn't satisfied. Markus offers him some beef and I pass him over a chunk of monkfish; he has a job of work to do. Paul isn't much of a drinker, and instead endeavours to have as many soft drinks as possible. With his sole he orders tomato juice: 'Nothing in it, just tomato and juice,' he tells the waiter. He talks quietly and precisely in English, with the occasional mispronunciation.

Early in the conversation I tell Paul that later in the year I'm doing a wedding in Jersey for some friends of mine. Has he got any advice for me? He isn't impressed. He says that what he does is very different to a wedding DJ: 'I don't play the obvious music and technically I have to be perfect.'

Paul's set at 'Time Flies' starts in just over an hour. Henry's phone rings. The Scouser tells him all the tickets have been sold for tonight. 'Anticipation is huge' is the message he asks Henry to pass on to us all. We have coffee, but Paul has to leave the table; before he plays he has a couple of things to do, including a photo session. He puts his coat on for the photos: 'I look better with it on,' he says.

If I was DJ-ing in an hour, I'd take the phone off the hook, run a shower, have a drink, take it easy, but Paul is different. For him, DJ-ing is not just about playing music for a few hours a couple of times a week. Between DJ-ing in clubs and recording in studios, he does an endless round of interviews, photo sessions, business meetings and travelling, getting on planes and checking in and out of hotels. On his *Out There and Back* LP there's a song called 'Pikes', inspired by a hotel in Ibiza, and a song called 'Travelling'. As the latter track begins you can hear the air stewardess doing a safety drill, apparently recorded on a flight from Berlin to New York. Paul considers his life: 'People think the life of a DJ is just playing records at the weekend, being pissed and off your head, and then doing nothing and sleeping. I work all the time, seven days a week.'

A few weeks earlier he'd been at 'Gatecrasher' in Sheffield, and before the gig did some interviews at the Swallow Hotel at Nether Edge. On his trail that evening were six German journalists, five French and two English, and he tried to give them each a good twenty minutes of his time. Even in the car on the way to Cardiff he was being interviewed by a journalist. Before dinner he did a photo shoot. All through dinner I've been lobbing questions at him, and he's politely answered them.

He's not had much time to think about tonight's gig, or to get nervous, although he never gets very nervous: 'No, I'm always really excited. I am maybe a little bit nervous but I'm too excited to feel it. The first gig I did in front of people I was very nervous, and many other gigs when I was starting out.'

I hang about the hotel lifts. Music is blaring from one of the function rooms. There's a posh party going on in there, a reception and black tie dinner with a disco. From behind the doors one of the DJ's selections can be heard loud and clear. 'Crocodile Rock' by Elton John. I have an urge to go and check the party out, but the security on the door won't let me in. I try to blag it. The guy from security and I discuss my obsession with DJs. 'I'm writing a book, and I'd love to meet the DJ in there tonight,' I shout above the sound of 'Blue Suede Shoes', but he's not having it. I'm just starting to row with him when Henry Blunt grabs me. It's time to go.

Outside 'Time Flies' there are a few people milling

about – a couple of doormen and Nicola with the guest list. Paul the Scouser greets me like a long lost friend; takes me to the small stage at the front of the club and gives me a big bunch of drinks vouchers. Soon Paul van Dyk arrives, walking through the club, following a doorman and Markus who have his records. There's not much time for socialising; he has just ten minutes until the resident DJ, Richard Hitchell, finishes his set. I position myself just to the right of the decks. In front of me the club is clearly very full (what Paul van Dyk calls 'big time packed'). It's claustrophobic, crowded with clubbers. You can feel their energy, caged, but ready to be let loose.

Paul looks across the dancefloor; at the far end of the club another stage, filled with clubbers waving, dancing, just visible through the dry ice, cigarette smoke and rising sweat. It's very hot. It's probably twenty degrees warmer in here than outside in the cold Cardiff night. Henry appears with a bottle of Smirnoff, a dozen cans of Red Bull and an ice bucket full of Red Stripe. He pours us all some drinks. The ice bucket starts steaming.

The Scouser flicks through the slides beamed onto a screen at the back of the stage until he finds the one with the biggest 'Time Flies' logo on it. Richard Hitchell is on his last record. Markus takes Paul's coat from him. Richard seems very young to be DJ-ing at a big night like this but Henry says he's not as young as he looks. The same is true of Paul van Dyk. He's one of the few DJs who don't seem to age, the ones who don't go to seed on a diet of late nights and booze. It's nearly eight years since I first met him when I DJ-ed at a club called E-Werk in Berlin, and since then he hasn't grown a beard or developed a beer gut or even a champagne double chin. He's always clean shaven.

He was born in 1971 in Eisenhuttenstadt (literally translated as 'Metal Hut Town') near the East German border with Poland. When he was two the family moved to East Berlin, although his father walked out on them soon after. In his teenage years he tuned into radio broadcasts from the other side of the Wall and dreamed of escape. A station called 2Eitklang was one of his favourite channels, and it featured a show playing indie music – New Order and the Smiths. What he heard on the radio worked a kind of magic, became a lifeline: 'Since I grew up in East Berlin we couldn't really go to the clubs or buy the records so I heard everything on the radio and my whole musical education was through the radio. This music was so different. I was addicted to it.'

The music inspired him and, eventually, led him into DJ-ing:

The thing is, it more became like an accident. I didn't plan it. When I was a kid I wanted to be a journalist, in fact. I wanted to study journalism but I couldn't because I wasn't politically in the right direction in that Communistic state, in East Germany, so I couldn't study that. But I still didn't want to be a DJ or anyhow involved in the music industry and I never thought about it. It just became. When I was about twelve years old I got a guitar and I learned a bit playing guitar, but in the guitar lessons they were making me playing old German shit folk songs and I wanted to play like Johnny Marr! So I skipped that pretty soon. Once I started out DJ-ing it felt right, I thought that's my thing, yes, even before I knew I had any talent for it.

His musical direction was also influenced by another show on the station which played electro and hip hop, and the kind of records that would form the foundations of house: 'In about 1985 I heard electronic dance tunes on the radio. It wasn't house; it was very danceable, progressive dance music all done by electronic instruments and I always thought that was the most interesting thing then. I never had found the Smiths energetic in that way –

their music didn't move me like a party record, although it moved me inside my emotions – but I was looking for music which does both.'

He was unsettled in the East. 'The only good thing about East Berlin was that West Berlin was next to it,' he says. The authorities allowed Paul and his mother to leave for the West just a week before the Wall came down. 'It was a lot of hassle. We were allowed to leave with one suitcase each and I actually stood in line for more than two days to be allowed to take my dog with me. We had two suitcases and a dog, that's all.'

After the Wall came down, he finally got the opportunity to witness the club scene for himself. People already in West Berlin in the middle of the 1980s recall that techno had started to make a small impact in clubs like UFO. Mark Reeder had been going out to the clubs in Berlin since he arrived there in the late 1970s, and would later run Paul van Dyk's first record label. Before I interviewed Paul I talked to Mark and heard how this small scene exploded when the Wall came down and a huge constituency of young people, especially the kids from the East, embraced it. 'The techno scene symbolised the revolutionary excitement of those times,' he says. 'There was a revolution taking place and here was a revolutionary music that was beginning to appear and it broke all the rules. It was their music. It broke all the rules of rock & roll. It was pure energy and it seemed to express everything for the kids of that moment.'

Paul liked what he heard, but he also had some reservations: 'The first thing I did when the Wall came down was to go to all the clubs and at that time all the music in Berlin was hard, Detroit-oriented, like tough, banging techno, and I really enjoyed the power and the energy but there was one part I felt was missing – since my favourite bands had been the Smiths, New Order, and stuff like that

– and I missed the emotion in my favourite bands, something which makes music different to just a bass drum, a hi-hat.'

He began DJ-ing using two old turntables and a battered mixer, and concentrated on trying to track down the right records: 'I was buying records that combined energy with a melancholic feeling and I made tapes for myself and for friends so we could listen to it in the car when we drove to parties.'

Paul's personal taste in music wasn't shared by the bulk of Berlin clubbers at the time, as Mark Reeder testifies: 'Techno in Germany at that time had to be hard, or very hard. It was like you could have categorised it to tekno with one "k" and tekkno with two "k"s and tekkkno with three "k"s and the amount of "k"s determined the hardness of the track.'

Paul's friends passed a tape on to a guy called Dimitri Hegemann who used to run a club called 'Tresor'. In March 1991 Paul got a gig at 'Tresor'. It was a big deal to get a gig there at that time, especially as Paul had little experience of DJ-ing, but his first set was well before peak time. It was virtually a warm-up set, so there was no big pressure on him, but no big chance to shine either, although he was happy with the way he played. The gigs didn't come pouring in, but that was less to do with his ability, more his music taste: 'I was playing completely different music to everybody else so it was tough for me over the next six months. I was really into the music I played and I didn't want to change that just to be able to play somewhere more often. I knew the music I enjoyed and that was the music I wanted to play.'

Six months or so after his gig at 'Tresor', Paul made contact with other promoters in Berlin, including 'Dubmission'; as an unknown DJ, he volunteered to do his first gig for 'Dubmission' for free. He also attracted the attention of XDP – Ecstasy Dance Project – who ran a night called 'Brain'. XDP had a reputation for developing new concepts for their parties, for pulling together the visuals and decor with hypnotic music, and Paul's imaginative, subtle sound suited the 'Brain' parties: 'The music that I was playing there and at the "Dubmission" parties was so different from everything else in Berlin there was some quite good press coming in. It was good that I stayed with sound I loved which was different from the others.'

A little magazine called *Thousand*, named after the old Berlin postcode, sent a journalist to profile Paul; the journalist was Cosmic Baby, and their meeting triggered a brief but fruitful partnership. They DJ-ed together at 'Dubmission' parties, and Cosmic Baby, who had begun recording for Mark Reeder's record label, took Paul to meet him. Reeder had built contacts at the East German record company Omega, and had persuaded them to set up a dance label, which Reeder called MFS. MFS, Mark maintained, stood for Masterminded For Success, but it also echoed the name given to the old East German security service – the *Ministerium fur Staatssicherheit*; at the fall of the Wall, the letters were always in the news, with people being discovered as ex-MFS, and he hoped the resultant publicity would rub off on his label.

Mark Reeder had been aware of Paul's DJ-ing ever since his first set at 'Tresor', but hadn't met him until Cosmic Baby took him into the MFS office. Mark remembers that 'Paul seemed like a nice lad, and I liked the idea of having a DJ who was young and good looking on the label.'

Once he'd made a point of going to hear him DJ, there was no going back. Paul fitted the MFS vision: something different to tekkkno, music that Mark had taken to calling 'trance' on the DJ reaction sheets and press releases that he sent out with records. MFS was beginning to specialise in hypnotic, melodic dance music, and giving the music a generic label encouraged taste makers in Germany like Juergen Laarmann who ran *Front Page* to latch onto MFS and Paul van Dyk.

From the outset, Paul was making the kind of music he was championing in the club. His first releases were 'Perfect Day' and 'How Much Can You Take?', both collaborations with Cosmic Baby under the name Visions of Shiva. The German trance sound of 1992 was the precursor to the trance sound of today, with its roots in an ongoing dialogue between electronic music-makers in Europe and America. When Giorgio Moroder stripped out some of the funkiness of dance music and gave it an overtly computer-generated sound in the 1970s, it upset the purists, but that Euro disco sound, plus German acts like Kraftwerk and DAF, and New Order and Cabaret Voltaire, began, in turn, to influence American music-makers, especially those involved on the edges of black dance music who were developing a stripped-down, electro sound. Afrika Bambaataa was inspired to make 'Planet Rock' by Kraftwerk's 'Trans Europe Express', and, a few years later in Detroit, techno innovators in 1985, 1986 – people like Juan Atkins – were looking for a new start, something that took them away from Motown or Philly disco. They embraced the machines, the repetition, the clean spaces of Kraftwerk, especially.

Detroit techno made an impact in Europe. Thanks to labels like Network in Birmingham and R&S in Belgium, the work of the Detroit innovators became more well-known here than at home in America. It was picked up by kids in the UK and Europe who started making bastardised versions of these techno records. So by 1990 a handful of techno originators in Detroit had unleashed the creativities of dozens of people in Berlin, in Sheffield, in Frankfurt. Techno in Europe took many different forms, some more brutal than others, including a speeded up, extreme form of techno dubbed 'gabba'. Some releases were a lot harder than others, but German techno generally revolved around huge flanged breakdowns and pulsing basslines.

In the early 1990s, German techno was beginning to find an audience in Britain. In 1993, the Orbit in Morley booked DJs Westbam, Mark Spoon, Frank de Wulf and Sven Vath, and featured live appearances by Cosmic Baby and Hardfloor. The sound was feeding into bands like Underworld and being championed by DJs like Steve Bicknell, and labels like Rising High and Guerrilla. In April 1993 Cosmic Baby headlined at Tribal Gathering. Later that year, though, Cosmic Baby left MFS and moved to Logic Records; Reeder redoubled his efforts to achieve success with Paul van Dyk.

Paul's profile built steadily. MFS had released a compilation called *Tranceformed from Beyond* mixed by Cosmic Baby and Mark van Dyk, and followed it with *X-Mix 1*, this time using Paul van Dyk on remixing duties. In 1993 his mix of 'Love Stimulation' by Humate was a near perfect record: Giorgio Moroder meets New Order, drenched with ecstasy.

Paul, ambitious and eager to learn, was becoming more proficient in the studio, taking time to study and experiment. Mark Reeder says that Paul was always very ambitious: 'I had no problem with that, and, in fact, I thought it was one of his better traits. It helped me that he wanted to help himself; being an ambitious person, I didn't have to force things on to him or explain things to him, that you have to do this to get there. He wanted to be the best DJ ever, and I always believed that Paul had the ability and the ambition and the aura to do that. He wanted to get to the top.'

That's not to say that Mark always found it easy working with him in the early days: 'Little things would irritate me, like the way Paul would not be very positive about his peers. Not in interviews, but, personally, just between us, and I'd try to explain to him that just because they weren't as proficient as him or they have a different box of records to you it doesn't mean they're not better people or shitty DJs. He'd find fault a lot in other DJs, and also label colleagues.'

As an ex-pat Mancunian who counted Mick Hucknall and New Order's Bernard Sumner among his friends, Reeder was able to pull in some favours for Paul. As a birthday present for Paul in 1993 he convinced Bernard Sumner to give him the opportunity to do a remix of 'Spooky'. Remixing New Order gave Paul credibility. In 1994 he released two EPs under his own name – 'The Green Valley' and 'The Emergency' – and then the *45 PM* LP, which contained the first version of 'For an Angel'.

My visit to E-Werk came in 1993. It was a brilliant club housed in a huge former East German electricity plant and crucial in the development of the German club scene. The majestic, brutal building, with a massive main room with a very high ceiling, dense pillars and rough brickwork, was a startling venue for a club. Huge dials and switches on the walls, and metal grilles, relics from the venue's previous incarnation, gave proceedings an industrial, futuristic feel. As the clubbers started arriving, filling the spaces, the hulk of a building was transformed by the sound of Paul van Dyk's chosen records – throbbing bass-kicking rhythms meshed with melodies.

Berlin was an amazing place to be at that time. The Wall had just come down and the annual Love Parade had helped galvanise a German house nation; at the first Love Parade in 1987, 200 people danced on the streets. By 1993 the crowd was 25,000; a few years later, the demonstration on Berlin's Kurfurstendamm had become an even bigger event, pulling a million people onto the streets. It's right to call it a 'demonstration' rather than a festival because it literally demonstrates the size and unity of the club crowd, and because there has always been a political angle to it, given Berlin's destructive history. The floats, love-mobiles and banners proclaim fraternity and freedom.

On the day I played at E-Werk I spent a lot of time hanging out with Mark and his business partner, Torsten, and they took me to the MFS office which was situated in the old Reichstag building. The symbolism of this was inescapable: Love Parade was reclaiming the streets, E-Werk was transforming the East German power station, and MFS were sending out trance compilations from the Reichstag building. It was only three years since the fall of the Wall and you could feel that Berlin was being remade and redefined by a new generation, the techno generation. It was a new start, the city and the culture like an old building that had just been taken by squatters; the void was being filled with new attitudes, new ideas, new music.

Paul's visibility in the industry was rising, at home and abroad. He'd become a monthly resident at 'Disco 2000' at New York's Limelight Club, a night hosted by the ill-fated Michael Alig. He'd got this gig after having first been invited to New York by a German institute promoting German culture and doing a night at the New Music Seminar. Through that he met Howard Chafer, Keoki's agent. Keoki was then resident at 'Disco 2000', and Michael Alig was the promoter; Alig was the flamboyant face of the New York club scene, an all-week, non-stop party person.

Michael Alig's career and the so-called New York club kids has become a very controversial clubbing story, and

Paul tells me what he can remember about his days at 'Disco 2000':

> For probably the first year or so I played there I didn't see Michael Alig at all, because he must have been somewhere else in the club or whatever, and then when it became very crazy with ketamine and everything else they took I didn't play there any more. Michael Alig was a really nice bloke, but he was doing too much drugs. It was gross at the end. I remember one really shit night when they booked me as a guest DJ and they had an Abba revival band playing the same night there and I just thought 'What the fuck am I doing here?' I hated that.

Alig's drug-propelled demise was frightening and spectacular: he was convicted of killing and dismembering Angel Menendez in his apartment (the same apartment van Dyk used to stay in on his trips to New York). 'I didn't really relate to it at all,' says Paul. 'I never took any drugs with them and I was never involved in the drug scene. I have to say, my whole experience of New York, aside from Twilo, has always been the same; that it wasn't about music. At "Disco 2000" it was about being seen, about fashion, about drugs, about club kids. The people didn't give a shit about who was playing there. For them it was all about being trendy, being more out of it. They weren't interested in the music at all.'

He doubts whether Michael Alig was even much interested in who was DJ-ing, recalling one night when he'd been flown over to play and was wandering through the venue when he bumped into Michael Alig who was wearing just a dress and no shoes. 'He said, "Hey Paul, what are you doing here?" And I said, "Well, because you booked me!"' That was the last time he saw him. At 'Disco 2000' the club kids were in the back room, and, according to Paul, the rest of the people were mainly interested in the next daft stage act, usually, he says, 'some cheesy slappers winning a hundred dollars for getting undressed onstage'.

Paul van Dyk's career confirms the showbiz cliché that it takes years of hard work to become an overnight success. The sound that was around in those early days at MFS was only doing moderately well in Germany and a few places beyond, although some important DJs – notably Nick Warren – were obviously into it; it wasn't until 1998 that it suddenly became all the rage in Britain. For Mark Reeder, in the meantime, it was just about hard work and trying to raise Paul's profile. Paul's first LP was released in 1994 to fairly positive reactions in Germany, but it was very difficult to convince people. It seemed as if distributors in Germany were solely into the heavier techno. Mark says they would dismiss Paul's music as 'fluffy'.

Together they faced another setback when the parent company, Omega, collapsed and Reeder had to start back at the beginning. Reeder linked up with Rob Deacon at Deviant, whom he had known since the 1980s. After a trip to hear Paul van Dyk play in Berlin, Deacon realised Paul's potential and did a deal to release the *Seven Ways* LP in Britain. In 1996, 'Words', one of the singles from it, came close to breaking the UK Top 50.

The UK crowds, volatile and always eager to move on, had been getting into records like the Future Sound of London's 'Papua New Guinea' and Jam & Spoon's 'Stella' – dancefloor records with a tingling ambience. This seemed to help BT, Brian Transeau, who emerged with a softcore, emotional trance which Sasha began to champion – the music was then dubbed 'epic house' – and BT's 'Embracing the Sunshine' became a big Sasha tune. Paul Oakenfold was also a BT fan, and had been playing similar music, although in his case, influenced by the Goa psychedelic trance scene. In 1994 BT remixed Grace's 'Not

Over Yet' for Paul Oakenfold's Perfecto label. BT had also made a link with Paul van Dyk and they began to work together. BT wasn't a DJ so Paul helped focus the music towards the demands of the dancefloor. One of their collaborations, van Dyk's mix of 'Flaming June', is reckoned by Mark Reeder to be 'a fantastic all-time anthem'.

These were the kind of alliances that were changing Paul van Dyk's career: a group of like-minded DJs who were pushing the music Paul had been playing and recording. An influential DJ can spark an interest in certain records, but DJs all moving in the same direction can achieve more. DJs hunt in packs.

Over the next couple of years, into and through 1996, the trance sound gathered momentum in big Northern clubs like 'Renaissance' and 'Cream'. Nick Warren's Way Out West project made a number of key tunes, including 'The Gift' (halfway between 'Papua New Guinea' and 'Bullet in the Gun'), and then Robert Miles had a commercial hit with 'The Children'; 'dreamhouse' was another label doing the rounds at the time. With a big following in countries like Holland and Germany, Sasha and Digweed premiering the music in New York, and the American west coast taking to the mystical, euphoric ingredients with enthusiasm, trance was fast becoming an international sound in the way purist New York disco or underground Detroit techno never had.

Paul suffered a delay with the third LP because of legal wrangles; he'd fallen out with Mark Reeder, and then with Torsten, too. The dispute over rights and contracts took over eighteen months to resolve. Meanwhile, ironically, Paul's profile soared. In 1998 he released a triple CD of remixes, *Vorsprung Dyk Technik*, and a remix of 'Binary Finary'; his reworked version of 'For an Angel' became his first Top 30 hit, with the video – recorded at the Love Parade – getting heavy play on TV.

The rise of trance in Britain was linked to 'Gatecrasher' in Sheffield. In Yorkshire in 1996 there were some great nights: 'Love to Be' and other clubs in Sheffield were booking garage and vocal house; the Orbit in Morley was still playing hard techno; 'Hard Times' had been bringing over premier New York garage DJs; and 'Back to Basics' was established as a haven for the party people. 'Gatecrasher' followed its own vision, booking DJs like Paul van Dyk, the Dutch DJ Tiesto, and DJ Taucher from Frankfurt. Resident DJ and booker Scott Bond followed this influence in his sets.

'Gatecrasher' became the home of trance in the UK and the most influential club of 1999. In the late 1970s and early 1980s Sheffield had housed a generation who were into electronic music and experimentation: bands like Cabaret Voltaire, Human League, Chakk and Hula had absorbed the industrial environment into their music, the concrete architecture, engineering works and steel factories of Sheffield belching out smoke, roaring noise. From their early singles like 'Nag Nag Nag', Cabaret Voltaire seemed to reflect this well: aggression, fading industry, the politics of no future.

Between Cabs and 'Gatecrasher' a lot had changed. A new generation was on the dancefloor, painting their hair lurid colours, spiking it up, dressing up in silver, gold and fluorescent spray-painted clothes, carrying kiddies' toys and sporting 'Gatecrasher' and Mitsubishi tattoos. Paul van Dyk was their hero. On his birthday they gave him presents, and when they found out he had a rabbit called Gromit, they started giving his rabbit presents, too.

If you wanted to trace the history of electronic music in Sheffield, then the bridge between the post-punk Sheffield generation and 'Gatecrasher' is probably Warp Records. In 1989 Richard Kirk from the band Cabaret Voltaire was spending a lot of time in clubs and in the studio with Parrot, a DJ who was then running a club night in the city called 'Jive Turkey'. They made a minimalist, bleepy record, as Sweet Exorcist, called 'Test One', which Warp, a shop where everyone bought electro, hip hop, On-U Sound and weird American imports, decided to release. Warp released 'Test One' in 1990, and by the end of the year they'd scored two Top 20 hits with LFO and Tricky Disco. Warp records were pretty varied, but they generally avoided banging beats and explored spacey, bleepy sounds. When I played at E-Werk, Mark Reeder and Paul van Dyk got excited about a record they'd never heard anyone play in Berlin before – 'France' by THK, a Warp release.

In 1999 Paul's sets at 'Gatecrasher' gained maximum exposure, especially in the wake of his success with 'For an Angel', and a blinding remix of 'Binary Finary'. 'Avenue', the follow-up to 'For an Angel', was less catchy but maybe more subtle. Paul had established a sound to his records; they had the requisite breakdowns and pulsing basslines, a rollercoaster of rush and dip in stark contrast to slower, chugging, classic New York house. The emphasis was on emotional melodies and shimmering ambience. He wasn't after an abrasive, urban music; instead the music suggested smooth lines, warmth, blue skies and open spaces.

The difference between 'Nag Nag Nag' and 'For an Angel' is like the difference between cheap speed and the clean rush of Mitsubishi; it's to do with drugs and changes in the zeitgeist. In the 1970s there was a rawness about life; it was the decade of polarised politics. Britain has now blanded out, and 'Gatecrasher' is part of a regenerated Sheffield, based on leisure and pleasure, on the service industries rather than manufacturing, call centres rather than coal mines.

During 1999, when trance seemed to dominate clubland, Paul van Dyk was labelled 'man-of-the-moment' by the British press. Paul Oakenfold also benefited; he'd been playing a similar sound for a number of years, and during his two-year residency at 'Cream', before it had any profile. '1999 was the year of trance, and about fucking time,' he said at the time. 'I've been with it for years and everyone used to slag it off. Magazines and other DJs would slag it off. The clubbers have always been into it; they love it.'

Paul van Dyk's faith in his music has never wavered, and it's brought him a lot of respect, but I felt it might have limited him as well. He claims it hasn't. He admits that his records have a distinctive sound, but his live sets, he says, cover a broader range. Before the gig he was adamant that I would be surprised by the range: 'What I play can be housey things to techno, to break beats. I might play something considered cheesy, but mixing it with a tough, minimalistic techno tune is different to playing cheesy tunes non-stop. It's like painting a picture. Just painting pictures in blue is boring after a while. I like to have all colours in.'

I wondered how far he would take this, whether there have ever been records that he would like to play but just couldn't fit in, maybe something by Lauryn Hill, something that was quite downtempo, syncopated, or whatever. 'There's definitely some music which doesn't fit into my DJ sets that I still like to listen to when I'm at home. But the thing is, when I DJ the music has to be energetic and moving, and if you take Lauryn Hill, then for me it doesn't move with that kind of energy; it's more a vibey kind of thing. I like to listen to that in the car or at home chilling out but I wouldn't go to a dance club to listen to that kind of music.'

People do, though.

'I'm sure people do. That's the wonderful thing about

different kinds of taste and individuals. People do that, for sure, and I'm not judging it, but to me clubbing and going out is more about energy and letting it all out, rather than having a joint and a whisky and chilling out.'

For someone who has DJ-ed for ten years and earned good money, Paul van Dyk has an image of being self-confident and focused. He's not as cynical as he might be, and certainly not flakey: 'The thing is, you always have to know why you're doing what you're doing. When I started being a DJ it was far away from being rich and famous or something so for me it's really pure, the music, and it still is. And the people I'm surrounded with and I work with, to them the music is the same way important as it is to me.

'In this business there are always going to be flashy, loud people around who never seem to do anything except be loud and flashy. But I don't really care; the most important thing for me is the music and everything else is second.'

A guest DJ on the circuit could begin to feel like a product, a name hired to play music to people so pro-moters can make money.

'No. I've never felt that way. And right now, it's the other way round; the promoter is really glad that I have the time to go to his place.'

Paul is making up for lost time, going to places he's not played before. Because of the time-lag before trance became commercially successful, old records and new remixes were released; 'Cafe del Mar' was five years old before it was a hit in the UK. Naturally, some DJs were scathing about the way British clubbers had suddenly taken to a kind of music that had been around for years. Laurent Garnier told *DJ* magazine that 'Britain has a more developed club culture than anywhere else in the world, which is why you're always starving for new sounds so that clubland can reinvent itself. The problem is that it's got to a point where there's nothing to reinvent and people are lost. The British are dancing to records that are nine years old, music that was called trance in Germany eight years ago, music that the British used to shit on.'

Other, especially older American DJs considered that real club music, with its roots in the classic New York sound – vocal garage – was music for the true house connoisseurs, and believed the faster, trancier music of DJs like Paul van Dyk and Paul Oakenfold was less valid. Paul reacts with scorn: 'It's like they're making good and bad people countable in bpms. Anyone who is dancing to something less than 130 bpms is a good person but anybody dancing to something above 130 bpms is a kid and a kid is bad. Maybe they're scared of getting old.'

Paul's first release of 2000 was a track featuring Sarah Cracknell from St Etienne – 'Tell Me Why (the Riddle)' – which was followed by the LP *Out There And Back*. The second single from the LP, 'We Are Alive', was released in the first week of October 2000. The same week, Simon Raine – the man behind 'Gatecrasher' – went on record talking about trying to move the club away from trance. Raine had signalled his intent a year earlier when he'd opened 'bed' – a 1,200-capacity club playing mellower house for an older crowd – and had tried to broaden 'Gatecrasher''s music style during their Ibiza nights in 2000 by including DJs like Roger Sanchez: 'We'd been tagged as the club to bring in the trance sound and it's been good for two, three, four years and it's got bigger and bigger – but we felt we'd gone over the brow of the hill with that now.'

The drugs were also having an effect in Britain and the USA. It wasn't just Home in Leicester Square that attracted problems as a result of the growing links between Ecstasy and club culture. There was a drug-related death at Twilo in New York in July 2000 when James Wiest, a student from John Hopkins University in Baltimore, collapsed during a set by Paul van Dyk. A few weeks later, police raided eleven New York clubs including Twilo, Sound Factory, the Tunnel and the Roxy. If it wasn't mainstream as early as it had been in Britain, then ecstasy culture was now hitting America in a big way, and not just in clubbing hotspots: in Florida, deaths associated with ecstasy and GHB had risen twenty-fold, while the number of ecstasy tablets seized by police had risen from only 196 in 1993 to over 200,000 in the first six months of 1999. In response to the growing use of ecstasy, in July 2000 the US Drug Enforcement Administration (DEA) held a specially convened conference on the problems of 'club drugs'.

In June 2000 Ian Scott died at a 'Sundissential' night in Leeds, the fourth ecstasy-related death at a 'Sundissential' event in six months ('Sundissential' had already temporarily shut its Birmingham event after deaths there earlier in the year). 'Cream' was raided in May 2000 when 140 officers and dog sections took away drugs worth £1,000 and arrested five people. The pressure on promoters was increasing as a minority of their customers seemed unable to hold their lifestyles in check; drug use becoming drug abuse. When Elizabeth Wood died at 'Cream' in 1999, the coroner reported that she'd been taking ecstasy for five days, during which time she'd not slept, before taking ecstasy and speed at the club.

Paul van Dyk DJs at 'Gatecrasher' straight and sober; all around him there are kids with tattoos, t-shirts and badges extolling Mitsubishi and other club drugs, and they love him, and the music clearly connects with them. Says Paul, 'I wish they maybe would take one less Mitsubishi and try to get really into the music rather than rely on the Mitsubishi, but I'm not there to tell them how to behave in their life, but they can see me as an example because I DJ without drugs and have as much fun as they do.'

By the beginning of 2001, it was becoming hard to separate trance from basic Euro synth pop. In interviews, Paul van Dyk tried to distance himself from some of the successful pop trance – like Ferry Corsten and ATB – although onstage he would still play Ferry Corsten's mixes. Trance had gone all the way from metal hut town to *Top of the Pops*, but the sound had become diluted and commercialised, and Simon Raine wasn't the only person who felt the edge had gone and the sound had had its day. There's always a fast turnover of styles in clubland; what DJs play has to be fresh to keep people coming back. Trance was still huge, but it wasn't talked about with the reverence of just a year or two earlier. There were other contenders for the music of the moment, none of them brand new: UK garage, for instance, or the harder sound of Timo Maas, or the twisted, funkier stuff by Tenaglia and Steve Lawler, or the breaks and beats of DJs like Adam Freeland, or the tech-house of Layo & Bushwacka.

Not being flavour of the month doesn't bother Paul. And whatever the critics may or may not be writing, he is still filling dancefloors. Another factor in the music's appeal is that it's primarily instrumental; this helps it to cross boundaries. Paul has new territories to explore, more gigs to do. One week South America, New Year's Eve in San Francisco, and then the Far East.

When he's at home in Berlin with his itinerary in front of him – say, one night in Israel, and the next night 'Gatecrasher' – he takes a set that he thinks will fit wherever he happens to land: 'If I go straight to Miami from Frankfurt or straight from Israel direct to "Gatecrasher", the records in the box are the same. It's not always like this, but there's a section of records which I really like and which I know well, and there's lots of new stuff there as well and I have to try to remember what's on the records and try to be ready and it just clicks and I think maybe it could fit now, and I just play it and hope it works.'

He'll take between 150 and 180 records on a trip like that. He tries to analyse why he can go from Israel to Sheffield and the same music can work: 'There are two points. One thing is that right now after ten years doing it, people know what to expect when they hear the name Paul van Dyk, so I pretty much have the opportunity to play what I like to. The general sound is in the box.

'The other thing is . . . Um, the other thing; what was it? Oh, yes: this music is a universal language, people understand it, from Mexico, South America, across Asia to the Philippines. On my Asia tour I played in South Korea and I was the first DJ to be invited to play in a club in South Korea. It worked, people were open-minded enough.'

In Cardiff, at 'Time Flies', it's one o'clock. Some of the clubbers down at the front are taking pictures of Paul, and hands reach up for him to shake. The clubbers are pleased, enthusiastic, and when he grabs their hands, totally radiant. He begins to sign autographs on scraps of paper, the backs of tickets and flyers handed to him by the crowd. He signs autographs all through his set, and hands keep appearing from the crowd right next to his decks. I keep thinking someone's going to knock the records, but they never do. Two girls wait patiently, and eventually he signs a cigarette packet for them, writing a message on one side and his signature on the other. He shows me the message: 'Smoke Me'. When he hands it back to the girls, I can see them scrutinising it. Somebody else leans out of the crowd and shouts at me, 'Anyone ever told you you look like Fatboy Slim?' Next time the music drops to a breakdown, instead of clapping or putting their hands in the air, a small section of the crowd start chanting at me, 'Norman Cook, Norman Cook.'

Richard Hitchell moves his boxes away and Paul puts his down. He flips open the lids, and his boxes are packed with records with no sleeves, records in wrong sleeves, white labels. Whereas Sasha spent time sorting out his boxes, Paul has had too many other things to do. It's surprisingly untidy, I tell him. 'This is what it's always like,' he says.

His first record goes on and it's quite downbeat. Approaching his set in a similar way to Sasha, he doesn't go for the epic, symphonic tunes from the outset. The crowd stamp their feet, clapping rhythmically. Paul turns to me and tells me what his plan is: 'I am going to calm them down and then go for it.'

He has no set plan, but he knows what records are in the box and responds to crowd reactions and his own instincts when deciding what to play. He has three decks to work with, and occasionally begins to cue a record up, then seems to change his mind and puts it back in the box, anywhere. His untidiness, compounded by the amount of white labels he has – with no sleeves and perhaps just a scrawl on the label – means that sometimes, in the heat and chaos of a night, he can't remember exactly what all the records sound like. 'I try to know my records well, but I forget which is which. I look for records I can't find, or I try records and they don't sound right in the headphones.'

While the music plays, he flicks through the records in his boxes, or cues up the next tune. There's no cutting or scratching, just mixing, blending. There's a photographer on the stage, and Rob Deacon and I exchange glances. With all of us cramped on the stage and Paul deep into his work, it's clear that the photographer is not going to get much of a shot. Rob confirms that photographers who track Paul usually fall short of capturing the crackling energy of a club. You either get lively pictures of the audience – sweaty dancers, happy faces, mad girls – or Paul stood next to his decks, or hunched over his records. Rob: 'They call me, tell me the photos are great, but then I get to see them and it's just another photo of Paul with his headphones on.'

Paul acknowledges the crowd occasionally, but there's not much to his performance, and although he's not po-faced, his naturally downbeat personality seems to hold him back from bouncing about, punching the air, hugging the punters. That's what a DJ like Brandon Block would be doing if he was here. Paul Oakenfold would stand with his hands outstretched acknowledging the love of the crowd; the first DJ I ever saw doing that was Mike Pickering at the Haçienda, high up in the DJ box (I think he used to think he could fly, that if he dived out of the box he'd be buoyed up by the crowd's enthusiasm and energy and his feet would never touch the floor). Fatboy Slim smiles and waves and boosts the visual element of his performances by going on tour with slides and videos. Paul van Dyk is clearly aware of the crowd but he's not a natural showman. He signs autographs, he smiles, and says that just because he's not bouncing about doesn't mean he doesn't care about the crowd: 'I respect the crowd, and it's important when you're creating the atmosphere to work with the people. You have to feel the energy from the crowd.'

You can practise DJ-ing forever in your bedroom, but when it comes down to playing live you have to know how to tune in to a crowd. 'I know many DJs who are technically not that good but have a great ability to actually feel the energy and play the right records at the right moment and I think that's much more important.'

So you're saying it's more important to be able to work a crowd than to be technically very good?

'Yes, but the best thing obviously is if you can be both.'

Paul is still signing autographs. He's half an hour into his set and he takes the music up a level. We start getting the odd record with snatches of vocals, some rolling breakdowns. An hour into his set and he unleashes a huge mix of his 'Tell Me Why (the Riddle)' single. I've never heard it so loud before; it sounds like a jet plane taking off. He is definitely spending too much time in airports.

I'm not quite convinced I've heard as eclectic a selection as Paul promised me before the gig. To my ears, he's not taken many unexpected turns, or slowed it right down, or played a pure vocal track or something with anything other than a 4/4 beat; what he plays is bubbling, fast, a layer of simple melody and very few vocals. Maybe I'm just not attuned to the nuances of what he plays, but maybe it's also down to the reality of 'Time Flies'. I'm not sure they would be too pleased if he started playing r&b, say, or disco cut-ups. They've come to see Paul van Dyk. They've heard his records, and they haven't paid to hear Trevor Nelson or Spoony DJ-ing; they're expecting a certain something from Paul van Dyk. He's like a brand, and it would be perverse, I suppose, for him to undermine that. The good people of Cardiff haven't paid fifteen pounds just so he can play a load of records they don't want to hear. Putting Lauryn Hill or Jill Scott or St Germain in there isn't part of the deal. Paul, I expect, is painting his picture, but it still has to be something recognisable to these people.

To our right there's a small podium along a wall at right angles to the stage. The dancers there are very hot. We have a fan and an ice bucket onstage, and I take it upon myself to throw ice cubes to the dancers on the podium. A girl near the front catches them and puts them down her top. Someone else grabs the fan and tries to turn it out towards the crowd but it won't budge.

At the beginning of his set, the first dozen or so dancers directly in front of the stage are girls. Most of them have staring eyes, big smiles, and bright pink clothes or vest tops, light green or grey. It's like a scene from *Human Traffic*, the 1999 film, set, of course, in Cardiff. As the set progresses, enthusiastic boys jump about and one by one the girls are elbowed out of the way. After an hour, the front of the stage is almost completely made up of lads, some with their tops off. They shout things at Paul like 'You're number one', or they turn to the crowd, arms aloft, encouraging the others. 'Come on!' they scream.

To our left are people trying to get onto the stage. It wouldn't be difficult, except that there's a doorman controlling access. You need to have a special pass and there's only a few of them. But late on, things start to get messy. Two girls manage to get up. One of them is wearing lime green hot pants and a bikini top. On the edge of the stage she goes into a dance routine that involves a lot of stretching, pouting, waving her legs around, and turning round and bending her backside towards the crowd. Paul is downbeat on stage, and the 'Time Flies' slides are interesting as far as slides go, but in the midst of this lack of anything much to look at, the dancer gets a lot of attention, which she milks. At one point she stretches her right foot high and grabs it with her hand, holding it up next to her left ear. It's like porno ballet. The crowd down the front are cheering her. Paul looks at her with a blank look. She turns to him. 'Smile!' she shouts, pulling a face. He turns his back on her and she flicks a 'v' sign at him. 'It's always the ugly ones,' he says to me.

It's getting hotter but Paul still isn't sweating. The crowd are having a fantastic time, but the end of the night is approaching. Paul is building towards a finale. He still has his first big hit, 'For an Angel', in the box, so far unplayed. He's saving it. He plays the 'Playing With Stone' bootleg. Henry Blunt gives me another can of Red Stripe from the ice bucket. The ice has melted, and the lager tastes like cappuccino.

At 4am Paul is supposed to finish. He's certainly not drunk and he's not been necking pills; nevertheless he's a bit carried away, and lines up some more records to play. The club is still packed. He plays 'For an Angel' then 'Avenue'; it's like a rock band leaving their greatest hits for the encore. Then it's his last tune: Alanis Morissette v Hybrid. 'I think I'm the only DJ who likes Alanis Morissette,' he says to me, and then he says something else, but I can't hear him; the crowd are cheering so loudly. They're happy but reluctant to go home, even when the house lights go on. Two dozen or so hang around, hoping to talk to him. A girl walks up to him with the cigarette packet he signed earlier. 'Does this say "Smack Me"?' she asks.

Paul packs his records away, then makes his way out of the club, back to the hotel and to bed. He's got an early start. First thing in the morning he's going to Norway; 'Same records, different set,' he tells me.

He could have taken a crowd of people back to the Cardiff Hilton tonight, but he avoids them all. As he makes his way to the door, people accost him. He has his picture taken one more time and then he hurries on.

A DJ's encounters with the audience can be fraught, or funny. DJs in the bigger clubs can be insulated from the audience while they play, high up in the DJ box, and they miss out on hearing things people shout or say. Like when a crowd of people, maybe an office party or something, who should really be at a different club altogether, implore you: 'Have you got anything we know?'

When a few people who are totally sober arrive and wish they'd stayed at home: 'Is it going to be like this all night?'

When the dancefloor has been full for three hours, everybody is cheering and clapping and someone comes to the DJ box to ask: 'Have you got anything good?'

When you're playing Masters at Work and somebody asks you have you got any proper dance music, and you ask them like what and they say: 'Like "Encore Une Fois".'

When there are loads of drugs in the club and the records are bouncing along at 130 bpm and a lad with his top off and his eyeballs halfway out of their sockets grips your arm: 'Harder, mate, play something harder.'

When there are no drugs in the club, somebody asks: 'Have you got any pills?'

When a seventeen-year-old lad on his fourth night out ever hasn't stopped dancing and comes up sweaty at the end of the night, shakes your hand: 'I fucking love you. You're the best fucking DJ ever, mate.'

CHAPTER 2

C'mon Taste the Noise
DJ-ing in the Early Days

His reputation as an odd-ball character precedes him, but the first thing you notice about Jimmy Savile when you meet him is the jingle jangle of his jewellery and his laughing voice. You hear him before you see him. Sir Jimmy Savile OBE was, in his heyday, Britain's first superstar DJ. Whereas the first big American jocks had gone to the dance halls off the back of their radio shows, Savile was a product of club culture; he built his reputation as a club DJ before he was offered radio work. In this sense, he is closer to today's big names than pioneers like Alan Freed.

Savile was born in Leeds in 1926. By the age of twenty-eight he was famous, having helped to originate the whole idea of dancing to records in dance halls, and then embarked on a hugely successful career in TV and radio. Although his name has faded among music lovers of today, in the 1960s and 1970s if you had asked people to name a famous DJ, ninety-nine per cent of them would probably have said Jimmy Savile. For two or three generations he practically defined who and what a disc jockey was. In 1964 he won Best Disc Jockey in the *New Musical Express* Readers' Poll (the previous year the award had gone to David Jacobs). It was a category he went on to dominate; in fact, he won the award every year from 1964 until 1972 when John Peel won it. His career bridged that huge gulf between Tommy Steele and Led Zeppelin; between Merseybeat and LSD; between the cosy, restrained world of David Jacobs and the mind-expanding, unshackled world of John Peel.

When I first met him at Christie's Hospital in Manchester he was there to open a therapy room for young people and make a tour of the wards. Much of his time is now taken up with all kinds of charity work, but he's always been happy to find time to talk to me about his DJ-ing days. He's wiry, very fit looking for his age, and, at Christie's, was wearing a red athletics vest, orange tracksuit trousers and green Fila trainers (his clothes tend to clash). He was also wearing dark glasses and heavy gold jewellery. Everywhere he goes he smokes a cigar. If you want him to be your friend, here's a tip: buy a box of cigars. And call him Sir Jimmy.

It was back in the 1940s that Sir Jimmy realised the potential of hosting dances and playing records. During the war he was declared unfit for life in the armed forces due to his poor eyesight, and instead was drafted to work in the coal mines. One day he was badly injured in an accident underground at Waterloo Colliery. He spent three years recovering, and while an invalid had time to consider various career moves, eventually settling on launching the idea of people paying in to a venue to hear someone play records, even though he suspected there might be some resistance to it:

Invariably people put records on – the old 78s on wind-up gramophones – in their front rooms on the carpet, it was like a party thing. And I thought, hang on, there are all these marvellous records by all these big bands like Joe Loss, Glenn Miller, and Artie Shaw and all those people, it would be a sensible idea to dance to their music but in a bigger place. But normally when they went out they danced to a live band. My idea of having people dancing to records was literally laughed at; people thought that at the dance halls you could only dance to a band.

Fired with enthusiasm and ambition and using his experience of working at a dance hall when he was a young teenager, he set up a gig to try out the idea: 'I wrote out the tickets myself. I wrote on them "Grand Record Dance" – everything I did was grand – "Admission 1/-". The very first one I did was at a place that's still up in Leeds, at the small branch office of an insurance company in a big detached house, with a big upstairs dining room which I then booked for fifty pence, which was ten shillings in those days.'

Back in the 1940s the technology and equipment required to host a disc-only dance night wasn't available in a big box by the cash tills at HMV, so Savile and a pal of his had to make do and improvise. They contrived to wire the pick-up arm of a wind-up gramophone to the innards of a valve radio set, which meant that the sound came out of the speaker of the radio rather than the box of the wind-up gramophone (so you could actually turn the volume up or down). They humped the equipment to the hall and laid it on top of a grand piano. Jimmy takes up the story:

I sold twelve tickets for that dance and the equipment lasted about forty minutes because the wires melted at the soldered joints, scarred the top of the bleedin' grand piano and it all finished up in a big round of silence. But everyone had had such a good time in forty minutes and obviously I was very enthusiastic and nobody asked for their money back, and the fella said, 'It was a brave effort; you can give me the ten bob whenever you're flush.' And I still owe him ten bob. And I'm telling you that that was by far and away the number one, world ever, disco.

As this was well before the days of double decks and the practice of blending records together in a seamless beat mix, as one record finished there was a long pause before the next one could begin. Between records Jimmy started entertaining the crowd with a bit of patter: 'I used to shout. I had no microphone or anything like that. It was only a smallish room, it fitted about a hundred people. I just shouted.'

He was, in effect, a mobile DJ: 'After ten years I ended up with arms like an orangutan because I dragged a bag of 78s and all this equipment around, all over the Yorkshire Dales, whenever I could get a room. I got rooms in cafés, I got rooms in tea places, I got rooms in shops where they put chairs round the provisions on the wall; people let me have these rooms because I was so enthusiastic.'

Sir Jimmy's primary concern with the technology is easily explained. Until amplification, live bands were always going to make a bigger noise than the first gramophones ever could, but once the technology to make records sound as loud as bands began to appear, the simplicity of the idea of gathering together and dancing to recorded music appealed, especially to poorer communities in small towns, or those areas of big cities inhabited by people traditionally excluded from the big city nitespots, like the black population, or the teenagers. These were the kinds of communities that had always pursued dynamic, cheap entertainment, and their enthusiasm led to the spread of various traditions based on dancing to records, from house parties to jukeboxes.

In Jack Kerouac's novel *On The Road*, set in the 1950s, Sal Paradise and Dean Moriarty visit a Mexican whorehouse bar where a jukebox plays loudly. They're stoned, and they shake, shiver, sweat and dance with the whorehouse girls. The bar owner cranks up the volume and plays some classic mambo numbers. 'This is the real way to play a jukebox,' think the two friends. 'We had never dared to play music as loud as we wanted, and this was how loud we wanted.'

Jukeboxes weren't pushed into the corner of neighbourhood 'juke joints' to provide background muzak – they were focal points, belting out dance music far into the night. Jukeboxes boomed in the 1930s in America, especially once the repeal of Prohibition in 1933 led to a rise in the number of tavern and saloon premises; it's reckoned that there were half a million jukeboxes in America by the end of the 1930s. The jukebox took its name from the black American slang term jukin', meaning wild or wicked behaviour (and, commonly, having sex). As jukeboxes began to play a more important part in a night out, jukin' came to have a more precise meaning: dancing.

Jukeboxes were stocked with records, of course, prerecorded music, whereas most dancing, up until then, had been done to live bands. The young were ever eager to find places to gather and pursue their devotion to loud dance music. In the 1920s, the jazz age, there had been a huge boom in dance venues in America and Europe, but the entertainment was always provided by live bands. The beginnings of a power struggle between DJs playing pre-recorded music and live bands in dance halls began as the technology to amplify music developed, but, at first, venues without live bands were a rarity.

The notion of a discotheque – dancing to pre-recorded music – began to take hold in various places during the Second World War, specifically in Paris, where the German invaders had banned jazz (they thought it was degenerate) and closed many of the dance clubs, breaking up the jazz groups. Deprived of their usual live music fix, local jazz fans took to gathering in hidden cellars to listen to records. One of these venues – on the rue de la Huchette, a small street on the Left Bank of the

River Seine – was the first to call itself a discotheque, an echo of the French word meaning 'library' (*bibliothèque*).

Discotheques struggled to thrive in Paris in competition with the rest of the city's well-established night-time network of clubs, cafés and theatres, but in the post-war era, Paul Pacine took the disco idea upmarket. He opened the stylish Whiskey-A-Go-Go, where dancers would take to the floor accompanied by a disc jockey playing records on a phonograph. Over the succeeding decades the importance of music generally was downplayed in Paris as the clubs concentrated on getting their decor right, and developing ornate design and marketing aimed at the rich and beautiful. Chez Regine opened in 1960, for example, catering to an exclusive crowd. Regine's, like most high profile clubs in cities around the world up to the mid-1960s, featured live bands rather than pre-recorded music. This was also true of the Peppermint Lounge in New York, the most famous nightclub in the world in 1961. The celebrities – Tennessee Williams, Norman Mailer and Noël Coward – and the socialites, sailors and salesmen who sweated it out together in the noisy gloom, doing the Twist, posing, cruising, ogling, were entertained not by disc jockeys but by live bands, primarily Joey Dee & the Starliters.

But customers in less fashionable surroundings were popularising the idea of dancing to pre-recorded music. Record players were perfect for parties in the home. In 1942 Malcolm X had just arrived in the city of Boston, straight into a world of zoot suits and reefers. By the time he was sixteen he would be a regular at big jazz venues like the Roseland Ballroom, and so hooked on the scene that he would give up his first job – as a shoe shine boy – because he couldn't find the time to shine shoes and dance too. But in his autobiography he recalls that his first introduction to dancing had come at 'pad parties', nights spent round somebody's living room, 'with alcohol and marijuana lightening my head, and that wild music wailing away on those portable record players'.

Sound systems were first formed in Jamaica in the late 1940s, by a team of record selectors, MCs and technicians, and were tightknit, community or family-run enterprises that would take the music to the people. The sound systems would play outdoors, or at house parties, halls or venues, often in competition with other sounds. In Britain in the 1950s the first sounds would play Fats Domino, Jimmy Reed and calypso, then it was mostly ska and bluebeat, but by the late 1960s and through the 1970s dub reggae ruled.

The way sound systems had developed out of a heartfelt need to hear records that weren't being played anywhere else, run for and by people shut out of the mainstream, was also the model for other developments in the rise of the disc jockey. The 1950s saw the emergence of the radio DJ, linked irrevocably with the emergence of rock & roll.

Disc jockeys were a key factor in delivering rock & roll to the world. Rock & roll was rooted in marginalised black American dance music – records produced by the black community through the 1930s and 1940s which were known as race records and seldom reached a wider audience. They were made for and by black people, recorded by independent labels like Chess in Chicago, King in Cincinnati and Atlantic in New York, and sold through record shops in black communities. Black music was thus segregated from the white world.

The disc jockey was the primary means through which the rich tradition of black music was desegregated and disseminated, at first solely through the radio, but eventually also through live DJ shows. By the late 1940s there were dozens of small, independently owned radio stations throughout America, staffed by specialist DJs who tailored their playlists to reflect the make-up of the local community; in ghetto areas or black townships this meant the sounds of jazz, blues and raw R&B. The stations showcasing black music encouraged more independent labels, and more sales, and formed part of a thriving infrastructure away from the pop music mainstream. All kinds of music-loving characters were drawn in to become DJs, many going on to use their base as a radio jock as a springboard to further involvement in music. Sam Phillips, who went on to run the hugely influential Sun record label in the 1950s, took his first job as a radio DJ on radio WLAY in Muscle Shoals, Alabama in 1942. WDAI in Memphis was the first black-owned radio station and featured DJs including BB King and Rufus Thomas, both of whom were to go on to have successful recording careers.

As the music and the culture evolved, race records became known as rhythm and blues, a phrase coined by Jerry Wexler at *Billboard* magazine in 1945 to free the music from racial stigma. The high sales of black music had already been acknowledged by the magazine, who had instituted a 'Harlem Hit Parade' in 1942. The sales curve kept rising; rhythm and blues was the future. In 1947 there were said to be less than twenty black radio DJs in America; by 1955 there were probably 500, all breaking records, enthusing, hit-making, many in the big cities like Chicago, Detroit and New York which were attracting a growing population (in the decade up to 1950, a million and a quarter left the South to look for work in the promised land, the Northern cities). In the cities black stations picked up white listeners turning their radio dial, while down in Tennessee, white-owned stations were beaming programmes aimed at black audiences but which also attracted eavesdropping white kids.

Segregated in their social life – in schools, at dance halls, even on the sports field – and for all practical purposes in their neighbourhoods too, the young, especially, saw radio as a liberating influence. Young Elvis Presley was one of the white teenagers who tuned into WDAI, turned on to artists like Big Bill Broonzy and Arthur 'Big Boy' Crudup as the DJs reached out across the tracks, beyond boundaries.

These DJs weren't just spreading music, they were helping to take black culture overground. Black radio DJs used jive talk as an unashamed expression of their culture and as a contrast to the more staid traditions of white radio announcers, and their style would define the way DJs spoke. A bunch of hip to the tip daddios, the meanest cats with the hottest sounds, these jive talking radio disc jockeys – the likes of Lavada Durst (alias Dr Hep Cat), Daddy-O Daylie and Douglas 'Jocko' Henderson (a.k.a. the Ace from Outer Space) – were funny, crazed, poetic, street-slanging. They influenced not just other radio DJs, but also disco DJs in the 1970s, and sound system MCs; it would also be hard to argue with Berry Gordy, the man behind Motown, who calls the black radio DJs from this era 'the original rappers'.

The reach of some of these stations was far and wide. When WLAC in Nashville, which played country music for a white audience during the day, started playing R&B during the evening, the signal was picked up from the Gulf of Mexico to the boroughs of New York. It was a big – but by that time inevitable – step forward when, in the early 1950s, these minority musics began to fuse, and rhythm and blues took on ingredients from hillbilly traditions. Alan Freed, then working as a radio disc jockey at WJW in Cleveland, Ohio, began to describe the music as rock & roll. He had become aware that the music had begun to cross over and R&B records had become popular among young whites, and instituted a show called 'Moondog's Rock & Roll Party' in 1951.

There was clearly a growing market among white record buyers for the accentuating rhythms of R&B. Bill Haley, recording for Decca, used the sounds of black music but sang with an undisguised white voice. He had a hit with 'Shake, Rattle and Roll' in September 1954, and the music made further inroads into the mainstream. Sam Phillips at Sun Records was meanwhile nurturing the talents of Elvis Presley. In 1956 rock & roll broke through; Sun had a hit with 'Blue Suede Shoes' by Carl Perkins, and Elvis had hits for RCA/Victor with 'Heartbreak Hotel' and 'Hound Dog'; Elvis had hits before he went out playing live, after his records were played to integrated audiences on Radio WHBQ across Tennessee.

White stations and DJs were playing rock & roll, but DJs like Alan Freed continued to champion the original black versions of any songs covered by white rock & roll groups, as well as great black artists like Little Richard, Chuck Berry and James Brown (who released 'Please, Please, Please' in 1956). In the process of taking the music to the people, the radio DJs extended their influence via record hops. DJs were now going live, into venues and clubs, dance halls and sports halls.

The big record hops were the ancestors of today's mobile DJs, the guest DJs, and the radio road shows. Like sound systems, record hops in America were itinerant shows, featuring a big name radio DJ on tour with his records, his sound equipment and his favourite bands. In March 1952 Freed planned an R&B showcase at the Cleveland Arena. Record hops were different to tuning into the radio; they encouraged young music fans to congregate, to feel a sense of community, to interact, to dress up, and to defy convention. The arrival in town of a character like Alan Freed would create a stir, and often controversy, as we shall see later in the book. A predominantly black crowd, possibly twice as big as the 10,000-capacity Arena could hold, turned up, sending the authorities into a panic. They cancelled the show.

The record hops cemented the power of the big personality jocks of American radio in the 1940s and 1950s; as a result of their activities and the trust they built up with the audiences, they wielded huge influence over trends, sales and the hit parade. Alan Freed has been widely credited for popularising rock & roll. Or, as Ulf Poschardt put it in his book *DJ Culture*: 'Rock & roll began with a DJ, and pop music began with rock & roll.'

Despite the clear expansion in the influence and power of DJs since the mid-1980s, DJs have played a significant role in pop music history for the best part of sixty years, on radio and on the road. They have been seen by the music fans and the music industry as taste makers, on the front line, gatekeepers of the culture. They were courted by the record labels, important to the radio stations, and heroes to the young. Their activities had already attracted the contempt of the authorities and the interest of journalists and social commentators. In 1964, writing about Murray the K, Tom Wolfe described DJs as 'culture makers'.

While Freed was working his magic in America, Jimmy Savile was on his way to fame and fortune. Savile had been augmenting his income from providing the music at parties with farm work, but then he was offered a job as assistant manager of the dance hall in Leeds where he'd worked as a schoolboy. From there he was taken on by Mecca to be the general manager of their dance hall in Ilford and at last he was able to bring all his ideas to fruition: 'From the start in 1942 it was a good ten years before it took off, but it wasn't for the want of trying. And then it took off all-of-a-sudden at the Palais in Ilford.'

By the middle of the 1950s disc jockeys had become accepted on radio stations, but they were still travelling, via various networks – record hops, sound systems and one-off parties in tea shops near Harrogate – and were only very slowly beginning to establish themselves permanently in various clubs and dance halls. You might find DJs doing a spot on Monday nights or Friday afternoons in various venues, but it was to take twenty years, until the late 1970s, for the bulk of the nation's old dance halls – built to feature live bands – to transform themselves into discotheques featuring DJs.

Nothing changed overnight; old venues had old ways of doing things, but small steps were taken in the long evolution. Savile, for instance, instigated various innovations when he arrived at Ilford, including installing two record players so he could play one song straight after another. When he ordered two record players from the local equipment suppliers, the sales representative was perplexed: 'Why do you want two record players? They're very good, they won't break down.'

Jimmy explained, 'Ah, when one record plays I'm getting the other one ready.'

'Are they in that much of a hurry?'

'Yes, my people are,' said Jimmy.

But as Sir Jimmy remembers, things still weren't quite right. When he arrived in the afternoon they were setting up the decks in the projection box at the very back of the hall – if they ever employed anyone to play music in the gaps between the bands it was the electrician or the lighting engineer who took on the job – but Savile told them he wanted them on the stage: 'And I told them on the stage I wanted a small rostrum about three foot six inches high with the two decks on and that's all I needed, and I wanted the biggest speakers that they'd got, one each side of the stage.'

It wasn't how things were meant to be done. Firstly, Mecca managers were supposed to be low profile, and to wear evening dress. They were not supposed to climb on the stage unless they had an announcement to make. Secondly, if any recorded music was to be played, it was not by somebody spotlit on a stage. But Jimmy was on a mission: 'The old order was to be destroyed.'

One Tuesday he hung a sign outside the Palais: 'Grand Record Dance; Bring Your Own Records; ADMISSION FREE' (he put 'Bring Your Own Records' because he didn't have many of his own). At about ten to eight there were 600 people inside and the stage was awash with 78s. The night was a great success, except that with free admission, it wasn't doing well financially. So Savile put on an LP – a ten-inch LP with a continuous tune called 'The Hucklebuck', which he describes as 'a beautiful medium-tempo jazz-feel number' – and dived off the stage, got a magic marker pen, went outside to the poster and wrote 'UNTIL 8pm, THEN ADMISSION 1/-'. And another 700 people came and paid a shilling each. He'd hit the jackpot.

His reign in Ilford was a huge success and he moved on to another Mecca-owned hall, the Plaza on Oxford Street in Manchester. 'By this time,' he says, with typical understatement, 'I had made myself the most unique dance hall manager in the world.'

By the time he moved to Manchester, rock & roll had arrived. Carl Perkins, Elvis Presley, Bill Haley soon became big heroes, says Sir Jimmy. He was playing rock & roll records, but not just rock & roll. He was also playing jazz and swing; he'd pick up on anything that filled the dancefloor: 'I was playing everything you could dance to. It had to be medium tempo, so that you could actually jive to it from start to finish. If it was too fast, it was out. Some of the great artists who brought out superfast records, I couldn't play them because the tempo was wrong.'

He spent three and a half years at the Plaza, and won two awards from the dance hall business for his success there, but his next residency was in Leeds – another Mecca venue in need of a boost. Savile used all his magic tricks to turn the situation around. From the first day he got there he put up 'House Full' and 'Sold Out' signs, even though the club was rarely busy apart from weekends, but the people who got turned away didn't know the place was half-empty, and so the legend grew. Reputation was everything. 'That's where the success came from,' he remembers.

The key to Savile's success was not only that he was a born entertainer, but that he had keyed into a growing culture. These were the early days of the teenager, when rock & roll triggered teen rebellion and pop singles started to sell by the million. It was an era in which club DJs had an important role to play. A club DJ doesn't have to guess what an audience's reaction to certain records or certain sounds might be; it's there in front of you every night you play. Radio DJs, on the other hand, are at one remove, playing records in a darkened studio, trying to imagine what the audiences are thinking. A club DJ can move quickly, chop and change playlists. The growing teen culture in the late 1950s was music-driven. DJs were willing and able to respond to the demands and desires in a way that TV, radio and magazines were slow to do.

From the late 1950s, what particularly fuelled the demand in Britain for what were then called 'disc-only sessions' was a demand for music from abroad; American rock & roll and rhythm and blues weren't being played on the radio or TV by obstinate, old-fashioned broadcasters like those at the BBC, so the young British teenagers took to dingy cellars, coffee bars and Co-op dance halls to hear their samizdat sounds. If they wanted to hear the music of Elvis Presley, Chuck Berry or James Brown, they had to go out clubbing. In Britain, La Discotheque had opened in Wardour Street, and by 1960 clubs like the Place in Hanley and Savile's Plaza in Manchester had instituted disc-only sessions. Soon the inability of national radio to provide the music young people wanted to hear also led to the rise of pirate radio.

There was now a general, inexorable shift towards specialist disc jockeys playing dance records in clubs. It wasn't just that the clubs were playing the right music; they also gave the teen consumers somewhere to meet, parade and socialise, celebrate their fashions, their creativity.

Once, going out dancing had meant going out and listening to live music – whether it was ragtime, swing, trad jazz combos or beat groups playing cover versions – but now even the most old-fashioned club owners realised that they had to move with the times. The economic reality helped change minds; it was cheaper to put on a DJ than hire a whole band, and if the DJ could fill the hall, then hefty profits could be made. They called upon the likes of Jimmy Savile to give them advice: 'I finished up having a hand in the music policy of fifty-two Mecca dance halls. I'd send out a list of ten records of the week that were good to be used, and at that time I suppose you could say I was overseeing four hundred disc jockeys. That went on for about a good five or six years, in the late 1950s into the early 1960s.'

The status of the club DJs and music history are intertwined. DJs have been important at times when a particular style of music is not catered for anywhere else. In the early days of house music, for instance, you could only hear it at clubs like 'Shoom' and the Haçienda, or on pirate radio stations featuring club-based DJs. There's often a time-lag before the music is accepted onto commercial radio or mainstream TV; it's usually at clubs and dance halls that new sounds break through. Once the breakthrough is made, the DJs become key characters, and radio stations rush to secure their services.

Savile was one of the first DJs to make the move from club to radio. Decca executive and Radio Luxemburg DJ Pat Campbell heard Savile play at the dance hall in Leeds and Luxemburg took him on. The station bosses took some convincing that his Yorkshire accent would work on pop radio, where transatlantic accents had predominated as a by-product of the American dominance of rock & roll radio. Eventually he started a pop programme there in 1963, and within weeks the listening figures had topped two million from a base of half a million. At Mecca he was earning sixty pounds a week in his proper job; working for Radio Luxemburg on his day off he was earning £400. In 1965 £400 could buy you fifteen hand-made suits or twenty 24ct gold bracelets. You could get a second hand Lambretta for £65, and a semi-detached house in Chorlton for £3,000. Within a matter of five months Savile was doing five different shows a week.

For about a year and a half he counted his cash and juggled his various jobs. Then he was asked by producer Johnny Stewart to front the first ever *Top of the Pops*. First broadcast in January 1964 from an old church hall on Dickenson Road in Manchester, *Top of the Pops* was a massive hit for the BBC, and Savile's profile was further boosted. He was important to the credibility of the programme and the BBC establishment knew this; he was someone, they would say, that the kids could dig. He was unconventional. He dyed his hair tartan for a while, and at other times sported a two-tone look. Savile went out on a limb when the vast majority of the public were restrained and conservative, especially in their clothes.

On one occasion he asked *Top of the Pops* to tie his feet together and haul him up so he could do the whole show upside down. His hectic lifestyle and his playful stage presence, he now admits, 'branded me some sort of a nutter'.

I once suggested to Sir Jimmy Savile that in many ways he was more outrageous than the groups, and, characteristically, he was inclined to agree: 'Oh, very much so. When Mick Jagger was taken to task for long hair he said "What are you talking about; Jimmy Savile had long hair when I was at school."'

He went out of his way to wear way-out gear on TV, at a time when many top pop bands dressed like their dads. You'd get a group like Brian Poole and the Tremeloes, all eager in their smart suits, neat ties and tidy hair, and then you'd get Savile; he went on prime time BBC TV wearing a Roman legionnaire's outfit; a kaftan before the hippies had discovered them; and, on one occasion, he presented *Top of the Pops* wearing a suit made of bananas.

He wasn't trying to make a fashion statement: 'The important element for me always was fun. If I thought anything was a bit of fun, I'd have a go; not fun at anyone's expense, but just pure fun.'

Most of the groups at that time wore suits, but Savile was different: 'Oh yes, I was always odd. Which is a good word to describe me, odd.'

Despite that oddness, people didn't treat him warily: 'No, they weren't wary because there wasn't anything to be wary of. I was never odd at anybody else's expense, and that made a lot of difference. It's not like today when everybody is trying to get everybody else into trouble. In those days it was a happy time. When I turned up, the first thing people did was smile.'

And they still do.

'Yes.'

Did you have a lot of groupies?

'No, groupies follow groups. This was something different.'

You had women flock to you though, didn't you?

'It's to do with recognition, and being on the stage and the TV screen. Even weathermen on TV get fan mail from the females. A man could walk on stage with a nut and bolt through his neck like one of Frankenstein's monsters and some girl from the audience would fall for him.'

In his glory years he met a lot of singers, managers, bands. Some would come to him for advice. He knew all the stars, including the Beatles, who asked him to compère their run of Christmas shows at Hammersmith Odeon. The first night, and every night, the noise from the screaming fans was so great that Jimmy realised there was no point even shouting down the microphone because he still wouldn't be heard over the noise the audience were making, so he decided just to mime the words. Everyone obviously knew why he was there, and that he'd be saying something like, 'Right, you've been waiting all this time . . . Here are the Beatles', so he just mouthed some words and waved them on. 'You couldn't hear yourself think; you could actually taste the noise. It was the most amazing gig; one of the world's greatest non jobs. I never uttered a sound; ten days of that and it said in the *New Musical Express*: "You wouldn't say that Jimmy Savile is overworked on the Beatles Christmas Show"!'

He also met Elvis Presley half a dozen times in America. 'We became quite good acquaintances,' says Jimmy. 'And one year when he won the Best Singer title in the *NME* Poll he sent a recording over as a speech of thanks and on it he mentioned the fact he'd met me.'

Then a bizarre moment occurs: Jimmy Savile imitates

Elvis Presley. Sir Jimmy curls his lip and recounts the words Elvis used in his speech of thanks. 'Once again this year we've been pleased to see Mr Savile with us over here' he says, proudly.

Savile was the highest profile DJ in the mid-1960s, mixing with the stars and appearing incessantly on radio and TV. His career had already revealed how influential and lucrative DJ-ing could be, but there are always time-lags in pop culture, and the potential role for a disc jockey took time to filter through to mid-1960s Britain. But one by one other young music lovers started taking up a career on the wheels of steel.

Jimmy Savile progressed through the TV schedules, doing adverts, Government Information Films (notably the 'Clunk Click Every Trip' road safety campaign) and *Savile's Travels*. In the 1970s he was in his forties, and his days as the great representative of the young had gone, but he had already begun to reinvent himself. Even while he was still a regular on *Top of the Pops* he'd started *Speakeasy*, in which he chaired a discussion of social issues with a panel of experts and a studio audience. He walked from John O'Groats to Land's End and filed reports for the TV evening news programme *Nationwide*. He also busied himself raising money for a host of good causes, and visiting the old and the sick. Once he went into an old folks' home run by some nuns, and while he was touring the day room an old lady had a fatal heart attack. He was clearly upset at this turn of events, but one of the nuns comforted him: 'Never mind, Jimmy, we were very overcrowded anyway.'

The dance hall revolution that Sir Jimmy had helped instigate was complete by the late 1970s. Early in the decade clubs had employed DJs on quiet nights of the week, but many had stuck with bands at the weekend; by the end of the decade the position was reversed. The disco revolution eventually completed this reversal. Until 1978 and the arrival in Britain of the hit film *Saturday Night Fever*, clubs were more likely to employ DJs at the weekend and book bands midweek. Big operators like Mecca had spent huge amounts of cash to give dance halls facelifts to become discotheques.

What drew the clubbers to all these venues was the soundtrack, but also the buzz; key to the discotheque experience is the atmosphere, the spirit of excitement and camaraderie generated in the halls and clubs. In urban areas clubs became focal points for the community, and clubbing became an addictive lifestyle. Discotheques began to boom as the 1960s turned into the 1970s, a time when many cities worldwide underwent major changes, slum clearance and job losses. In an era of fragmentation and isolation – and a retreat into private lives, private housing and private space – the dance hall and the discotheque became progressively more valuable, a rare public place. This was something Jimmy Savile recognised himself in 1975 when he told the readers of the *Top of the Pops* annual, 'It looks like this country and the world generally is going into a decline commercially. And when it comes to periods of decline, entertainment comes into its own.'

The disco era, socially, was fed by a mass craving for partying, escape, release, and an addiction to the ritual and opportunities to congregate and mingle afforded by clubbing. Musically, the foundations were laid by dance music down the decades, especially the continuing genius of soul and funk labels like Motown, Stax and Atlantic. The biggest contribution to the creation of the disco sound, however, came from Philadelphia producers Gamble & Huff. They eschewed radio play and aimed straight at the dancefloor with tracks like The O'Jays' 'Backstabbers' (1972) and MFSB's 'Love is the Message'

(1973). The Philadelphia sound – Gamble & Huff's lush strings, surging rhythms, instant choruses and positive messages – dominated dancefloors in the mid-1970s and became the staple diet of DJs, from the progressive soul DJs in Britain to the DJs in New York's club underground.

This was the beginning of disco. The idea of a disco as a place of entertainment and delight was fully established, but in the 1970s disco became a sound, and 'disco' became a genre of music; disco music used certain sounds and formulas which made it perfect for the dancefloor. It had been clear to working DJs from the start – from Jimmy Savile to Brian Rae – that the rhythm, the tempo, the feel, the vibe of a record was all important. That certain records had the right groove and did the business on the dancefloor. DJs keyed in to this, searched out the records that worked for them, and disco music developed and distilled this.

The mid- to late-1970s witnessed the height of disco fever, and featured some genuinely inspirational musicians breaking or rewriting rules – Chic's Nile Rodgers and Bernard Edwards, and Maurice White of Earth, Wind & Fire, for instance – and creative visionary producers – from Giorgio Moroder to Patrick Adams – but it also featured the somewhat less illustrious careers of Amanda Lear and the Village People, for example. At the commercial end of the disco market it was often hard to work out where the tackiness began and ended; Cerrone, a French disco star, released some of the era's best records in some of the era's worst record sleeves. The creative focus was on musicians, producers, influential record labels (like Casablanca and Salsoul), the important clubs and, of course, the clothes, the attitude and the lifestyle. These disco DJs in underground clubs in New York, and a handful of DJs playing to soul, reggae and funk crowds, were creative, inspirational figures, but they were exceptions as the numbers of DJs rose but the quality didn't. By 1978, apart from a few figures who were still championing innovation, DJs were mostly out there on a Friday or a Saturday night playing to packed crowds despite, not because of, their performances. A lot of the music was great, but on the high street the worst thing about the disco era was the DJs.

It was the way the DJs presented the music in clubs, more than anything – as an extension of radio. An influential DJ through the 1970s in Britain was the Emperor Rosko. Born Mike Pasternak in California in 1942, he grew up listening to R&B and dreaming of being a radio DJ. His career took off in Europe when he began working for Barclay Records, fronting their sponsored radio programmes. In 1966 he went to the pirate station Radio Caroline, and then moved on to Radio Luxemburg, based in Paris. By this time he was probably one of the highest paid DJs in the world. He'd also started taking a big mobile show on the road around Europe, often to places where they'd not had a disc-only night out before. He'd be onstage playing his dancefloor selection, with a light show and the by now obligatory go-go girls.

Rosko left Radio Luxemburg in 1968 after a disagreement with the station bosses, who wanted him to tone down his programme during the student uprising in May of that year. But by then he was established at Radio One, and the Rosko International Road Show was out playing Top Ranks and Mecca halls, and even Wembley Stadium. He took his radio personality onstage with him, jive talking his intros, whooping during the songs, and seldom letting up with his barrage of choice phrases: 'It's moody, moody'; 'Don't wear it out'; 'The platters that matter'.

Emperor Rosko could carry off this kind of performance because he was an original, with good taste in music. But the high street DJs in the 1970s – chatter-boxing and interrupting the flow of the records with jokey banter – were giving the profession an embarrassing reputation. By this time everybody recognised what a DJ was, but they didn't always like what they saw. In 1974 Radio One DJ Noel Edmonds was complaining that the worst thing about being a DJ was having to play records every day ('I'm really a frustrated TV comedian,' he admitted); Dave Lee Travis had started out DJ-ing at a Manchester club called the Oasis (where he met his beautiful blonde Swedish wife Marianne) but he was happy to have moved on: 'I'm not just a DJ, I'm a really dedicated all-round entertainer . . . I'd do anything to get a laugh.' Kenny Everett had started out running trendy mod nights in the West End of London, but left his musical roots behind and became a full time, larger than life, mad-cap comedian. Very occasionally some of these high jinks were amusing on radio, but what works on radio doesn't mean much in a club, and in the hands of your average club disc jockey it was excruciating, and it was killing dance music.

Getting on the microphone still survives, of course, here and there. Hip hop DJs used MCs to vibe up the crowd and namecheck the DJ. The hip hop set-up clearly owed a debt to reggae sound systems, where the guy putting on the records – the selector – would have a box of tricks and techniques like dubs and rewinds, and he'd work with a guy who vibed up the crowd, toasting. The sound systems have never gone away, and in some cases evolved into hardcore house collectives or UK garage pioneers. On the UK garage scene, characters like MC Creed and MC Neat have risen to prominence, deftly providing a bridge between the audience and the music, adding texture to the beats and basslines.

Getting on the microphone also survives at the other end of the clubbing spectrum, a long way from the raw cutting edge. If you're only used to clubs like 'Cream' and Fabric, you forget the strength of that image of the old-style personality DJ. In the 1970s there wasn't much difference between radio DJs and mainstream club DJs; they all followed the personality DJ model, and always seemed to be talking over the music. That image still has a very strong hold: onstage, doing requests, nattering and chattering.

That there's some confusion isn't surprising given that the 1970s style DJ is still out there. You can find him at weddings, hotel receptions and commercial nights on the high street. He's not interested in playing a cutting edge role, he's having a laugh. He's still getting work, talking over the records, trying to get his audience singing along, not to Mud's 'Tiger Feet' any more, but Alice Deejay. He's living in the shadow of Jimmy Savile and the Emperor Rosko. Even the biggest DJ superstars have to work hard to shift that 1970s image. Fatboy Slim once told me he would do anything to avoid using a microphone: 'I figure that as soon as you get on the microphone you're in Dave Lee Travis territory.'

Bad versions of Emperor Rosko prevailed, rather than the influence of the New York underground. By 1977 and 1978 you'd go out to dance to Earth, Wind & Fire and the Real Thing and end up spending half the night listening to some inane DJ. It was like being stuck on a bus with a drunk. DJs were in your face, unavoidable, always shouting. The personality and individuality Savile had introduced to the role of the DJ was mangled. DJs were striving not for musical excellence or creative programming but purely to outdo each other in contriving odd-ball personalities: 'I'm so mad.'

'I'm so wacky.'

'I'm the hairy cornflake.'

CHAPTER 3

Pills, Thrills & Bellyaches
Tales from the Mod Underground

If Jimmy Savile was the highest profile DJ by the mid-1960s, there were other DJs in Britain then who'd also made a considerable but unacknowledged impact on music tastes and the club scene. Prominent among these underground heroes was Guy Stevens.

Stevens was resident at the Scene in Soho from 1963. It wasn't the most glamorous club in the world, but Guy Stevens had never conceived of DJ-ing as a route to glamour. For him, DJ-ing was an extension of his natural enthusiasm for music, particularly black American R&B. He was an evangelist who had a passion for the power of music, a hunger for records, and a desire to share his obsession. He knew loud music can change your life. He believed clubs mattered.

The Scene is remembered, just. Kids would gather outside, idling near the scooters or propping up walls, hanging around in the nocturnal shadows, judging the right time to make a move inside. There would be dealers selling pills in the streets of Soho and the West End, in coffee bars, and in the club itself. You'd go downstairs, through a door wedged open with a brick, into the club, a bare, dark room with a stage at one end and a DJ area in the corner. The walls and the floor were concrete. It was very, very dark in the basement; this was before flashing lights, slides, oil wheels and mirrorballs. You leant against the wall or danced in the middle of the room. The sound, from tiny fairground speakers on the walls, was loud but not particularly clear. There was a touch of sensory deprivation. Guy Stevens would be playing raw R&B. All you could do was feel the music banging through your body.

He wasn't surfing some DJ-ing wave; when Guy Stevens started out he was going against the grain, particularly in an era when disc-only nights were rare and R&B DJs in Britain were unknown. Playing at the Scene did give him an advantage, though: it was situated in Soho, an area with bohemian traditions, an area of strip clubs, gay clubs, late night coffee bars. One of the attractions of the nightlife in boho Soho in the early 1960s was that going to clubs was still a secret adventure; at that time there was no media coverage of what happened late at night out on the dancefloors. Clubland was a world of secret languages, clothes, codes and, at the Scene, strange music you couldn't hear on the radio.

In 1963 Guy Stevens was the first DJ to play rhythm and blues in Britain, moulding tastes, inspiring other DJs and a multitude of bands. Like the best DJs of our era, Guy Stevens had an influence on music that went far beyond the four walls of the club. He played a key part in the early career of the Who by turning Pete Townshend on to American soul and R&B; he ran the legendary label Sue Records, releasing classic tracks like 'That's How Heartaches Are Made' by Baby Washington (later covered by Dusty Springfield) and 'Harlem Shuffle' by Bob & Earl; he went on to help establish Procul Harum, to manage Mott the Hoople, produce Free, and, finally, to produce *London Calling* by the Clash. But his story also has a darker side, and his heavy drinking and addiction to amphetamines contributed to his death in 1981.

Unlike the best DJs of our era, his work was largely unrecognised. There are few sources, very little documentation relating to the life of Guy Stevens, even in the furthest corners of the world wide web and the dustiest archives of the music press. Many of the tales about the Scene are contradictory, most mangled by time and the effects of the chemical substances around at that time. I made a pilgrimage to the site of the Scene nearly forty years after Guy Stevens DJ-ed there, winding my way from Piccadilly Circus tube up Great Windmill Street for a meeting with Dave McAleer at a pub called the Red Lion.

The Red Lion is near Ham Yard, an enclosed little dead end road off Great Windmill Street. You had to go down Ham Yard to get to the Scene – which was in a basement – but exactly where the front door was I'm not sure, so while I wait for Dave McAleer I have a scout about. On the corner of Ham Yard and Great Windmill Street there's an old pub, the Lyric. There's now an exit for a big NCP car at one end of Ham Yard, and apart from that there are just the backs of a few buildings, some nondescript fire exits, air conditioning vents and a few people going about their business. There are no front doors, certainly no front doors to anything resembling a club.

I stand for a while across the road from Ham Yard. A tour guide appears right next to me, surrounded by a dozen or so tourists, eager young Americans wearing baggy shorts and hanging on every word the guide says. He's wearing a jacket with The Big Bus Company stitched on it. He turns and points to the Lyric: 'On the site of that pub there used to be a club called the Scene and one evening the Rolling Stones played here and all the Beatles turned up to see them play.'

I wasn't sure he was exactly right about the site of the Scene, but the tourists were very excited. Photographs were taken and then the group moved off. 'Now we're going to see Soho's own church, St Anne's,' said the guide, as he led them down Archer Street. Dave McAleer appeared and we went to the pub to compare notes.

Guy Stevens was eleven when he heard 'Whole Lotta Shakin' Goin' On' by Jerry Lee Lewis, and it made an immediate impact, as he later recalled in an interview with Charles Shaar Murray: 'I was never the same again. That intensity of feeling. I've seen performances by Jerry Lee Lewis that were just unbelievable. It was when he was at his most unpopular, two hundred people in a two-thousand seater, and he played his heart out, and that's always stayed with me. That electricity, that manic intensity.'

He was at Woolverstone School at the time, and he started a rock & roll club. Even then he'd become a selector, a taste maker; his rock & roll club would meet after lessons and he'd charge the other boys a shilling a week for the honour of hearing his choice of tunes: 'Peggy Sue', 'Bony Maronie', 'Great Balls of Fire'.

In the austere, buttoned-up 1950s, devotion to rock & roll was considered dangerous, and a clear threat to authority. Guy Stevens wasn't fitting in at his rugby-playing boarding school and was expelled at the age of fourteen in July 1958. He moved to London and eventually took a job at Lloyds, the insurance market. He was entering the job market in an era of full employment. The teenagers who left school in the late 1950s enjoyed money and opportunities. They distanced themselves from the sacrifices and hardship of the War and the years that followed it, when it wasn't just essential foodstuffs and fuel that were rationed; to some people in the 1950s it felt like fun – ideas even – were held in check. The new generation wanted to spread its wings.

At first, the soundtrack to this rebellion was rock &

roll, with Bill Haley, Elvis Presley and Jerry Lee Lewis exploding onto the scene with life and energy in the years after 1956, but the mainstream success of these early rock & roll heroes stimulated the more adventurous music fans to dig deeper, and it soon became obvious to them that the white rock & rollers owed a great debt to black American R&B. Thus, by the beginning of the 1960s, among serious music lovers, R&B had become a passion.

These rhythm and blues enthusiasts were forever seeking out obscure records on small, black-owned independent record labels, the original versions perhaps, or the records which inspired the commercial versions, the records that never made it beyond the ghetto-ised world of race records, overshadowed by the white-owned labels with their superior marketing and promotional clout. In 1960 Dave McAleer was fifteen. He'd begun to subscribe to *Billboard* magazine and order new R&B records direct from America: 'I was playing records to my friends and trying to convert them, and all the time no-one at school knew anything about what we were talking about. Part of the fun was going into record shops and asking for something you knew they hadn't got, or you'd ask for the original version and they'd pass you the British release and you'd be dismissive, like "Nah, not that one!"'

In the meantime, Guy Stevens had amassed a phenomenal record collection. Like McAleer, he obtained most of his records via mail order from obscure record shops in Louisiana and Tennessee. He even visited America and toured Memphis in 1963, including a trip to see the Stax record shop and recording studio. Not that Guy Stevens was leading the high life; he was living in what he later remembered as a 'one-room, no-water flat' in Leicester Square when he got the job at the Scene.

Gary Brooker was an R&B fan growing up in Southend. He formed the Paramounts, who played gigs round the dance halls and ballrooms of Southend before starting their own club, Shades, in 1961, aiming to provide themselves and their fellow R&B enthusiasts with someplace to meet. Cover versions of records in the jukebox at Shades, stocked by Tony Wilkinson, a local R&B collector, began to find their way into the Paramounts' repertoire.

There was a gap between the pop world and the underground world of R&B. You couldn't hear these songs on the radio or read about them in pop magazines. Most of the records were available on import only. Getting to hear songs by Ray Charles, Bobby Bland or James Brown was an adventure in itself. We take for granted our access to music via the high street or the Internet, but forty years ago devotees of the best music would go to great lengths to pursue their devotion. People would travel from all over to hear the right records on a jukebox. On one occasion, Brooker and his fellow music lovers gathered at the club to listen to the radio: 'We discovered that Ray Charles, then on tour in Europe, was being broadcast live on French radio from the Paris Olympia. We got hold of a good radio set, plugged it into the amps, spread the word, and about a hundred and fifty of us settled down in Shades to listen.'

Cover versions formed the staple diet of most young bands of the time. The Beatles, the Rolling Stones and the Animals all started out doing covers of Chuck Berry, Bo Diddley and John Lee Hooker; the Stones made their recording debut with Chuck Berry's 'Come On'. Guy Stevens, incidentally, founded and ran the Chuck Berry Fan Club in the UK.

Over a number of years, anyone who had the original records was an important figure for the fans, and also a source of inspiration for the groups. Guy Stevens' collection was unequalled and irresistible, and to hear the records you had to be at the Scene. The Scene opened at the beginning of 1963 and was run by Ronan O'Rahilly. O'Rahilly was born to wealthy Irish American parents with extensive family interests in manufacturing and shipping, but Ronan was a maverick who had no desire to work in the family trade, and instead took himself off to London where he carved out a career in the music business – he became the manager of Alexis Korner's Blues Incorporated. Even in London the real R&B scene was small, so O'Rahilly's club venture was far from an obvious commercial move. 'At that time in London there were only a tiny, tiny number of people who were into R&B. I knew Guy had a large record collection, so when I opened the Scene I offered him Monday nights,' he later recalled.

The basement housing the Scene already had a small place in music history. In the 1940s the room was used as a rehearsal space by jazz musicians until it was opened as Club Eleven, a jazz club run by Ronnie Scott and ten of his jazz friends, although Club Eleven moved to a venue on Carnaby Street after a year at Ham Yard. At their new home, Club Eleven suffered the first London club drug bust, in April 1950, when around forty police raided the club. They searched the 200 or so customers, arrested ten men and discovered an empty morphine ampoule, a small packet of cocaine, some prepared opium and a large number of cigarettes containing Indian Hemp (Ronnie Scott himself was one of those charged under Raw Opium Regulations and the Dangerous Drugs Act the next day at Marlborough magistrates court). Subsequently, the papers were full of stories of 'drug-crazed beboppers', and Club Eleven folded soon afterwards.

Meanwhile, the basement in Great Windmill Street went on to house Cy Laurie's Jazz Club – the first British all-nighter – and then, immediately prior to its incarnation as the Scene, it was the Piccadilly Jazz Club, run by music-biz mogul Giorgio Gomelsky. Jazz clubs were all over Soho and the West End of London, and modern jazz was the smart music to be into, as opposed to skiffle or trad jazz; it was from the term 'modern jazz' that the mods got their name. They were inspired by the cool style of jazz star Miles Davis, and West Coast musicians like Gerry Mulligan and Chet Baker in both music and fashion; they were almost rat pack in their look, with a penchant for Italian and French designers (skinny ties, tighter suits, short jackets, narrow pants). Their sharp, Continental look stood out in dreary Britain, just as their music was a million miles from the likes of Matt Munro or Rosemary Clooney.

In 1963 the mod movement hadn't become a cliché. There were pills around – the night-time scene in Soho was awash with amphetamines – but taking them still felt like a secret adventure known only to the few. The mods were the sharpest dressers in town, but Guy Stevens wasn't interested in the look; he would never have considered himself a mod. Dave McAleer tells me that 'Guy was the student-type, with a baggy jumper. He would have even looked right in a trad jazz club.'

He wore a duffle coat?

'No, not quite that bad, but he wasn't dressing to impress, and he didn't dress to the latest trends; he dressed like a student.'

So what did McAleer wear?

'We weren't scruffy because we were there to get birds! I can't remember what we wore in each era, it was always changing, but I guess it would be "mod" in a way. It would be sharp Italian suits.'

Whatever the latest trend, mods would be on it ahead of the rest. At His Clothes on Carnaby Street owner John Stephens favoured bright colours and sharp clothes. His styles changed regularly: monthly, weekly, daily even. He had a number of shops, but the one on Carnaby Street encouraged other shops to open alongside his, and it was also one of the first stores to be called a 'boutique'. It was a new start, a new vocabulary. Boutique sounded right – like 'discotheque'.

But the word discotheque wasn't yet common currency; the idea was still a good few years from catching on, and most nightclubs and dance halls at that time – the Scene included – had resident and live bands on every night of the week apart from Sundays (when most clubs had to be closed), although Mondays at the Scene were now billed as 'R&B Disc Night with Guy Stevens'. To have no live band during the evening was still a relatively rare state of affairs, but it suited Dave McAleer and his friends: 'Most of the live bands were crap. Most R&B fans didn't want to see British groups even if they were singing R&B covers; it would be, what's the point, we'd rather hear the real thing. We'd rather hear the records.'

McAleer started going to the Scene in 1963 when he was eighteen and Guy Stevens had just started DJ-ing. Friends of McAleer's, lads about town, told him about this wonderful place with this DJ playing great music: 'I went down on a Monday night and it was the first time I had met anybody with the records I had, and the worst thing was that he had things I didn't have, or things I'd read about. I got on with Guy because I didn't know anybody else who knew this material. If he was playing something I didn't know I'd go up and ask him what it was and when it was finished he'd hold up the record so I could read the label and I'd make a mental note of it. Sometimes I would take things in for him.'

It wasn't the only disc-only night in London – DJ Ian Samwell had originated lunchtime sessions at the Lyceum in 1961 – but what marked Guy Stevens out was the quality of his tunes. He knew the right records to play, and would go looking for them in the specialist record

importers like Transat Imports in Soho, or obscure music
shops, or secondhand stalls. One rhythm and blues
enthusiast would sell a box of his records every Friday
morning in the basement of a shop on Lisle Street in
Chinatown, just round the corner from Guy's flat. By
lunchtime they would all be sold. Guy made it his business to know where to look, which shops to trawl, which
dealers to befriend. If he wanted a record like 'Money' by
Barrett Strong, he would spend all day looking for it, all
week. A year, if necessary.

The Scene on Monday nights was never mad busy,
although as well as a handful of serious music aficionados
like McAleer, there would also always be a sizeable crowd
of dancers who just got into it, uninterested in the who,
when and what of the records. Stevens himself was
low-key, and there was no sense of hero worship. Dave
McAleer had some great nights in the Scene, but had no
idea that history would remember Guy Stevens: 'I mean,
we never looked on him as a DJ; I don't think we even
knew what a DJ was. To us, he was just a guy playing R&B
records. He was quiet, and he was usually there on his
own. It wasn't a technical thing; it was no precision stuff,
and he wasn't like the "personality" DJ at all, performing
or leaping around.'

McAleer also says that Guy Stevens didn't talk
between the records – 'one record would finish and he'd
start the next one' – although others remember that he
did announce which songs he was playing. There would
be a lot of Chuck Berry and Bo Diddley, which might have
been construed by some as a bit old-fashioned, but
generally he wasn't doing a retro thing; he was mostly
playing current R&B from America. Big tunes at the Scene
included the jazz-tinged instrumental grooves by Jimmy
Smith and Jimmy McGriff, the soulful sounds of 'I Gotta
Dance to Keep From Crying' by the Miracles and 'It's

Alright' by the Impressions. Like other collectors, he would sometimes order two copies of a record on import and sell on his spare.

Celebrities didn't go down to hear Guy Stevens play his records, but some of the people who did went on to become celebrities. Musicians and aspiring music industry heads were now viewing the Scene as the most influential club in Soho. Chris Farlowe became a big fan. Eric Clapton used to go with ace face Lionel (no-one can remember his surname). Guy wore this interest lightly, didn't act cool and had no conspicuous ego.

In 1963 Gary Brooker met Guy Stevens at the Crawdaddy Club, where he also used to play the records. Brooker began to go round to see Guy Stevens in his flat and rummage through his huge record collection, and thus Guy Stevens replaced Tony Wilkinson's jukebox in inspiring the Paramounts' repertoire; they'd borrow a pile of his records for a week, and learn another fifteen or so numbers. In this period more people began to drop by at the Scene, or invite themselves back to Stevens' flat to listen to records, including Steve Marriott who would go on to play in the Small Faces and Humble Pie, and also members of the Who, who were introduced to him by Pete Meaden.

Pete Meaden was a Scene regular: a cool dresser; always neat and smart, although he lived in a tiny flat in Monmouth Street containing just a chair, a phone, a sleeping bag, an ironing board and a filing cabinet (the flat doubled as his 'office'). He was a freelance publicist who worked with Rolling Stones mentor Andrew Loog Oldham. The Rolling Stones were also part of the Scene scene when they were nobodies; they used to meet at Guy Stevens' flat, sit and listen to Jimmy Reed and Bobby Bland records and then crash out on his floor. But Dave McAleer shares my scepticism about the Scene playing host to a Rolling Stones gig with the Beatles in the audience: 'That happened, but I think it was at the Crawdaddy. I really don't think it was at the Scene.'

Meaden was sacked by Andrew Loog Oldham because he got too out of his head at a Stones reception. For Pete Meaden, mod living was a continuous party, and he loved what Guy Stevens played. The Scene, he once said, was where 'the greatest records you can imagine were being played'. He used to go to the Scene with another ace face, Phil the Greek. Meaden called everybody 'baby'. People who knew him at the time recall that if you bumped into him at the Scene he'd be 'How are you baby, too much, what's happening, great, keep cool, can you dig it?' In other words, he spoke like a DJ.

Pete Meaden began to work with another group – the Who. He persuaded the band to take on board a mod image and to establish a sound that was harder, angrier and sharper, mimicking the kind of records he'd been hearing Stevens play at the Scene. He told them the effect the music should have: it should have an edge. He recommended that they change their name from the Who to the High Numbers, and they did.

Meaden took Townshend to the Scene in order to introduce Townshend to the music Guy Stevens was playing and the culture which had found a focus there. For Meaden it was part of his grand plan: 'All I knew was that I had to get the band established in the West End in a way that would be recognised by the hardcore cult centre, which was the mods that used to hang out in the Scene Club, you know. You can't get any more authentic than that. So I had to give them the golden seal of authenticity.'

Mods had begun to gravitate in large numbers towards the Scene. They had a disdain for anything mainstream or obvious, and they liked to be exclusive, in their dress sense and their music taste, which by now wasn't confined to modern jazz. They would enthuse about early bluebeat music and Caribbean culture in general; they were looking anywhere for inspiration – anywhere other than staid old England. They liked frothy Italian coffee rather than dishwater English tea. Many of them professed a fondness for the beat writers emerging from the United States – especially Jack Kerouac – but didn't share the bohemian scruffiness of the beatniks of the time; the mods wanted to be smart, in control. In Manchester, a beatnik hangout called the Left Wing Club was replaced by a club playing R&B and soul and reggae; the club was called the Twisted Wheel.

There were other hang-outs and other insalubrious basements. The Flamingo on Wardour Street, underneath the Whiskey-A-Go-Go, was another unlicensed Soho dive, with a reputation for hosting all-nighters on Fridays and Saturdays and for pulling a multi-racial crowd. One of the regular DJs at the Flamingo was the Lyceum's Ian Samwell, who used to fill his Flamingo sets with nothing but R&B and bluebeat. It was a particular favourite with black GIs stationed at American military bases in Hillingdon and Ruislip, and visiting jazz musicians would also drop by. These days, the twenty-first century celebrity haunts quiver with excitement at the arrival of Martine McCutcheon, but back then the hippest hang-outs attracted a cooler selection of VIPs: the great Muhammad Ali, for example, paid the Flamingo a visit in June 1963. Later that year, though, there was a stabbing in the club which led US Airforce chiefs to ban servicemen from going there.

Tribalism was becoming key to understanding teen culture; music lovers defined themselves by what and who they didn't want to be, how they stood, how they walked. Mods carried an uptightness, an air of don't touch me. The first mods – the 'faces', as they called themselves –

would soon be contemptuous of the late-comers – dubbed 'the tickets' – the post-commercialised mods. For the original mods black dance music was a passion, and they started turning up to the Scene on their scooters. Guy Stevens never considered himself a mod, but the mods' desire to stay up all night, dance, live outside the mainstream drew them towards the kind of music Guy Stevens was championing. The Scene was now the quintessential mod hangout, and Guy Stevens the mods' greatest DJ.

Townshend understood, studied the look and the dance moves, the clothes, and the tunes, and appreciated that the Scene was unique: 'The Scene was really where it was at, but there were only about fifteen people down there every night,' he said later. 'It was a focal point for the mod movement. I don't think anyone who was a mod outside Soho realised the fashions and dances all began there.'

The Scene was unlicensed; you could only get an espresso or a soft drink at the bar, and the sweat would start rising early. Apart from when the front door swung open, there was no ventilation. When Guy Stevens started there the night would finish at 2am or 3am. You'd then have to hang around until 6am and the first tube trains. Your parka would be your sleeping bag.

Amphetamines had been part of the night-time scene for a couple of decades, favoured by jazz musicians who were doing three or even four sets a night. Pills were also used by a wide selection of the general public in the early 1960s: in 1961 two and a half per cent of all prescriptions written by British doctors were for amphetamines, and many of the pills leaked onto the streets. Most of the pills taken by mods and their nightlife companions were manufactured drugs, not pills from illicit laboratories. In fact, many of them bore the manufacturer's name, SKF (Smith, Kline and French).

The trade in pills was controlled by dodgy geezers in and around the clubs, either involved in running the clubs, or part of other illegal activities in Soho. Although Ronan O'Rahilly ran the Scene, it was part of an empire operated by the notorious Nash gang who also had a hand in one of the other clubs frequented by mods and speed hungry dancers in the early 1960s – La Discotheque in Wardour Street – and it was never far from the attentions of the unpredictable police force. Ace face Johnny Moke remembers, 'Guy would play all these great rhythm and blues records and we'd groove all night. Of course, nearly all of us were doing pills – you had to if you were dancing all night. Same way they take ecstasy now.'

There were dealers in the Scene, but they were one or two links down the chain of supply. Most of them got their drugs from a club in Frith Street which sold them in big batches. For a while, two cousins ran the door and rigorously searched the customers as they came in, confiscated pills, then passed them on to authorised dealers who recycled them in the club. Some ex-regulars also claim that the soft drinks bar sold straight coke and expensive coke; expensive coke had something in it, probably amphetamine. At clubs like the Scene during the Guy Stevens era you could buy Drinamyl pills (the 'purple heart' tablets that were actually blue, slightly heart-shaped triangles) for around 7d (3p), although they were usually bought in batches of five, ten or more. Pete Meaden later recalled the effects of Drinamyl, the 'sustaining power' you needed if you were going to be up for three days at a stretch. The pills, he said, liberated him: 'You lose all lack of confidence, you lose all guilt.' In fact, Drinamyl was originally prescribed to counter anxiety, and Meaden confirmed it made you feel free, 'unburdened by chains of resistance'.

The average clubber would start the evening with

three or four purple hearts, and then have a couple more every time they felt their energy flagging, and then an extra one or two as back-up. By the end of the night, unsurprisingly, the Scene had its share of casualties, propping up the door, a faraway look in their eyes, foam flecks around their mouths.

When the TV show *Ready Steady Go* began broadcasting in August 1963, it featured pop acts but also American artists like the Miracles, James Brown and Stevie Wonder. The show's producers would scour the clubs looking for audience members, and the show's dancers, including Sandy Sergeant, Teresa Godfrey and Patrick Kerr, were all regulars at the Scene. According to Richard Barnes, the 'ideal mod' would spend two or three nights a week at the Scene, one of which was always Monday.

For Guy Stevens a career was developing, in a haphazard fashion. Word spread about the Scene and Guy's sessions. According to Ronan O'Rahilly, people would travel from all over the country to hear him play his selections, and from France and Holland, too: 'It was that good.'

The Who were also developing a career. In the summer of 1964 the band, still called the High Numbers, had a five-week residency on Wednesdays at the Scene. Their sets were reliant on tunes they'd heard Guy Stevens play, and included covers of 'Heatwave', 'Smokestack Lightning' and 'I Gotta Dance to Keep From Crying'. In July 1964, the High Numbers released 'I'm the Face' which drew heavily on a record Meaden had borrowed from Guy Stevens' collection: Slim Harpo's 'Got Love If You Want It'. The single flopped, although 'I'm the Face' was big at the Scene, which Meaden considered a good omen. 'If they could turn these kids on, they could turn on the world,' he said.

Dave McAleer began DJ-ing at his own club night for a while, at Ready Steady Go on Dean Street, but it wasn't too successful. The venue had been called Ready Steady Go in the hope that the punters would connect it with the TV show: 'The gist of our publicity was that it was a chance to impress the people who made the show and get yourself on TV. But really we had no connection at all.'

It was a scam?

'Yes! I had the DJ-ing name Hamilton Lee: "R&B with Hamilton Lee". Mickey Most was a doorman – his father-in-law owned the club – and his wife collected the coats. I was the only non-Most family member. But the club was too far off the beaten track. It was only on Dean Street, two or three streets up from here, but we couldn't get any decent passing trade.'

They would hand out flyers to tourists, anyone in the vicinity, but they never got more than fifty people. Even Dave McAleer's South London mates wouldn't go, although the legendary Gene Vincent paid more than one visit: 'He was going out with one of the Most girls and he came down, although he never sang, he just came down with his mates and they'd have a drink and fall about.'

The Scene's Ronan O'Rahilly broadened his involvement in the pop world in March 1964 with an audacious move: he launched Radio Caroline, an illegal radio station broadcasting off the coast of Harwich. Within three weeks a Gallup survey revealed that the station had seven million listeners. Together with the American Forces Network and the Dutch Radio Station Hilversum, Radio Caroline was integral to the spread of soul, R&B and the new pop sounds. The first track on Caroline was the Scene classic, Jimmy McGriff's 'Round Midnight'.

The success of Radio Caroline proved the culture was no longer just about a few people leaning against the walls of the Scene while Guy Stevens played records by the Impressions, and the mod movement hit the front pages when the first incidents of what became the summer of mods versus rockers battles were tracked by an hysterical press during Easter 1964. The media hyped up the situation and made further battles and confrontations with the police and the authorities inevitable at seaside resorts like Brighton, Hastings and Margate right through Whitsun and into August. Mod was becoming a cliché.

Media coverage wasn't limited to graphic accounts of bank holiday skirmishes, and in May 1964 the *Sunday Mirror* ran an exposé of the scene at the Flamingo and La Discotheque. Reporters had gone undercover and witnessed pill-popping and all-night partying, and described the 'drug menace' said to be sweeping Soho's 'all-night clubs and dives'. The cognoscenti, unfazed by tabloid interest, moved on from La Discotheque (or 'the Disc', as it was called) to clubs like the Last Chance Saloon on Oxford Street where a purist soul playlist was soon in place on Friday and Saturday nights. Dave McAleer remembers how this process of being mainstreamed killed off modism: 'Mod was only interesting for me when it was something the man-on-the-street wasn't interested in and had never heard of. By the time mods and rockers began fighting on the beach it was all over, and it wasn't the real thing any more.'

Once mod had gone overground, the early pioneers were sidelined. On Sunday 2 August 1964 the High Numbers appeared at the Florida Rooms in Brighton at what was billed as an 'All Night Rave'. A friend of Meaden's invited entrepreneur Kit Lambert to the show. Lambert, and his business partner, Chris Stamp (brother of Terence), took over the management of the band. They paid Meaden off with £500 and the band reverted to the name the Who.

Meanwhile Guy Stevens left the Scene at the end of 1964 and went in search of a new challenge. His manic energy and informal involvement with bands – playing them records, lending them records, opening their ears – led him closer to the music business, and he became involved with a label, Sue Records, an imprint of Island. Island Records had been launched by Chris Blackwell in 1959 to tap into the great creativity of Jamaican music, ska especially. Blackwell wanted to begin to license recordings from Sue, the American R&B label, and decided to employ Stevens to run the company. Sue had been started in New York by Juggy Murray, and the British version of the label began by putting out tracks emanating from its American counterpart – like Jimmy McGriff and Bobby Bland – but also reissued tracks from previous UK labels like Top Rank, Parlophone and London, and picked up tracks from American labels like Modern, V-Tone, Kent and Ace. Sue soon had a wide roster of blues, R&B and soul, including recordings by Ike & Tina Turner, Rufus Thomas, James Brown, Screamin' Jay Hawkins and Etta James.

Stevens ran the operation with huge enthusiasm. He wasn't noted, however, for sitting in the office, forward planning or attending meetings. If he was at Island HQ in Baring Street he'd be dressed in tight skinny trousers and suede brothel creepers, hair everywhere, jumping around, holding forth, enthusing about records he'd heard the night before or bands he was going to see later in the evening. He loved being out and about; in 1964, in the early days at Sue, he flew to America to meet Chuck Berry.

As label boss and the public face of the company, he was good PR for Sue. On the front of the first label compilation, *The Sue Story*, he's pictured on the telephone, playing the part of hip young record company executive, while on the front of *The Sue Story vol. 2* he's there with a pile of records. In reality, he had an informal attitude to contracts and legalities, although in the vast majority of cases Stevens sent advance royalty cheques to the artists and labels in America. There were, however, one or two records released by Sue without the knowledge of the original artists. Likewise he released a number of records by fictitious groups, including 'The Whip' by Alexander Jackson and the Turnkeys which was actually a song called 'Flea Pot' by Lala Wilson. 'The Whip', nevertheless, was a minor hit.

The label ran from autumn 1963 to the summer of 1968, although Stevens split from Sue before the end. Their biggest successes were probably 'Mockingbird' by Charlie & Inez Foxx, and several releases by Ike & Tina Turner, including 'It's Gonna Work Out Fine'. Another, 'I Can't Stand It' by the Soul Sisters, was the first hit for the Spencer Davis Group. Stevens' releases on Sue fed back into the burgeoning DJ culture in a similar way to those dozens of DJ-controlled labels of our era – from Perfecto to Paper Recordings – and became important songs for a generation of DJs. Stevens was no longer behind the wheels of steel, but he was still having an impact in R&B and soul clubs around Britain. He became friends with Roger Eagle, the influential DJ based at Manchester's Twisted Wheel. Roger Eagle was one of a select number of DJs Stevens would service with pre-release copies in order to popularise the records before they hit the shops. London, Manchester and the rest of Britain had also watched as dance nights and DJs became part of the leisure landscape.

In 1965 Chubby Checker recorded a song called 'At the Discotheque'. He had built a career with numerous releases and reworked songs eulogising the Twist, and was eager to find his next big cash-in. On release, however, 'At the Discotheque' was B-sided in favour of 'Do the Freddie', a song inspired by Freddie Garrity, the lead singer of Freddie & the Dreamers, who had had a series of hit singles in the United States from 1963 onwards. In 1965 Garrity, who leapt about onstage, had been asked by journalists in America what the name of the dance was. It had no name, it was just spontaneous slapstick, but Garrity claimed it was called the Freddie. Chubby Checker, it has to be said, suffered a severe lapse in taste to ever think the Freddie would catch on; within months of Garrity's pronouncement and Chubby Checker's single, the Freddie disappeared to whatever heaven dead dance crazes go too. In contrast, 5,000 discotheques had opened in America by the end of 1965. The days of live bands exclusively providing the soundtrack for a night out were over.

The word 'discotheque' had entered the English language and with it the notion of the DJ as a star. In most of the coverage of pop culture in the 1960s it had been the bands or the fans or the fashions that had caught the eye of the social commentators, the press and the media, but early in 1967 Tom Wolfe visited Tiles, a basement discotheque in the heart of London, and realised that all eyes were on the DJ. Tiles drew crowds day and night eager for soul music and non-stop partying, and was a prototype superclub; the dancefloor was the focus of a lifestyle and the base for a variety of commercial opportunities (attached to the club, just off the main room, there was an arcade of boutiques, a record stall and a beauty parlour, all literally underground). A good proportion of the crowd were office girls, as well as bank clerks and shop assistants, and most of them were in their late teens. Wolfe was investigating the mod lifestyle – 'the Life', as Wolfe calls it; he dubs the scene at Tiles 'the Noonday Underground'. It was as busy in the day as it was at night, especially on bank holidays. The DJ, Clem Dalton, says Wolfe, is 'the idol of the boys; they all want to be DJs'. The DJ, reckons Wolfe, leads 'the Total Life', living all day long in a world of mod style, drenched in music.

The particular pleasures of club DJ-ing were becoming apparent. It wasn't the same as being on the radio and talking to a faceless audience. Many DJs did both, but being in a club was something special. Clubs were becoming the front-line of the music scene.

In the rise of discotheques and disc jockeys, innovations in technology have been important – equipment facilitating an increase in volume, the seguing of records, vari-speed, and so on – but not as important as the ongoing creativity of the music, specifically music from black America. As recognised by the likes of Sam Phillips, Alan Freed and Guy Stevens, from ragtime through boogie woogie and jump blues, to R&B and beyond, there has been a strand of black American music that has accentuated and developed dancefloor rhythms (although this is not the only tradition, as evidenced by the variety of other genres: work songs, doo wop, slow blues, gospel and free jazz, for example).

Out of all this beat-heavy dance music, it would be hard to overestimate the importance of Motown in the rise of the discotheque. The pure, driving upbeat soul records released by Motown sounded phenomenal in a club, and were glorious two-and-a-half-minute gifts for the first generation of club DJs. Motown exploded onto the music scene, partly via the British groups who made no secret of their debt to the label, partly because it gave a sparkle and a sheen to raw, original R&B, partly because of the way Motown was picked up by Radio Caroline and *Ready Steady Go*, but mostly because it was perfect dance music, made for the world of the all-nighters.

The pop world had caught up with the pioneers.

Bands like the Paramounts were now regulars on TV shows like *Five O'Clock Club* and *Ready Steady Go*.

The Paramounts split in September 1966; according to Brooker, their repertoire was 'no longer sacred'. Now that discotheques were favoured places, record companies were licensing American records by the van-load and even DJs in pop discos were plugging the latest R&B and soul; those British bands relying on versions of black American records were suffering in competition with the real thing. 'You could play at a club, and perform a song, and five minutes later they'd play the record and wipe you off the floor,' Gary Brooker remembers. 'And that couldn't have happened in the earlier days because only Guy Stevens had the record!'

A restless music lover like Guy Stevens was never going to run with the mainstream – even a mainstream he had helped to create. His interests shifted away from soul and R&B, Island Records began to invest in the career of the Spencer Davis Group, and Guy Stevens began to do some studio work. He got involved with a band from Carlisle called the The V.I.P.s who were signed to Island. They were renamed Art, and then became Spooky Tooth. His productions for them include 'In a Dream'. He summed up his theory thus: 'It built up. All my records build up.' He had a DJ's addiction to riding the rush. If you listen to some of the great records around at that time, like 'Wade in the Water' or Kenny Burrell's 'Burning Spear', you can hear what he means.

Before the break-up of the Paramounts, Guy Stevens had introduced Gary Brooker to Keith Reid, and Brooker and Reid started writing songs together, originally without any plans to form a group. Stevens persuaded them otherwise, and together they worked on finding a sound for the new group, influenced by Guy Stevens' huge enthusiasm for Bob Dylan's *Blonde on Blonde* LP, based on two keyboards and the addition of other instruments, saxophones and strings. The group took the name Procul Harum, which Brooker has always said came from the pedigree name of a cat belonging to a friend of Guy Stevens. Guy Stevens supervised the recording of some songs, including the first recorded version of 'A Whiter Shade of Pale'.

Meanwhile, involvement with musicians continued apace. Stevie Winwood got him involved in the first Traffic album *Dear Mr Fantasy* and he went with the band to a country house in Berkshire, took all his records, smoked dope with them, and eventually they recorded the LP, although it was Jimmy Miller who took all the producer credits. Out in Berkshire with Traffic, Guy Stevens couldn't avoid getting into scrapes. A difficult, manic side to his character was beginning to emerge. He took to regularly breaking into a neighbouring cottage and making off with food and drink; Chris Blackwell had to intercede to avoid the police pressing charges. He kept going on binges. He fell asleep in a hotel room and his electric fire burned the hotel down.

In 1967 he took 'A Whiter Shade of Pale' to Chris Blackwell who turned it down. The track slipped through Stevens' hands and ended up being released by a subsidiary of Decca; 'A Whiter Shade of Pale' has gone on to sell more than forty million copies.

1967 was a turning point in the culture, when psychedelia arrived. Ex-Tiles DJs like Jeff Dexter were now running sound and light 'happenings', and psychedelic clubs like UFO on Tottenham Court Road and Middle Earth in Covent Garden were the new hub of the town. Stevens got involved in one of freak rock's most infamous projects, contributing to and producing the 1967 album *Hapshash and the Coloured Coat featuring the Heavenly Host and the Heavy Metals Kids*. Side two, 'Empires of the

Sun', filled the whole length of one side of the vinyl LP, inspired by side four of his beloved *Blonde on Blonde*. An unstructured LSD-inspired trip out, the LP was filled with repeated riffs, vocal chants and bits of percussion.

Around this time, Guy Stevens caught the attention of Patrick-Campbell Lyons of the 1960s group Nirvana, who later recorded a monologue about Stevens called *The Indiscreet Harlequin*. He'd seen Stevens out at various hippy haunts, and then bumped into him at the Island Records office. Stevens, wearing a sheepskin coat and a long rainbow scarf, passed him a joint. One day they went to the Ace café in West Ealing where there was a jukebox full of Prince Buster singles and they got pilled up on black bombers. They ended up in the Limbo club in Soho still dancing at 8 o'clock on Sunday morning.

Generally, DJs didn't play such a key role in the new psychedelic scene; aside from the odd all-nighter in Soho, Guy Stevens and the rest of the cognoscenti were down at the Roundhouse watching Soft Machine. There was a change in the drugs and the music. Out went the sharp, soulful, three-minute songs and in came tripped-out journeys into sound, live bands, dope and acid. At UFO or Middle Earth there were likely to be a few customers engaged in some ungainly dancing, but most of them would crash out, get into the oil wheels and the patterned lights.

Guy Stevens had a bad 1967 and was reported to have suffered a nervous breakdown, partly due to business frustrations like the loss of Procul Harum, but also to the adverse effects of drugs and drink and the loss of his record collection in a break-in at his mother's house. The thief sold the records for ninepence each (less than 4p in our post-decimalisation days). They were priceless to Stevens. The collection included every Muddy Waters record, every Miracles record, every Chess release from 001. His Chuck Berry collection was so complete that some early reissues were cut not from master tapes but from records in Guy Stevens' collection.

Stevens was still working at Island, and soon became involved with another label signing: Free. On the advice of British blues legend Alexis Korner, Free began work with Guy Stevens during the summer of 1968 when they had just begun recording their first LP. Drummer Simon Kirke remembers that the band were experienced at playing live but had little clue how to capture their sound in the studio. Guy Stevens calmed their nerves: 'Guy sensed that we were struggling and he pulled us aside. He told us to relax and just play the two forty-five-minute sets that we had been playing in the clubs. It was ninety-five per cent live. Guy was just zooming about the place, saying, "Great, great"; it was a fabulous vibe.'

The album, *Tons of Sobs* (a title coined by Stevens), was released in November 1968, but Guy Stevens wasn't around to enjoy its relative success. In the summer he'd been arrested for possession of cannabis and sentenced to a year in jail. One of his colleagues at Island, David Betteridge, later explained that 'in those days they nearly shipped you out to Australia for carrying a joint'. While Stevens was in jail he read a book by Willard Manus called *Mott the Hoople*.

At the end of his term he was met at the gates by David Betteridge and he returned to work at Island. Stevens nursed the idea of bringing a band together, a cross between Jerry Lee Lewis and Bob Dylan, something intense, and something using the name Mott the Hoople. He found a group called The Silence but he wasn't happy with the singer so he held some auditions. Ian Hunter, who was working in a factory at the time, turned up, having come from Archway in London expecting just another dodgy demo session. He sang Sonny Bono's

'Laugh at Me' and Bob Dylan's 'Like a Rolling Stone' and Stevens hired him. He asked what the band was called and Stevens told him Mott the Hoople. He went, 'Whaaat? Mott the What?!'

Guitarist Mick Ralphs remembers when they started work on the first LP:

> Guy was good at getting the most out of people in an unconventional way. We'd go into the studio, get drunk, have a huge meal sent in at great expense, all before we'd play a note. Then he'd say, 'Right – let's wreck the studio.' I could see the method in his madness. It was his way of getting people to release their emotions. If there was anything he thought would be artistically viable then he'd go along with it.

Sales of their first album were poor, but Mott the Hoople were a huge success on the live circuit. The personnel were not handling things well, though. For Mott the Hoople, having Guy Stevens as a manager was a liability. On the road, particularly, it was nerve-racking for the band; their manager needed a manager.

Stevens decided to record Mott's second album 'live in the studio', to try to capture the flavour of the gigs. The result, *Mad Shadows*, didn't work out. The session was dominated by the pills he insisted the band take in order to keep awake, and studio time degenerated into all-night boozing and bantering. His belief in capturing artistic passion rather than technical perfection began to weary the group; jams that sounded good at three in the morning sounded a mess in the cold light of day.

His role as a taste maker had drawn him inexorably into the music business, but he lacked the interest to see things through. He was a motivator and an instigator, but he soon got bored and wanted to move on to the next new thing. By 1971 Mott's career was a shambles, and during the recording of another LP Stevens dressed as a highwayman and then attempted to set fire to the studio.

Island boss Chris Blackwell had clearly lost patience: Mott the Hoople left Island, and Guy Stevens disappeared. For Mott there were better times ahead, and they hooked up with David Bowie who helped them to success with some amazing singles, including 'All the Young Dudes'. But for Guy Stevens some dark years followed, from that Mott the Hoople LP through to 1978 (a time he later described as 'a very mixed-up period of my life'). He made a return of sorts when the Clash's manager, Bernie Rhodes, who had been a Scene regular, brought him in for the recording of the LP *London Calling*. Once in the studio it was as if he had one hand on the faders and the other on the self-destruct button; no-one knew which was going to win out in the final mix. The band never thought his contribution was negative or destructive, though – he gave the recordings a looseness and an edge, conjuring extra chaos and noise and channelling it into the music – and always acknowledged he was integral to the huge success of the album on its release. He also steered the Clash towards a far more eclectic sound than they'd pursued in the early punk-thrash phase. The record included a cover version of 'Brand New Cadillac', and 'Train in Vain' provided the band with their first American hit. The LP went on to be declared the best LP of the 1980s by *Rolling Stone* magazine (it came out in 1979, but there you go).

During the recording of the LP he often left the studio comatose, and would then disappear. Once out of the studio, he was having trouble keeping his life together. Patrick-Campbell Lyons was at the launch party held by CBS records for the release of *London Calling*. 'It was obvious to me that Guy did not know where he was, what was happening, nor did he care,' says Lyons. Just before Stevens died he saw him again, and Guy had become a dishevelled figure: 'The last time I saw Guy it was a sad and shocking experience.'

Some of his followers had also had a hard time. In 1967 Pete Meaden was working with Jimmy James & the Vagabonds, and then acid turned his world upside down. He remained on the periphery of the business – he set up the first UK dates for Captain Beefheart – but he died in 1978. A few months earlier he'd said this to interviewer Steve Turner: 'My own feeling is that the debt you have to pay for drugs is too much to compensate for taking the drugs in the first place. I always say don't take any drugs whatsoever. A few smokes, a few beers, speed a little bit now and again, be careful with anything else. That's all.'

Stevens himself died on 29 August 1981. He'd effectively stopped DJ-ing in the mid-1960s, when he moved on from following soul and R&B and embraced psychedelia, but the energy, ideas and influence of the music didn't disappear. Clubbers in the North of England, especially, rejected psychedelia and maintained their passion for soulful sounds, creating the Northern Soul scene. The best disco DJs maintained clubland's devotion to black music from America just as Guy Stevens had brought R&B to the first London DJ-only nights.

The key role of black American music continued as the 1960s turned into the 1970s. Big soul and funk records from Motown and beyond – from Sly & the Family Stone's 'Dance to the Music' (1968) to Stevie Wonder's 'Superstition' (1973) – began winning over a wide constituency of fans. Some of it was heavier – influenced by America's involvement in Vietnam – and some of it crossed right over into the commercial mainstream; acts like the Four Tops, the Temptations and Marvin Gaye were featuring high in the national charts as well as the specialist R&B charts. As the sound of black America became the sound of young America, black British groups also began to have success with dancefloor-oriented records; the mid-1970s would witness chart hits from bands like Hot Chocolate, Sweet Sensation and the Real Thing. Then the Philly Sound began to dominate and DJs entered a new era: disco.

Stevens and Savile never met, and their stories illustrate the difference between paths taken, roads missed. Savile had gone from being an enthusiastic party host in obscure Northern venues to one of the biggest radio and TV personalities of his generation. Guy Stevens was still looking for recognition in the wake of *London Calling*, sixteen years after his DJ-ing career, and throughout much of the intervening period had been skint and on the skids. Yet Guy Stevens was an influential DJ, more so than Savile, possibly not in terms of fashion and image, but certainly in terms of music; his inspiration contributed to the sound and success of some of Britain's greatest bands.

Just as mod went overground and lost its charm for many of the characters who had kickstarted it, so disco lost something too when it went overground. In 1978 disco music was flying in the charts, but the aficionados believed that disco had lost its way; discotheques were booming, but creativity was ebbing away and commerciality and glitz were advancing. Studio 54 in New York had become the quintessential club of the disco era, a night out for the beautiful people, attracting international hype and interest through its door policy and the antics of its favoured celebrity crowd, but the music had been relegated. To the aficionados, Studio 54 and *Saturday Night Fever* had commercialised a culture that had already lost its vitality.

Through all this, dance music had survived and evolved, often hidden away in small clubs; the Scene was one of those intimate, independent places in which dance music has been created, often unheralded. In the early 1970s, similar small-scale venues stimulated the flowering of gay clubbing in New York, as a tentative sense of freedom developed in the city's gay community. Semi-public spaces like nightclubs, bars and bath houses were the perfect venues in these early days of gay liberation; the most notable was probably the Sanctuary, housed in an old Baptist church. Venues like this reflected the way successive generations of clubbers and hedonists have taken possession of unprepossessing, semi-legal, dark, noisy places and created a community and a glimpse of utopia there.

It was left to the underground DJs to keep the faith. Disco had its key spaces, just as R&B had and house would: clubs down a dead end perhaps, or in the basement of some derelict building behind a pub; a place where you could get hold of drugs, hear loud music, feel rhythm-heavy records through your bones. For New York's gay community, clubs were a place of entrenchment, but through the 1970s funky rhythms were casting a spell worldwide and many discos attracted a more pluralist audience than could have been imagined a generation earlier. The perception that the popularisation of dance music was breaking down racial, sexual and social barriers gave the disco movement its idealistic edge, its belief in one nation under a groove.

DJs were making a contribution to disco; support from club DJs was instrumental in launching the careers of artists like Gloria Gaynor and Barry White, for instance, and in New York, DJs like Francis Grasso, David Mancuso at the Loft, Walter Gibbons at Galaxy 21 and Tee Scott at Better Days (and younger characters like Larry Levan and Frankie Knuckles playing to gay crowds at venues like the Continental Baths) spent the 1970s and early 1980s taking the disco sound into new, uncharted territories.

They were the forerunners of a new generation of DJs who created new techniques and new ways of presenting records. If stage one was reached when public demand encouraged nightclub owners and dance hall promoters to dispense with bands and run disc-only nights, then the next stage in the rise and rise of the DJ arrived when DJs started doing without chat and instead concentrated on pioneering new sounds and developing creative ways to play the music, using techniques like cutting and mixing. Francis Grasso, the resident DJ at the Sanctuary, would blend and mix a funky, eclectic selection of Motown, James Brown, Santana, Osibisa, and even Led Zeppelin and the Doors.

There continued to be tension or incomprehension between the mainstream and the mavericks, a gulf revealed by the divergent paths that opened up for Jimmy Savile and Guy Stevens. Without trying, Stevens' career took a route later DJs would also travel: he licensed dance music from America to his label, and moved into production. His death, triggered by an overdose of the prescription drugs he'd been taking to lower his alcohol dependency, was a tragic waste, and means also, I suppose, that he was the forerunner of the DJs who succeeded him who were distracted and derailed by drugs.

The Scene days are now distant memories of a few ex-mods, Ham Yard nothing much more than a car park exit ramp, and Guy Stevens is largely forgotten, despite his pioneering roles as collector, evangelist, record producer and culture creator. He was one of the first superstar DJs, but no-one understood this at the time. You could argue that Guy Stevens was the first underground DJ in Britain, up on things too early to make a killing commercially; he DJ-ed at the Scene when it was barely full. A couple of years after he quit, the DJs at clubs like Tiles were the ones who cashed-in on mod. This was part of another emerging pattern: the way music, over time, moves overground. It would be the same in the house era; you'd see the ripples of interest and excitement spread. You'd have a DJ in a room with some records, then a bunch of people in a scene, then a revolution in music. And sometimes the originators would be forgotten. Ronan O'Rahilly recalls how much Guy Stevens cared about his records: 'He used to carry the records around in a huge trunk, and he was so protective of them that he used to sit on top of it while he DJ-ed. I've seen him sleep on it! It was like a religion to him.'

CHAPTER 4

The Bomb Explodes
Norman Cook, from the Margins to the Mainstream

Fatboy Slim is in Nottingham being interviewed by a crew from regional TV. We're all in an upstairs room at the Bomb – club offices which are doubling as Fatboy Slim's dressing room – watching as the interviewer adjusts her position perched on a desk and waits for a cue. A voice calls from just behind the cameraman, 'Ready everybody. Try it in two.' Then there's silence. Then another voice: 'OK, and, at speed.'

The cameras are rolling and the interviewer, Judy Shekoni, pitches in with her introduction: 'I'm here and I'm with Norman Cook, a.k.a. Fatboy Slim. How's it going?'

Norman Cook has only just arrived. He's been driven from his house in Brighton by his PA Ginger Tim, via London to pick up his manager Garry Blackburn. Also in the party is Gareth Hansome, Norman's mate who organises the Big Beat Boutique nights. They quickly checked-in at the Lace Market Hotel, and then sat down with me for five minutes in the bar with some beers and a bite each of Ginger Tim's sandwich. Norman rooted through his luggage to choose what to wear from a selection of his trademark loud, retro shirts. Then we walked down the hill, 200 yards, no more, to the Bomb.

Norman has the beginnings of a cold. It's nearly midnight, only a few minutes before he plays, and this TV clip is possibly one more interview than he really wants to do today, but he remembers his manners. He smiles back at Judy. 'It's going good, apart from my cold, so sorry if I sound a bit nasally.'

'And you're here at the Bomb. Why the Bomb?'

'James Baillie mainly,' says Norman. James Baillie is the promoter who runs nights at the Bomb, and Norman first met him at a Boy's Own party ten years or so ago. James is an enthusiast and a bit of a caner, with a legendary status in clubland (he started by promoting at nights at Venus in Nottingham); before I went down to Nottingham one industry figure told me that James Baillie has been 'involved in almost everything that's ever been good in Nottingham'. But although James Baillie is a legend in some club circles, he's not yet a household name among the viewers of Central TV. 'He's like a good old boy from the old days,' explains Norman. 'I've got a lot of respect for him. He was responsible for me not playing north of London for five or six years because every time I came to Nottingham I had such a good time that it took a day and a half to get back to Brighton!'

'So have you been promoting all over the world?'

'Yeah, DJ-ing, interviews; "promo" we call it. I've also been getting my photo taken a lot which I don't really like. All the bits of the job I don't especially enjoy. I love making records but I hate trying to sell them to people.'

Halfway Between the Gutter and the Stars, the third LP Norman has released under the name Fatboy Slim, follows 1996's *Better Living Through Chemistry* LP and the 1998 LP *You've Come A Long Way, Baby* which has sold four million copies. His singles in this period all made an impact on the charts, from 'Everybody Needs a 303' to 'Rockafeller Skank' and 'Gangster Trippin'', through 'Praise You', 'Right Here, Right Now', 'Sunset (Bird of Prey)' and 'Demons' with Macy Gray.

Norman is up near number one in all the annual lists, from top DJs to wealthiest people in music. After the success of *You've Come A Long Way, Baby* he was the highest placed DJ in a list of the world's fifty most powerful people in dance music published in *Muzik* magazine. His manager, Garry Blackburn, also featured. Garry tells me Norman's rise to fame has put his label manager and his accountant into the list, too. Since then his success has continued around the world. Sydney, Australia generally, Tokyo and America.

Although he's been a club DJ for nearly twenty years, unlike Sasha it's primarily releasing records that's given Fatboy Slim his status. His involvement in the music-making process – remixing, then producing, originating and putting out records – has put his name in the charts, his face in magazines and his videos on MTV. On the strength of *You've Come A Long Way, Baby*, he was the most successful British artist in America in 1999. It's taken his name out into the wider world, outside just the club magazines. Now he books into hotels under assumed names, including 'Michael Fish' (he says this works well in America because no-one has heard of the TV weatherman over there). According to the *Financial Times*, his annual earnings in 1999 were more than those of any other British pop act ever: six million pounds.

The club DJ fraternity had been tight knit; heroes like Colin Curtis and Norman Jay were known to the cognoscenti, but few names were familiar to the public at large. Norman Cook's name is widely known despite a confusion of identities: he records under the name Fatboy Slim and has had various bands, aliases and projects, from his years with the Housemartins in the mid-1980s, Beats International and Freakpower in the early 1990s, plus solo work under various names – including Pizzaman and Mighty Dub Katz – and his remixes for the likes of the Beastie Boys and Cornershop. As if this isn't enough evidence of shape shifting, he was actually born with the name Quentin, not Norman.

He's reminded of his celebrity status in different ways: being phoned up by Mick Jagger; checking in alongside Brad Pitt and Jennifer Aniston at the Chateau Marmont hotel in Los Angeles; going to TV Awards and joshing with Ricky Martin and Robbie Williams (or, more to the point, going to TV Awards and winning them); being pictured on the front cover of national newspapers (it made news when he dated the TV presenter and radio DJ Zoe Ball, it made news when they married, and it made news when their son, Woody, was born). The newspapers have covered other stories, too, like when Norman endorsed Ken Livingstone as mayoral candidate for London (complete with a photo opportunity at a fundraising club night, with Norman trying to teach Ken, unsuccessfully, how to cue a record). At his home town in Brighton, where he started his music career working behind the counter at Rounder Records, he is now one of the local celebrities, with a bus named after him.

Norman Cook is a hit-making DJ, a one-man band and a one-man brand. He enjoys the good times and the buzz of working, but he also can't escape the grind, doing 'promo', spreading the word, selling. The interview with Central continues, with Norman telling Judy about the one person he'd like to collaborate with ('Sly Stone, but he's kinda not match fit at the moment. I've tried before and his brother said that he was just a little bit unreliable'), and discussing Norman's use of a Jim Morrison sample, taken from a bootleg for 'Bird of Prey'. One or two Doors fans found it sacrilegious, but Norman tells Judy that the best response was from Ray Manzarek of the Doors when he was asked about it. Manzarek explained that the Doors had started writing it in 1967 and had never finished it – Norman had taken the sample from a bootleg of unreleased studio material – and he thanked Norman for finally finishing the track for them.

Norman takes a sip from a McDonald's cup, then quickly puts it down behind his back, aware of the inadvertent product placement. Judy has come up with something neat: 'I read somewhere that Jim Morrison was once quoted as saying that music in the future would be one guy surrounded by electronics. And that's what's happened.'

'Yeah, I heard that, too,' says Norman. And then he tells her about how everyone who's ever worked with Jim Morrison sees his ghost. But he hasn't. Yet.

'Are you going to do another album?' she asks.

'Yeah, of course.'

'What about DJ-ing?'

'DJ-ing I might have to cut back on as I get older, all the late nights and the shenanigans.'

'Can you not keep up?'

'I'm doing all right but every now and then I wake up in the morning and feel about fifty, so the DJ-ing I might have to cut back on. Also, being a father means I've got responsibilities. Making records is fine; I won't stop making records until they fire me, but I'll do the DJ-ing when I can.'

One of the crew is waving her hands about behind the camera, apparently hoping Judy will soon wind the interview up. But there are a few subjects not yet covered. 'How do you feel about having a crowd wanting to see you so much?' asks Judy. 'Do you like being a superstar, a bit of an icon?'

'I kinda do,' says Norman, 'but I try not to take it too seriously. I much prefer being the underdog having a laugh rather than having to live up to being a star. So I'm ambivalent about it.'

'Would you miss it if it wasn't there?'

'I'm sure I would. If it ended tomorrow I would be pining for the old days, when I was famous, when I could get a gig in Nottingham! Me and Zoe have got this scenario about our son when he's fourteen trying to get his head round the fact that once we were famous, "No honestly, we were," because by then our careers will have totally finished.'

'You don't see yourself and Zoe as Posh Spice and Beckham?'

'I hope we're not seen as the same as them, but I'm far too tactful to slag them off!'

'And finally, we've talked about fame, can you explain why is the album called—'

Norman cuts off the end of her sentence. 'You know what?' he says in a soft voice. 'Not again. I'm sure it's apparent. I've spent the last three months explaining it all.'

Norman's doing his best, but he has been plugging *Halfway Between the Gutter and the Stars* for months, and some of the more obvious questions are wearying him.

'Thank you very much, Norman Cook,' says Judy. The interview ends, the filming finishes. Judy hops off the edge of the desk, Norman cradles his coffee cup in his hands, and the researcher tells everybody, 'That was great, fantastic. Thanks.'

Looking at his watch and casting an anxious glance at Norman, Garry asks the crew if they would move downstairs, please, to give Norman some space to get ready. They do, leaving us alone in the room. Tim has found some drinks. Norman says, 'That was strange. My mind kept wandering. Halfway through a sentence I'd be thinking, "What am I doing here?"'

'Don't worry,' I say. 'Your lack of enthusiasm shone through.' They all laugh.

It's only a few minutes to show time and Norman is slightly stressed, on his knees looking through his record boxes, one yellow, one blue, covered with stickers and full of records. Gareth has been downstairs. Norman wants to know what kind of audience it is – heavy or fluffy? He wants to know what they're into.

'It's packed, they're happy, they're awaiting a superstar DJ,' says Gareth.

'Well, this superstar DJ doesn't know what he's doing!' says Norman, scrabbling about, still sorting his tunes out.

Gareth tells him that the DJ who's been playing up until now, Si Begg, is keeping it pumping, on a level, no peaks and troughs. We know it will be bedlam downstairs. 'The crowd are ready for the taking, Si's not unleashed the beast yet!' says Gareth.

It's time to go downstairs, back through the cloakroom and the club to the decks. I'm clutching the yellow box of records, Tim has the blue one; Tim has already told me the yellow one is the heavier of the two, so I'm suffering as we make our way through the cloakroom. We're in a convoy of six, with a doorman leading, then Norman (unencumbered by boxes), then another doorman, then Tim, then me, then a cameraman from Central TV. It's probably only fifty feet from the cloakroom to the DJ area, but there's a huge press of people in our way. The doormen try to slice through the crowd, but it's a squeeze. I can't manoeuvre the box, and it's like carrying a suitcase through a station during rush hour; I keep banging the box into people's knees. The rest of the convoy disappears from sight. The cameraman has given up following us. I'm wobbling and people are getting in my way, but as I pass them they pat me on the back. Finally I hear a big cheer, which I assume means that Norman has reached the decks.

The Bomb isn't big. It's a cellar, archways and a warren of rooms, and it only holds about 500 people in total, a far cry from the big festival gigs and stadium appearances Norman has made in the past; this is raw, intimate and intense. The DJ box is just a booth on the corner of the dancefloor. There's no stage. You simply walk off the dancefloor and into the booth. We put the boxes on the floor behind the decks, then the rest of the convoy heads back to safety and it's just me and Norman. He's sorting his records, I'm at the entrance to the booth with dozens of yelling faces all around. The crowd is pushing right up to the sides of the booth and I have to stand my ground. I'm not exactly sure what his fans would do if they got to him, but it would certainly disrupt his DJ-ing. He has some records, acetates, with phrases, soundbites, many from his songs, and he puts one on – 'Fatboy Slim is fucking in heaven' goes the a cappella. The crowd cheer, and I can sense a girl right behind me getting crushed against my back. A couple of photographers push their cameras into Norman's face and I wave them away. I've suddenly, accidentally, assumed the role of Fatboy Slim's bodyguard. The girl behind me shouts into my ear, 'I hope you're getting paid for this.'

Fortunately reinforcements soon arrive. Two doormen appear and between us we just about form a barrier in front of the booth. People are still pressing against us, though. Someone breaks something off the front of the booth, and a girl nearby starts hyperventilating. It's very hot. It's like the Bay City Rollers have come to town. It's nothing like dance music on TV or on the radio, it's just us packed tight in a dark basement. Like the Scene, that same sweaty sensory overload, an event. Like the Loft, but louder, faster, harder.

We're the heirs to what's gone before. Norman is riding the wave launched by those DJs in New York and in

Britain in the 1970s who reacted against the commercialisation of disco and the fripperies of the personality jocks, who moved away from talking over the records and championed relentless music in stripped down, unsophisticated clubs instead. In that period, pioneering DJs like Francis Grasso developed technical skills, a means to manoeuvre and maintain the energy of the crowd, mixing, blending and chopping the records, building and controlling the momentum. Through their efforts, club DJs were at the heart of the action. On the front-line, they had developed an instinct for what works on a dancefloor.

Guy Stevens had become involved with making and releasing music; sound system operators like Duke Reid had put big Jamaican records out in the early 1960s, and there'd always been special one-off dub plates in reggae circles; radio DJs had released singles (Jimmy Savile had released 'Ahab the Arab' – one of the more unfortunate episodes in the history of recorded music – and Tony Blackburn had recorded a Northern Soul cover called 'I'd Do Anything'), but in the mid-1970s the pioneering New York DJs were clearly gaining influence in predicting and creating hit records. They represented the future, and record companies recognised their growing power and began to give them a role remixing. Remixing grew directly out of the new working practices, the way someone like DJ David Mancuso would link two copies of the same record to make an extended version, blending them, mixing, or dropping the percussive section of one record into a break of another. DJs were changing the way music was listened to and recorded.

In this era of free-form dancefloor dynamics, the days of the three-minute dance record were ending. Motown seven-inch singles were being replaced as the standard tool of the DJ by extended disco re-edits and megamixes;

groups themselves recorded versions that would ride
the dancefloor groove ('Disco Inferno' by the Trammps
clocked in at a majestic eleven minutes). It was the arrival
of the twelve-inch single format in the mid-1970s which
boosted demand from record labels for elongated disco
mixes of favoured songs, commissioned not from the
artists themselves but from DJs like Tom Moulton, Walter
Gibbons and Larry Levan.

For these New York DJs playing underground disco
in the hardcore gay clubs, DJ-ing was already more than
just playing one record after another, but it was the
contribution of a different set of DJs, in the Bronx in the
mid-1970s, which did most to establish the creative new
future for DJs. The first hip hop DJs – like the experimental DJs at the gay clubs – were part of an isolated, hardcore culture away from the glitz of Manhattan disco
palaces like Studio 54 and the commercialism evident in
the success of *Saturday Night Fever*. Like the DJs in the
gay disco clubs, the hip hop DJs were trying to stay one
step ahead of the mainstream, steer a way into a new
post-disco era, introducing hundreds of new ideas into
the role of the DJ: a more active attitude to the decks,
mastery of the vinyl.

At block parties, house parties, old dance halls and
a host of dodgy venues, early hip hop DJs like Grandmaster Flash, Kool Herc and Afrika Bambaataa generated
a sense of discovery and excitement, developing various
techniques – back spinning, cutting and scratching, for
example – to radically alter the sounds of the records as
they were being played. Unlike the experimental DJs at
the New York gay clubs, the hip hop DJs weren't so much
into mixing and blending; instead they destroyed in order
to create, breaking down records and remoulding them.
The key development was the way they homed in on the
instrumental core of a song, a few bars of sax or a funky

drum pattern; these bits were what musicians called the 'breakdowns', shortened to the 'breaks'. They began cutting between two copies of the same record, repeating the break. This is what the hip hop crowd wanted to hear, and it was how they got their name: breakdancers. It was like cut and paste, cut and paste. A DJ was now the pilot and the engine, no longer passive. The days of waiting for the records to drop on the Dansette were long gone.

At the start of the 1980s, a number of DJs in Britain were beginning to feel the influence of New York and to move away from the 1970s DJ cliché, to take advantage of new technology – the arrival of Technics decks which had an instant stop-start facility, and the ability to speed up, slow down and match the beats of the records playing on any two decks, thereby making mixing possible. Down in the South of England, a DJ called Froggy was foremost among the DJs who popularised mixing, at clubs like the Regency Suite in Chadwell Heath in Essex. In the North hip hop and electro began to inspire DJs like Greg Wilson and Chad Jackson.

Chad Jackson grew up in St Helens and by the early 1980s had progressed from being a fan, a dancer and a collector to getting decks and beginning to work mobile and in clubs. This was just as the culture was changing; he was doing a lot of mixing and interspersing it with a little bit of chat: 'I thought that all the people should get is the music. I used to hate being surrounded by all these other DJs who were doing all that chatting and joking, and they seemed to like the sound of their own voice more than the music. At that time mixing wasn't very prevalent and if you mixed in the clubs and didn't talk on the mic then you were liable to lose your job. And that's what happened to me on more than one occasion.'

These changes in British clubs didn't happen overnight. There was an old guard – there's always an old guard – who didn't approve of what the new generation of DJs was doing. Despite the changes and innovations, the old ways have never quite died out. Out there in high street clubs and small town discos there's a commercial club world that's been unaffected by the transformations in club culture over the last fifteen years; it's hard to believe that back in the early 1980s, though, it was almost all that was on offer in most town centres. Back then most clubs had carpets on the floor, talking DJs and a dress code. The dress code for men stipulated a tie. And white socks and black shoes. And, it seemed, a moustache. But it wasn't as if the clubs were particularly good when you got in; usually they were less about being lost in music, more about being pissed on lager.

There was a new generation of DJs and clubbers who didn't want to be mainstream. These more obscure clubs had all the good ideas, and housed the people who would go on to frequent the first house clubs: the gay dance fraternity, the black jazz funkers, the soul heads and the New Order fans. If you were lucky, you might be in a town where there were people who had developed some alternative spaces, in hired halls, midweek. When it opened in 1982 the Haçienda was the only club in Manchester that would let me in. The culture was beginning to change, and in most of the best clubs in the North of England dress codes were out, music was in. 'Thank God it changed,' says Chad Jackson, who became a resident DJ at the Haçienda in the mid-1980s. Down in London, clubs like the Wag continued to have picky, exclusive door policies, but everything opened up in the acid house era. So much so, in fact, that it became hard to sort out the devotees from the tourists; by 1994, 'Golden' in Stoke was rumoured to have put on its flyers: 'No moustaches'.

By then, the changes, the new ways of doing things, the transformation in the mechanics of making music and the notion of the remix were slowly being accepted. It wouldn't be long before DJs remixed rock records for the disco crowd and indie records for ravers, before Paul Oakenfold remixed Happy Mondays, Andrew Weatherall turned Primal Scream's 'I'm Losing More Than I'll Ever Have' into 'Loaded' and before Norman Cook's remix of 'Brimful of Asha' by Cornershop went to number one. From DJs remixing, it was only a small step to DJs making records of their own.

The new DJs didn't suddenly break through into musicmaking. Hip hop DJs were making records by 1979, but even then it was three or four years after they had established themselves in venues in their own neighbourhoods. Among the pioneers, Kool Herc missed out on commercial success, but Grandmaster Flash released several successful records, among them, of course, 'The Adventures of Grandmaster Flash on the Wheels of Steel'.

'Adventures on the Wheels of Steel' put down on record what you could only have heard if you'd gone to a block party in the Bronx; according to David Toop it's 'as close as any record would ever come to *being* hip hop'. Hip hop was rooted in the DJ cutting up records, and once it reached the studio it kept that spirit – Grandmaster Flash used breaks and bits from Queen, Chic, Blondie, Richard Pryor, Spoonie Gee and the Sugarhill Gang on that classic track – but soon the emphasis changed, and the recording and marketing of the records began to focus on the rapper.

Throughout the 1980s and beyond, hip hop DJs were raiding records from the past, searching in their crates for new breaks, for bits of songs nobody else was using. Drum breaks from records by James Brown or releases on Stax or Blue Note were the staple diet of the DJs, but less obvious tracks also provided hip hop with some of its most well-used breaks, like Thin Lizzy's 'Johnny the Fox

Meets Jimmy the Weed', for instance, and a 1973 version of a song made famous by the Shadows ('Apache' by Michael Viner's Incredible Bongo Band).

Then came the sampler, a piece of computer equipment that built on what DJs were doing live on the decks; it could chop and repeat breaks, store, change and regurgitate riffs, notes, drum patterns, snare sounds, voices, horn blasts. Samplers have since become a key piece of equipment for musicmakers of all kinds – from the KLF to EPMD, Photek to Tupac, St Germain to Will Smith – and breaks – looped or fractured – have become the building blocks for most recorded music.

In a curious tug-of-war, dance music in the last fifteen years has introduced new sounds and noises, but at other times also mercilessly recycled old sounds: cover versions of old soul records by artists like Barbara Mason and Thelma Houston have appeared, funk and rare groove breaks are everywhere, and, in recent years, disco sounds have been sampled and filtered by the likes of DJ Sneak, Ian Pooley and Bob Sinclar. In some instances, this has appeared to obliterate the past, but has also resurrected careers; Bob Sinclar's 'I Feel For You' sampled a loop from Cerrone and led to a collaboration between the two. In the 1970s, says Sinclar, 'All the art, the music, the film, the design was really ground breaking. We take everything from this period because everything is a cycle.'

Norman Cook has used samples from many and varied sources, including 'Sliced Tomatoes' by the Just Brothers on 'Rockafeller Skank', the Who on 'Going Out of My Head', Joe Walsh on 'Right Here, Right Now', Camille Yarbrough on 'Praise You', Bill Withers on 'Demons', and Colosseum and Doug Lazy on 'Ya Mama'. He doesn't loot ignorantly. Like Guy Stevens, he's a collector, a fan (on the cover of 'Praise You' there's a photograph of shelves bending with the weight of Norman's record collection).

He knows and reveres his music (for Christmas 1999 Zoe gave him a jukebox stocked with Northern Soul singles from Manchester's Beatin Rhythm record shop). Once I told him I had a 1976 footstompin', hipshakin' disco mix LP by the Emperor Rosko. 'Oh, right,' he told me, 'I've got all four.'

Samplers made the recording process cheaper and, to some extent, easier. That it was now possible to create a hit song by putting together somebody else's drum pattern, a stolen voice, and notes and sounds from other records, however, was controversial. There were copyright issues, of course, but most opposition to the sampler came from traditionalists disturbed that technical mastery of the basic pop instruments – guitar, drums, bass and piano – was now a thing of the past. Samplers, computer technology in general, opened up music-making, created what writer Kodwo Eshun calls 'new sonic territories'. These innovations brought down the barriers to entry-level musicmaking and reinstated punk's call to create – 'here's a guitar, here's a drum kit, now make a band' – with a new emphasis: 'here's a turntable, here's a sampler, now make a record'. Samplers also unleashed the creativity of dozens of individuals who would never have made music with bands, and brought into existence that scenario prophesied by Jim Morrison: the solo musicmaker alone with his machines.

In the time-lags, the slow revolutions and reactions in popular culture, this new era of mixing, sampling, hip hop and remixing, and these new kinds of music and new kinds of DJ-ing filtered into the mainstream slowly. As the 1980s progressed, it went overground via the success of records which exploited the novelty of samplers – like Steinski & Mass Media's 'We'll Be Right Back' – and other records which did a whole lot more – the sonic assault and civil rights sensibilities of Public Enemy, and the ripped and torn hip hop of the Beastie Boys. Hip hop broke the door down, and the rave era burst in.

House music evolved out of disco and relied on the same basic 4/4 beat. It had its roots among the clubs and DJs that eschewed the mainstream sell-out of the disco era, especially Larry Levan, the DJ at the Paradise Garage in New York. The Paradise Garage thrived under his direction during but also after the disco boom, and Levan himself has since become mythologised; he died in 1992 but there are Levan worshippers almost anyplace you can find two decks and half a crowd. He had started out playing gay venues in New York, and, inspired by the Loft, especially early in his career, Levan was an eclectic DJ, playing Grace Jones and Talking Heads records in a set alongside Salsoul and Philly, but the beat was everything. There was a relentlessness and repetition built into the way Levan played. He plugged into the energy on the dancefloor and conjured music for the body and the soul.

House was relentless rhythmic music driven by emotion, but it took different forms in different cities. In New York it drew on the past, especially the Philly sound, and the feel and rhythms of some of the better New York disco labels like Salsoul, and also used vocals with a gospel influence. But house music also soundtracked the future; music-makers pioneered that branch of house music which would best be called 'techno', drew on hip hop breakbeats and electro, and European electronic bands like Kraftwerk. In Detroit, for example, Kevin Saunderson, Juan Atkins and Derrick May introduced a new stripped-down sound, reacted against soul and gospel which had soundtracked Detroit in previous eras, and distilled the music to pure rhythm and twisting noise.

In Britain, DJs were quick to pick up on this post-disco music from New York, Detroit and Chicago, especially those who had been following black American music for some time and were in the habit of buying imports. The first wave of interest in house music was DJ-led, by people like Pete Tong, who began licensing Chicago 'jacking' records to the London label, and Neil Rushton, an ex-Northern Soul DJ whose Network Label (based in Birmingham) supported the Detroit techno generation; Paul Oakenfold already had links with American labels through his work PR-ing Profile and Def Jam. Other DJs working in record shops made sure imports were readily available. House music wasn't being played on the radio, so you tracked it down to certain record shops and certain DJs in clubs: Mike Pickering, Graeme Park, Jazzy M, Danny Rampling, Paul Oakenfold and Jon Da Silva.

In Britain the acid house era felt new, but it also built on what had gone before; the devotion to all-night clubbing owed something to the Northern Soul scene, and the adventurous demand for import records echoed the early Soho R&B clubs. Its uniqueness lay in the textures of the computer-generated music and the high visibility of ecstasy in the clubs, warehouse parties and illegal raves. House music spread as the drugs spread. For some on the scene, the drug was their way in; ecstasy increased the attraction of the music. In 1990 Norman Cook's Beats International had a hit record with 'Dub Be Good to Me'. He had remained oblivious to the charms of acid house, but he started going to Boy's Own parties and there he heard DJs like Darren Emerson; he soon fell under the spell, and began wearing his smiley badge with pride.

The proliferation of DJ remixes and hit singles stemming from this period was a key reason why DJs reached out of the clubs and into the mainstream. There were landmark records from the mid-1980s onwards, records which boosted the profile and credibility of DJs. Soul II Soul grew out of Jah Rico, a London sound system operating around Finsbury Park, and was fronted by the charismatic DJ Jazzie B. Having made dub plates for the exclusive use of the sound system, the group was signed by Mick Clarke at Virgin in 1988. After a single, 'Fairplay', in May of that year, they had three massive singles in 1989 – 'Keep on Movin'', 'Back to Life' and 'Get a Life' – and chart success in Britain and America with the LP *Club Classics vol. 1*.

Soul II Soul were a collective fronted by a DJ, but individual DJs were credited with a rapidly increasing number of hits. The sampler, sequencer and computer set-up had simplified music-making, and DJs were at the front of the queue to take advantage. Many of these early tracks by British DJs were hip hop flavoured cut-ups; CJ Mackintosh helped put together the landmark record 'Pump Up The Volume' by MARRS; Tim Simenon, a DJ at the Wag club, had a hit with 'Beat Dis' under the name Bomb the Bass; Cold Cut released 'Beats & Pieces' – raw cut-ups of rare groove and funk riffs – and then remixed hit singles for Eric B & Rakim; Mark Moore of S-Express and Chad Jackson had hits. The Haçienda's Mike Pickering started T-Coy, an influential British Latin-house group. DJs making records were no longer novelty acts; they were hit-makers.

In that *Mixmag* front cover feature of 1994, Dom Phillips praised Sasha's technical skills, especially his mixing ('at times stunning'), but concentrated on his remixes and his single 'Higher Ground' which had just been released. This was the big difference since the 1991 feature: Sasha was now a music-maker. In 1991 he was a rumour, a DJ few had heard or seen – he hadn't even set foot in a recording studio – but by 1994 he was beginning to be known for his records, as an artist. He couldn't DJ everywhere, so his mix CDs, records and remixes took him to a wider audience.

Back then, though – and this was true up to 1995 or 1996 – DJs tended to have success with one-offs. Now they're building careers, keeping the hit-making going, and recording LPs: Sonique, Paul van Dyk, the Chemical Brothers, Basement Jaxx and Fatboy Slim. Sonique first became involved in dance music in 1990 when she met Mark Moore in a club and he asked her to audition for S-Express, and she sang and co-wrote hits like 'Find 'Em, Fool 'Em, Forget 'Em' and 'Nothing to Lose'. She started DJ-ing in 1994 when S-Express had come to an end, and practised at home for years until she ventured onto the decks. Her singing instincts took over, and she began to sing over the top of the records. In 1998 she released 'It Feels So Good', but it didn't do particularly well until a DJ in Florida started playing it and a buzz began Stateside. Eventually the single got to number five in the Billboard chart and to number one in Britain. When it came to promoting the single and the LP *Hear My Cry*, Sonique was on TV and radio with other pop acts.

In Nottingham, Norman's driver is nowhere to be seen. It's still just me and Norman, and I'm still standing guard around the outside edge of the DJ box alongside two doormen. There have been waves of overexuberance, and although the situation has calmed a little, there's still a press of bodies all around us. One of the girls behind me catches the eye of a lad twenty feet away and manages to blag a cigarette from him purely by sign language. The cigarette is passed along the front of the DJ box. Then a bucket of ice appears, coming over the heads of the crowd. I grab it and put it down on the floor behind the decks. There's not really any other place for it to go, but Norman falls over it. I move the bucket, but he nearly trips over it again. He looks down at the bucket, then at me. 'What am I supposed to do with this?' he asks.

We're joined in the DJ booth, our cramped, noisy,

pressure-cooker corner of the room, by a newcomer. I'm
on Norman's left, the newcomer is on Norman's right,
near the lighting controls. He throws the strobe switch
on and starts conducting the crowd in cheering, clapping
and shouting. He sweats, grins and encourages the
audience. When Norman's set finally ends – at around
2.30 – the capering, grinning strobe addict introduces
himself to me. It's James Baillie.

Norman gets straight off, propelled through the crowd
by the doormen. We pack away the boxes, and Si Begg
takes Norman's blue one as well as his own. Norman is
now upstairs, back in the dressing room; later he tells me
that some lads were making themselves at home in there
and started shouting 'Fatboy, fuck off!' when he got up
there. He and Gareth walked away, sat in a corner waiting
for the lads to leave. Later, I'm pleased to say, he also tells
me that one of the doormen confided this to him: 'Your
minder was good.'

The crowd disperse quickly after Norman's retreat,
and I stand talking to somebody who works at the Lace
Market Hotel who claims to have made Ginger Tim's ham
sandwich earlier in the evening. Once I get back upstairs,
Tim is there with Norman's yellow box. He asks me if I've
got the other one. I haven't. The room is suddenly thrown
into chaos. Norman and Tim panic. I am adamant that Si
Begg had it, but no-one can raise him on his mobile to
check, so we decide to leave for the hotel immediately
to see if Si does have it in safe custody. I walk back up the
hill carrying the yellow box. The heavy one.

James Baillie is with us, and two doormen also accompany us. Fortunately Si Begg is sitting in the bar, with
Norman's blue box, and without a care in the world. Tim
grabs the box and takes it upstairs to Norman's room.
Everyone gathers in the bar and gets some drinks in, but I
persuade Norman to leave so we can do a quick interview

in his room. We've met a few times before. Once when the Housemartins were recording in Stockport, I invited him over to the Haçienda to play a set with me – I think that must have been 1987 – and he also came up to play at one of my nights in Manchester, 'Yellow' at the Board-walk, in 1992. We have talked on the phone a few times, but I haven't spoken to him properly since 1995.

We were reminding each other of these various moments and talking about what he'd said about working with Macy Gray after being used to just a sampler and computers, and I'm thinking about him DJ-ing, the way he throws everything in – another noise, more sounds. With Norman Cook, it's not a controlled or linear style of DJ-ing, but explosions of sound, and his music-making is similar. Most post-sampler dance music eschews verses and choruses, and works as a collage of sounds. Samplers and computers have not only removed any responsi-bility to be diplomatic, but have led to a different kind of music-making.

'Yeah,' Norman nods, 'I just plug in my PC and I'm away. But the whole thing to remember about technology is that in the right hands it's a wonderful thing, but a kid with a sampler who hasn't got any imagination is just like a kid with a Telecaster who still plays "Smoke on the Water" and "Johnny B Goode".'

Norman is talking quite slowly. We both are. It's late. Norman asks me how to pronounce Wyclef Jean's second name.

'Jean,' I say. 'Like Jean Paul Sartre.'

He tells me about a TV programme he saw at the week-end, *Later with Jools Holland*: 'Wyclef Jean was on, and he was second to last on, and there's this big build up and then he goes and does this rock & roll medley. I was think-ing, is this ironic? It wasn't. And there was Jools Holland jamming along to "Long Tall Sally" and him and Wyclef

Jean doing that rock & roll medley thing that I thought was dead and buried.' Norman says that if he ever got invited on, he would have to stipulate that Jools stayed offstage. 'I would be like "All right then, I'll go on there but please will Jools not jam along doing boogie woogie piano".'

I try to steer the conversation back to Norman's career. I run through the potted biography – being a DJ in Brighton playing funk when he was in the Housemartins, his conversion to acid house in 1990, his great one-off singles like Pizzaman's 'Sex on the Streets' in 1995 – and wonder how he's not just survived, but thrived. I'm sure he's too modest to claim to be talented.

'I think I put it down to luck and perseverance. I mean, you must admit I've landed on my feet so many times. You know me and you know that I'm into it and I'm doing it for all the right reasons, but I do have this knack of landing on my feet.'

Why do you think that is?

'There are so many people who believed in the same thing and did the same things and never got lucky and never made it. I figure luck has had a big part to play.'

Do you think it might also have to do with your willingness to change?

'If there's a reason I've done well it's because I never did the thing that was of the moment, the latest thing. I've never jumped on the bandwagon. In fact, I've always tried to be on the last bandwagon or the last but one band-wagon, and I've figured that cycles would turn and in a couple of years it would all come round again.'

You've never tried to be up with the latest thing?

'I always think that if I tried to play the game I'd lose so I have to play a different game. I can't compete trying to be on it; if you try to do what everyone else is doing you've got to do it better than them. If you do something that's not quite right but interesting then you have a chance. I enjoy being the wrong 'un. But at the end of it I've figured that being the wrong 'un might just be the thing that attracts people's attention. If you do what everyone is doing it might not get you noticed.'

You told the TV interviewer that you're more comfortable being the underdog than the pop star.

'I'm the strange one, the weird one.'

I disagree with him, because I don't think he's that strange. I think he's weird only in a way people can identify with: he's human. In a DJ culture full of braggarts and blaggers, he doesn't come across like a precious superstar. He makes mistakes; he doesn't pretend to be infallible.

'I don't know. The only thing I know is that the only way to get noticed is to do something different. But, yeah, at the same time, it's about common decency as well, being nice to people. In America, even when we were really off our nut, we were still being really polite to people even when we're absolutely caned. We'd get in a car and ask, "Excuse me, sir, do you mind if I smoke?"'

And tonight, after your set when those guys invaded your dressing room, you just walked away?

'That's right. I was brought up as a pacifist so I've got this whole thing about being nice to people even if you're in a real mood and everyone's getting tense. We weren't going to make waves. It's that thing about turning the other cheek. If you're dealing with an idiot the best way to win is not to react.'

Is getting recognised a downside to your success?

'It's the best job on earth, so it's not for me to come over all tortured. There are some things you can't do, but on the whole people are quite nice to me and Zoe. Sometimes clubs are bad because you get people off their nut. When people are straight it's OK because they don't come bounding up to you, you can just hear whispers and feel fingers pointing at you and you have this sixth sense about it. But when people are off their nut in a club they jump about and shout and get you in a headlock and start pointing at you and shouting at their friends, "Look look!"'

Norman Cook is drinking vodka long after I've moved on to water. His excesses are well known; in 1999 he talked to *Heat* magazine about his cocaine use. In the 'Manumission' movie he's interviewed outside Space at four o'clock one Sunday afternoon looking very much the worse for wear, and only slightly intelligible, saying things like 'It's all gone right off, and it hasn't come back.'

He's got a reputation for excess, but then he's not the only one. DJ Brandon Block has won awards for his uncontrolled partying; dictionary compilers please note, he was also the person who invented the phrase 'largin' it'. And lived it. In 1993 he ran a Sunday night called 'FUBAR' (Fucked Up Beyond All Recognition). In 1996 he left Ibiza early and later that year checked into rehab to deal with his drug addiction. His DJ-ing is less bothered, less precious and less serious than many DJ superstars, but his fans are devoted, revelling in his antics: picking fights with Ronnie Wood and flicking v-signs on TV, falling out of boats, missing planes. He's the self-confessed biggest nutter in the world, though obviously not the hairiest cornflake.

It's hard to DJ stone cold straight and sober because at some point you need to feel in harmony with your audience, on the same wavelength; and the chances of them being stone cold straight and sober are non-existent. DJ-ing stone cold straight and sober is like trying to triple jump without a run up, but it's even harder to DJ when you're off your head – you lose your legs, lose the plot, lose your career. Cocaine seems to give DJs an exaggerated sense of their talent, and alcohol renders them senseless. DJ Derek Dahlarge has been hanging around at

'Manumission' in full-on party mode for so long that *Mixmag* has declared that he appears to 'have given up DJ-ing entirely in favour of a full-time position as "freak of nature"'. Dahlarge, on the other hand, does his best to dispel the myth that his hectic partying and nightmare hangovers cause him to miss his plane: 'It's not true. I just choose not to get on some.'

Philandering, drink binges and drug sessions don't have to be part of the lifestyle, but in true Brits abroad style, DJs often save their wildest behaviour for Ibiza. Others don't appear to be so locked into largin' it. Paul van Dyk, Pete Tong, Paul Oakenfold; they all seem more intent on looking after their careers and themselves.

Despite Norman's far from sober reputation, he's actually only once been too out of his head to DJ, and that was at a friend's wedding. It reminds me of my forthcoming date in Jersey and I ask him to tell me more. Apparently, the wedding was fancy dress, and Norman was dressed as a bumble bee: 'We walked through the town afterwards to the reception, and we'd done tons of acid. I ended up at the decks and I couldn't see them or work it out, like which record was playing and how it worked. What's the record? Who's that? That's the only time I've ever lost it.'

That's not bad considering the number of man hours on the decks and opportunities you've had to wobble.

He thinks about it. 'I've had so many times when I've been somewhere and I couldn't talk or walk, but when it's time to DJ it comes from inside. I've DJ-ed off my nut and it's gone really well and then at the end I've finished and I'm trying to talk to people and I'm walking into walls. While you're playing you don't realise you're twatted. Maybe it's some kind of self-preservation.'

Norman also DJ-ed at his sister's wedding, although the bulk of the entertainment was provided by his uncle

Denis. Denis was in pop bands in the early 1970s, and was a DJ then, too: 'His band used to rehearse in my nan's living room. When I was a kid I was convinced that they were the Beatles because I'd hear them rehearsing and they'd be doing Beatles songs and then I'd hear the Beatles on the radio and I told everyone at school it was my uncle's band! He was my guiding light. My parents used to say if I didn't watch out I'd end up like uncle Denis and I was like "Bring it on, Mum, bring it on!!"'

Did he make it as a DJ?

'Not really, but DJ-ing was new then. Now he's fifty and a double glazing salesman but he still does karaoke nights, and he's got this band and they do Dire Straits cover versions.'

Norman is into karaoke, although it was one band-wagon he managed to jump on before it was even a bandwagon. After the demise of the Housemartins he hosted the Norman Cook International Roadshow, with Billy Bragg and the Frank Chickens, which involved doing karaoke. If you ever want to get him crooning, by the way, his speciality is Charlie Rich's 'The Most Beautiful Girl'.

His enthusiasm for karaoke in the mid-1980s wasn't ironic: 'In those days, it was a weird, wonderful, cool, new Japanese thing to do, but then it became the domain of drunk idiots and then it got really hi-tech as well. When we did it it was just cassettes of really bad backing tapes; now they've video screens and subtitles. Anyway my uncle still does that as a hobby and he does it really well.'

Norman pauses. 'Where was I?'

Your sister's wedding.

'Yeah. Anyway, he was doing the entertainment for the wedding, and my sister asked me if I could play a few records and I didn't really want to, to be honest, but she's like "It's my wedding, tons of my mates from work will be there and it would be nice if they knew Fatboy Slim was going to be DJ-ing," so with three days to go I agreed, but under duress.'

On the morning of the wedding someone just happened to mention to Norman that the DJ equipment was set up for CDs only, which sent him into a mad panic; he usually only works off vinyl. So he and Zoe hunted around for some CDs, any CDs – a 1960s compilation, Blondie's greatest hits – and made their way there. The wedding ceremony was at midday but Norman didn't start playing until midnight, by which time he was just a little bit drunk. And he'd never DJ-ed using CD mixers before. It was a nightmare: 'It's a whole different kettle of fish, the whole way it works is completely different. I was absolutely useless! I was doing stuff like switching off the track that was playing. In fact, at one point I switched the power off completely. After half an hour people were shouting at me "Call yourself a DJ!"'

What was your problem – using the pause button?

'I don't know, I don't know if I got that far! When a track is playing you can't see it; with vinyl I'm always looking at the record that's playing, where the breaks are and how long you've got to go, but with a CD mixer you can't see anything. Is it cued up? Is it going to play the right track? I don't know!'

His confusion in the face of a CD mixer sounds typically Fatboy. Despite his use of samplers and computers in his music-making he doesn't trust technology, and doesn't have an email address. He's no gadget freak. On one occasion *Future Music* magazine, a specialist mag for techno boffins, invited themselves to watch him at work in the studio. They saw Norman using his old-fashioned Atari computer to programme his sounds and assumed he was having a laugh. He wasn't: 'That's what I use. They couldn't believe it. They said, "We heard you were old school but this is just wilfully old school."'

He never feels totally comfortable and at ease on the decks because he knows things can go wrong: 'Daft things like when you're doing a really big gig and there's too many people there and the decks start jogging and you can't calm the crowd down.'

Once at the Glastonbury Festival Norman temporarily lost all his records. The site was very muddy and, unable to carry the boxes through the mud, he'd put them in the back of a Land Rover which then got called away on an emergency. The next thing he knew, he was being told he was due on in five minutes: 'I was trying to explain that I hadn't got my records! I could be the best DJ in the world but without my records I am nothing! I've been DJ-ing for so many years; how stupid is it to be not with your records at the right time. The easiest bit of DJ-ing is just to turn up with your records.'

His records arrived fifteen minutes after he was meant to go on, but that episode explains why he got freaked out earlier when Si Begg had his blue box. Ever since that Glastonbury, Norman and Tim have this rule that they won't let the boxes out of their sight; they have to know where they are. He has learned his lessons: 'There are only three things about being professional as a DJ – make sure you turn up with your records, don't fall to bits before you play, and don't be rude to people.'

Norman thinks for a moment about times he's broken that last rule: 'I once snapped at "Cream" when there was this kid standing at the front trying to shake my hand, and every time I looked up he shook my hand. I'd already shaken his hand maybe three times, and then he reaches over again and his hand knocks the tone arm and knocks it off the record, and the music stops. I lost it then. And sometimes I've lost it with people down the front throwing things at me. It wasn't like that tonight.'

We talk about crowds, and how, rarely but scarily, you can have the odd person who's so mashed-up they can be a danger to themselves or everyone else. Norman talks about sometimes trying to reason with people: 'You can get some idiot who just doesn't understand what I'm trying to do, that all I'm trying to do is work the records and connect with the crowd and give everyone a great night, but what you're actually doing is making it hard for me and ruining it for anybody else, throwing stuff, or just making it difficult for me to DJ.'

When you do some of your big gigs in America you scribble messages to the audience and they get projected onto a screen; are you ever tempted to get on the microphone?

'I think it's OK just to shout at people, people down the front, but not get on the mic. The other day in Paris the crowd were just standing watching me like I was a band, and they weren't moving so I was shouting at them, "Come on you fuckers! Don't stare; dance", but that was just random shouting because I was frustrated. Your job as a DJ is to be able to communicate without microphones.'

It would be cheating?

'Yeah. I think defeat would be to actually have to talk to them. You should be able to communicate with them by the records you play.'

So how does that work do you think?

'Sometimes when it's getting a bit out of hand, like tonight, hot and a bit packed, instead of getting on the mic and asking them just to calm down and hold on a bit, you calm them down through your records. A good DJ can go in lots of directions, he can say, right, now we're going to go nuts, now we're going to calm down a bit, now we're going to go really nuts, now I'm going to finish. I think the start and the end are really important. There's no need to get on the mic; you can communicate without resorting to talking.'

He can only recall a couple of times when he used a microphone, including when he was at Woodstock in 1999. There were thousands of people there, and things were getting out of hand during his set, then somebody drove a van into the middle of the crowd. Some people climbed on top of the van and it looked like it would topple over and crush the people next to it. Norman had to stop playing and plead with everyone to get down. Later, just after he had left the site, Woodstock degenerated into fights and fires all over the field; his dressing room was burnt down.

We talk for a while about America. Although America got sick of DJs in the disco days and the mainstream has never accepted them again, this may be changing. At the beginning of the house era, people like Kevin Saunderson were unknown or marginalised in Detroit; New York DJs like Tony Humphries and Todd Terry got far more attention in Britain than they had back home. In America acid house had never happened; there were big r&b and rap industries, but no big mainstream club magazines, house music stars or widespread acceptance of computer-generated music. There was also no big ecstasy scene.

In the mid-1990s British acts – generally the ones who'd managed to fuse dance music with rock sensibilities, like Prodigy and the Chemical Brothers – began to break through with college kids, techno heads, fashion followers. The work of American artists like BT, Richie Hawtin and the Hardkiss label began reaching parts of the country that the early house music pioneers never had: Florida, California, Canada. Carl Cox and Fatboy Slim began playing to big crowds Stateside. Sonique had a hit, then another. Sasha's gigs at Twilo caught the imagination of New York. America also began to get turned on to ecstasy.

If the American club scene has the pioneers, Britain seems to have the passion. It's a worldwide phenomenon, but it's in Britain that DJ culture has the strongest hold in the world. Norman likes the travelling, and admits he's always up for a gig in some glamorous location like Japan or Australia, but that gigs in Britain usually turn out to be more fun: 'This country is the best. I've just spent two months doing America, Australia and Europe and last weekend I was in England again, and actually people in England just get it so much more, and you feel at home and it's so much better here, but then there isn't the glamour here to compare with going to places like Las Vegas.'

Are you saying that Nottingham isn't glamorous?

'Yes! If it's between travelling to Sheffield or Tokyo then you want to go to Tokyo, but the crowds in Sheffield will be better, and the crowds in Nottingham will be better.'

I finally pull myself away from Fatboy Slim's room at the Lace Market, say goodbye, shake his hand, wish him luck – more luck – and walk back to my tatty hotel across town, just before dawn, with the council rubbish vans touring the main streets. You never can say goodbye to Norman Cook, though; he's part of that inescapable soundtrack. Al Gore used 'Praise You' during his bid to become American President, football teams run onto the pitch to the sound of 'Right Here, Right Now', and Fatboy can be heard on a TV advertisement for the Halifax's Internet account; Zoe advertised Egg (the Prudential's Internet-only bank) so Woody is no doubt open to offers, too.

You also know that Norman Cook will be back, with

more Fatboy Slim, or perhaps in some other guise. And he will still be slightly dippy, never too polished. That night at the Bomb, Norman DJ-ing, the crowd bouncing and baying at him, was under control, but only just. There was noise, unpredictability and huge, barely checked energy. That's how it should be on the frontline of DJ-ing: you're never quite sure what will happen next.

The maelstrom at the Bomb was a clear example of the DJ as a star, but it also reinforced my belief in how much the crowd matters; a good night out is a two-way collaboration, with the DJ focusing and manipulating the energy of the crowd, teasing noise, reactions and emotions out of them. A DJ without a crowd is just someone with some records.

My night at the Bomb also reinforced my belief that small clubs are the scene's lifeblood. In the smaller clubs a DJ benefits from being close to the crowd, feeding off that energy, although in among the audience it can be very messy. At 'Cream' the mad lad who knocked the record was obviously too close or too out of control; Carl Cox had some problems at Home until they moved the DJ booth; Jody Wisternoff from Way Out West had a drink spiked with ketamine at a gig in San Diego and he collapsed behind the decks; Derrick May once snapped at a gig at Sankey's Soap when he was getting hassled and punched a lad who had to be carried out of the club by security.

DJ-ing, you have to get used to people talking to you, maybe hassling you; when somebody wants you to look after their coats because the cloakroom's full, or asks you to get on the microphone and put a call out to all their friends because they've lost them. Sometimes people come up to me and say, 'Why aren't you smiling?' At the Bomb a lad kept jumping in the air and shouting, of all things, 'Rock & Roll' at Norman. There are loads of daft things people say to DJs.

One Saturday in Glasgow, in the back room of the Tunnel, I was DJ-ing on a Radio One night; Pete Tong was in the main room and the crowd were losing it. I'd met up with some friends, I was getting well paid, and I was having a good time, too. A guy was yelling at me over the top of the DJ box, but I couldn't make out what he was saying. He didn't look angry so I assumed he was telling me what a grand time he was having. 'Yeah, thanks,' I said, acknowledging his praise. But he kept on shouting at me, still smiling. I played another record. He just stayed put. He'd been there about six or seven minutes when he held out his hand. I went to shake it, but he carried on shouting and gave me a five pound note. I realised what he was saying: 'Bottle of Bud, bottle of Bud.' He thought I was a barman.

CHAPTER 5

Hang the DJ
a Night Out at the Anti-Disco Disco

Dave Cotrill is a DJ. Every few months he goes to a function room upstairs in a pub on the edge of Manchester city centre, down the wide streets behind Piccadilly Station, under one of the iron bridges, well away from the bustle of the city's club and bar hotspots on Canal Street, Oldham Street and Oxford Road. He goes where there are few cars, no taxi ranks, no gangs of drinkers swaying down the pavement, to a pub on a corner of Fairfield Street called the Star & Garter. The main door is always locked, so he goes in the side entrance. When he walks in there are four or five customers congregated round the bar downstairs sipping pints. This is unregenerated Manchester, untouched by the digital, global, corporate world; there's no stripped pine, no chrome, no theme, no menu, no cloakroom, no Chardonnay, no champagne.

He goes upstairs to a room that's available for hire. It's nine-thirty. The decks have been set up on a trestle table on the stage. He clambers up onto the stage with his records. It's a one-man operation: he hires the room, does all the publicity and plays all the records. He has with him three boxes of records – not the swish metallic record boxes festooned with logos and airline stickers that the top notch DJs would have someone carry for them – just plastic crates, which he carries himself. His crates are full of records by the Smiths, and the records the Smiths singer Morrissey has made during his subsequent solo career. Tonight, as usual, Dave will be hosting a Smiths/Morrissey night, a one-man disco dedicated to the man who infamously called on the listeners to one of his songs to 'Hang the DJ'.

Dave also carries with him a slide projector and a bedsheet which he hangs at the back of the stage. He dusts down the in-house DJ equipment, turns on the power and checks the leads are plugged in. The Star & Garter's DJ equipment consists of two old-fashioned Citronic decks built into a crumbling black console with a mixer. The mixer has no crossfader, and the decks, needless to say, have no pitch control and no slipmats. There's a 20-pence piece glued on top of each stylus, weighing the needle down to prevent the records jumping. The set-up is state of the art 1978.

Dave has been running the Smiths/Morrissey disco since 1994. It takes place every few months. It's the only DJ job he's ever had; nobody has come down to one of his nights and headhunted him, snapped him up to do a festival or a gig somewhere else, although occasionally he has branched out and run a Smiths/Morrissey disco in London. The last one at the Liquid Lounge in King's Cross was OK, but not as good as the Manchester nights.

The Star & Garter doesn't have queues. When I get there I worry, not just because there's no queue, but there are also no doormen, and at first I'm not sure I've come on the right evening. At the bottom of the stairs there's a middle-aged lady in a purple anorak collecting the entrance money. It's £2 before 10.30pm. I pay and go upstairs. I can hear 'I Started Something I Couldn't Finish' as I walk through the door into the room, which is already half full. The hall holds maybe 200 people, with

Dave, his records and his slides on the stage to the left, chairs and tables to the right, and a bar in a room off to one side. There's no VIP bar (naturally; there are no VIPs). Somebody gives me a leaflet advertising the sale of a West Ham Boys' Club t-shirt; apparently Morrissey wore a similar shirt on his last tour in Britain. I ask the t-shirt salesman if it's the same design as Morrissey's. 'No, but as near as I could get it,' he replies. There's a fruit machine but it's been turned off.

Tonight, pints of Stella in a plastic pint pot are £1.30. I could probably buy a round for everyone in the room for the same price as drinks for four in some London bar. I don't though, although half an hour later I get Jane a pint of cider. She's celebrating her 26th birthday.

Jane has been coming to the Smiths/Morrissey disco for five years. She's on Dave's mailing list so she gets advance warning of when the events are going to take place (every couple of months, always on a Friday, and a special every year on the Friday that falls nearest to Morrissey's birthday). Dave has more than a hundred people on his mailing list, and most of them are in the room already.

I look for somewhere to sit. There's no room round any of the tables, but there's a bench running along the side wall next to the dancefloor, with a couple of spaces available. It turns out that this is where the true devotees sit. I'm next to Bill from Wigan. He's in his late twenties and he too is on Dave's mailing list. Something has gone wrong recently, though, and he hasn't been sent any information about tonight, but he ended up here anyway.

He was on a night out in Wigan with his mates, but they went looking for some decent music. They ended up in Warrington (Why Warrington? 'Don't ask,' he says). Eventually Bill and his friends found themselves in

Manchester, at the Thirsty Scholar. I didn't even know it was still open, I tell him. While they were there he picked up a flyer advertising tonight's Morrissey disco, so they came straight over.

Talking to Bill is difficult, and not just because the bench is down near the speakers. Morrissey fans know all the words to all the songs and throughout the evening they sing them raucously. As we sit chatting on the bench, Bill will suddenly start singing, so about one out of every four things he says are lines from Smiths songs. I choose what to respond to as it's clear he doesn't expect a reply every time. Dave plays 'Girl Afraid'. Bill gets up to dance, and I go and talk to Dave.

At home Dave listens to Scott Walker, David Bowie, Prince, some old soul, and French pop from the 1960s like Françoise Hardy. He's very disciplined about what he plays at the discos, though. Probably a good ninety-five per cent of the records he plays are songs sung by Morrissey, three per cent are by other groups, and the remaining two per cent are Smiths instrumentals. He has a clipboard on the table next to the decks on which he writes down the names of the songs. 'I sometimes forget what I've played,' he says, 'and I never like to play anything twice in a night.'

At the beginning he knew most of the audience, and they became friends and regulars, but he's been doing this for seven years and a lot of the original audience has drifted away. Now he doesn't know many of the crowd, although just as he tells me this a couple of lads come into the room and wave to him.

So how does he know what to play?

'There are certain things that I know are going to be popular.'

Like anything with Morrissey singing on it?

'Yes.'

There are a surprising number of younger people there. No toddlers, of course, but eighteen, nineteen year olds, which strikes me as a bit odd considering that it was 1986 or 1987 when the Smiths were at their height. Somehow the Morrissey cult is still strong enough to renew itself with fresh-faced new disciples. According to Dave Cotrill, it is in fact the more recent converts who are the most devoted and eager. They're the ones totally consumed by Morrissey: 'The younger ones are definitely the ones most likely to want to hear just Morrissey and the Smiths and the ones who have quiffs. The ones into them originally wouldn't have quiffs.'

I ask Dave if these older Smiths fans are broadminded enough to want to hear some house or garage or something. 'I don't know,' he says, 'I mean, I don't know what all those different dance things are called, but some of the older ones I speak to used to go to the Haçienda.'

The Haçienda seems like a long time ago and a long way away. Here at the Star & Garter there are photocopied A4 posters stuck up with sellotape on the blackwashed walls advertising punk nights. Also on the wall there's an advert for next week's Manic Street Mania, a night of records by the Manic Street Preachers, also £2 in before 10.30pm, but not organised by Dave Cotrill. He tells me that other people have hired the Star & Garter for tribute nights. There was one night that featured records by James. There was also a Belle & Sebastian night and, predictably, some of Belle & Sebastian actually came down to the night (it sounded horrendous).

Many of the gathering crowd at the Star & Garter are wearing genuine antique Smiths t-shirts, while others have come dressed in plain t-shirts, with scribbled tributes to Moz daubed in indelible black pen on them. The prevailing colours of the clothes are black and dark denim. Many of the girls are wearing skirts with flower prints, and some of them are dressed like Miss Havisham: gothic, I suppose, wearing long black dresses, clumpy shoes, widow's weeds. They dance in groups, rather than couples, or singly. There's one couple dressed in Gap light khaki combat trousers and canvas trainers sitting at a table about ten yards from me. They are clearly in the wrong club.

Dave plays 'Golden Lights' by Twinkle – a song which the Smiths once covered – but the dancefloor clears. Jane comes over to sit next to me. She arrived here on her own. After about four or five Smiths songs, Dave plays something by James. 'He never plays much else besides Morrissey and the Smiths, does he?' I say to Jane.

'No, not really, but he'll throw in the odd weird one.'

Like James?

'Yeah, or the Fall.'

What about Motown?

'No.'

A bit of disco or some funk, you know, something by the Fatback Band?

'No,' she says, 'you won't get any disco music here.'

We change the subject. She admits to me that her job is about as inappropriate as you can get for a Morrissey fan: she works in a McDonald's. Tomorrow she has a day off. When she asked her boss, the man had said, 'Why, is it another Smiths night?'

'Come back in two months,' she says to me, 'and it'll all be the same.'

Dave then plays the acoustic Sandie Shaw version of 'Jeane' and five people get back onto the dancefloor – a group of four girls and a boy, tall, with black floppy hair and Adidas trainers; he looks like Alex James before he met Keith Allen. The girls are smiling and doing a skippy dance but he's just standing there on his own, gently rocking and touching and hugging himself. It's a bit creepy. I go to the bar to get Jane a drink.

I have to bring the drink back across the dancefloor, which has filled now, to the strains of 'How Soon Is Now' (a song about leaving a club, crying and wanting to die). Everybody is singing along. Even the Gap couple are dancing, singing the words to each other; it turns out they're Smiths fans, after all. Then Dave plays 'Still Ill', and suddenly Bill weaves his way across the dancefloor to me. 'Does the body rule the mind or does the mind rule the body?' he asks me. 'I don't know,' I reply.

For the throng, dancing is a sideways swivel of the hips; their feet are everywhere and nowhere. Many of them twirl invisible gladioli above their heads. They dance with their hands and their hips, but primarily with their voices. When Dave plays 'Everyday is like Sunday' the dancefloor fills and the crowd roars the chorus. I nearly spill my pint onto Jane's lap.

Jane says that when the night first started it used to be full of Morrissey lookalikes. Back then, she remembers, 'All the boys looked like him and everyone brought flowers.'

Did they?

'Yeah, I brought daffodils.'

And then what happened?

'I grew up.' She laughs.

I'm still amazed at how young the crowd is. I must be one of the only people in the room old enough to have seen the Smiths play. Jane never saw them, although she has seen Morrissey during his solo career. The last time she was a bit disappointed, not by him but by the crowd: 'There were all these students there, who must have been into Morrissey for like a year or something.'

I ask her what she thinks would happen if Morrissey walked in now.

'Well, we'd all jump on him.'

A few minutes later I'm back bothering Dave as he

tries to cue the next record up through his headphones. I
ask him if Morrissey or any of the other members of the
Smiths knows that the night exists.

'I don't know.'

What would happen if Johnny Marr came in?

'I don't think people would leave him alone. I think
they'd ask him questions.'

What, like 'Why did you split the Smiths up?'

'Er, no. I don't think they'd ask that.'

Would you ask him to sign your records?

'I don't really bother with things like that.'

As we talk, a few dancers come over to the stage and
ask Dave to play certain tracks. It's all very polite. There's
no-one asking, 'Have you got anything good?'; nobody is
giving Dave any sort of a hard time. He's giving them
what they want. Do any of the audience get aggressive
when they ask for records?

'You can get one or two but that's usually because
they're drunk really.'

Do you ever get any shady characters down here?

'Um, once or twice we have had some shady people
in, but I don't think they were here selling drugs.'

So, what happened. Did these shady people start
fighting?

'No, they just stood there and then they left. We never
have fights. Sometimes it gets a bit rowdy and if somebody has had too much to drink they might start acting
daft and pushing people on the dancefloor, but nobody
would start fighting.'

Does anyone ask to hear something a bit different?

'No, they never want anything else, although somebody asked me once for Dinosaur Jr. But they didn't get
aggressive.'

He waits for the record to finish so he can put another
one on, and then he tells me about his proper job. He

works for a company that helps find work for people in places like Salford and Bootle. His employers know that he moonlights as a DJ: 'I have told them, yes, but I don't know what they think.'

Do you think their image of a DJ is somebody living a very glamorous lifestyle with dolly birds hanging around him?

'No, I don't think they think what I do is very glamorous.'

I take a quick look round the Star & Garter dancefloor. They would kind of be right wouldn't they, Dave?

Dave has played a few floor fillers but now he's playing one of the more miserable dirges from Morrissey's back catalogue, and the dancefloor has thinned out again. Dave is DJ-ing in a totally different way to the way Seb Fontaine does at 'Cream', or Steve Lawler does on the Space terrace on a sunny Sunday in Ibiza. If I was behind the decks I'd be looking to build the atmosphere, peak it, hold it there, take it down again, bring it up, climax, encore. But Dave's set isn't like that at all; it seems like he's just throwing the records on one after another. There's no underlying thread, no sense of programming or progression. But this is a different world. I ask him if he ever hangs out with other DJs. 'I don't know any other DJs,' he tells me. If Paul van Dyk walked in now Dave wouldn't recognise him: 'No. Paul van Dyk? No, I've never heard of him.'

Dave isn't on that loop – clubs, promo records. He's not interested in going to 'Cream', Fabric or 'Gatecrasher'. He's happy doing his own night: 'I used to go to indie clubs but not any more. The last club I went to was the Venue because it was all bottles fifty pence but it smelt of sick and everybody was about fourteen.'

The gaps between records are getting longer. He's like a jukebox, full of the audience's favourite tunes, with somebody pressing random buttons. But then why should he follow the disco rules? He's entirely matching the audience's expectations, after all. I guess if he started some nifty crossfading he'd be booed off. He's not even standing up; he's sitting behind his decks, only getting to his feet to change the slides. Next up, a picture of Viv Nicholson.

Morrissey doesn't like dance music, does he?

'I don't really know. I don't believe anything he says in interviews because he always seems to contradict himself.'

He's never said he likes dance music though, has he? He's still up for burning down the disco and hanging the DJ as far as we know.

'Yes, but I don't know if he means it literally.'

Do you think he would burn down this disco?

'I've no idea.' Dave is getting wise to me. 'I don't know if his limousine would find the Star & Garter,' he says.

Dave has been a fan of Morrissey's since 1988, just after the Smiths split up. The first record he heard by Morrissey was 'Suedehead'. 1988, of course, was the year of acid house, an episode stubbornly resisted by Morrissey. 'I could never begin to explain the utter loathing I feel for dance music,' he said.

Voices raised in opposition to dance music have been heard since people first started gathering in rooms to dance. Dancing was always connected with morals; the puritan strain in society has always found dancing, like fun, to be a suspect activity.

Decades before the disco era, and through acid house, a queue of people waiting to go into a room to dance – especially to dance to a DJ – has been an affront to the sensibilities of countless rock musicians, right-wing activists, left-wing social critics, influential academics, music magazines, Sunday newspaper columnists, police-

men, politicians and Church leaders. Their opposition to
what goes on every Saturday night in dance halls, discotheques and nightclubs has been ideological, musical,
ethical, and even medical: on occasions health experts
and doctors have warned against the perils of going out
dancing.

Throughout the last century, popular music, especially popular dance music, has attracted moral panics.
Jazz, in the form of ragtime, brought untamed rhythms
and widespread controversy to Britain. It arrived in
Europe just before the First World War and boomed over
the subsequent two decades. Jazz was modern and exotic,
but its major appeal to the young and the adventurous lay
in the fact that ragtime was instant dance music. It was
never intended that you would sit down and listen to it; it
was made for Saturday nights, nights out, dance halls.

Jazz initiated a change in social habits in Britain;
previously dancing had tended to be occasional or
seasonal (on May Day, at weddings or high society balls),
but dancing now became a regular activity. It was also
broadly-based in its appeal, cutting across class distinc-
tions. This attracted disapproval from the traditionalists,
but to the jazzers it was liberating. The dance styles themselves accentuated this sense of freedom surrounding
jazz; in polite circles anyway, dance styles had controlled
the body, kept emotions and limbs in check, but ragtime
changed this (the word 'jazz' itself was derived from a
slang term for sex). Jazz dancing was less formal, less
restrained. In comparison to what had gone before it was
all hot rhythms and sweat. Young hearts were running
free.

The establishment considered dancing to be just too
much fun, not contemplative enough, and providing too
many opportunities for physical indiscretion. They were
also suspicious of its African roots. Jazz wasn't European,

and certainly wasn't Aryan; it's no wonder jazz was outlawed by the German invaders in Paris. Furthermore,
dancing to jazz was a communal activity, jazz fans taking
strength from their shared pleasure in subverting the
authorities; any time the young congregate unsupervised,
the authorities are anxious.

The first discotheque on the rue de la Huchette wasn't
the only manifestation of the German persecution of jazz
fans during the occupation of France. In 1942 a group of
young French music fans were arrested in the Metro
dressed in 'flash, impertinent, provocative suits and
dresses, and wearing badges with the words "*une France
swing dans une Europe zazoue*"', which could be translated – not at all literally – as 'one French nation under a
Euro groove'.

One of the factors which brought jazz into disrepute
with the authorities was that for decades jazz and drugs
had been linked in the public mind, just as rave clubs and
drugs are now. The story of jazz through the twentieth
century was marked by the way, as each form of jazz
became mainstreamed, other forms arrived to take the
music back out onto the edge. There was a continual
turnover of styles and sounds, attempts to resist appro-
priation. Drugs intensified listening pleasure perhaps,
but were also part of this outlawed activity, this attempt
to get beyond control. Drugs seemed to be part of the jazz
lifestyle – bohemian, anti-authoritarian – for the musicians and fans alike. By the 1920s, marijuana – known as
'weed', 'reefers', 'muggles' (a title of a song by Louis
Armstrong) – was part of a jazz musician's world, as was
cocaine (the subject of 'Wacky Dust', a song by Ella
Fitzgerald).

Drug use among jazz stars of the 1950s was becoming
widely accepted, with the likes of Charlie Parker struggling with heroin addiction. Paris maintained its love

affair with jazz through the century, and by the 1950s the city still played host to a sizeable community of black Americans in exile. Faced with a segregated society in America, writers like James Baldwin and some of the best black American jazz players had adopted Paris as their home. In the 1950s the Musicians Union had effectively banned black jazz musicians from Britain, so British jazz fans would go to Paris to see their idols playing. Bruce Mitchell, a drummer, remembers Manchester musicians would go over to see them play clubs over there, and return trading stories about what a state some of them were in. 'Bud Powell stands out because it took him something like ten minutes to walk down the room. He was a tragic case, but enormously talented; a lot of them were.'

By the early 1950s, it was rock & roll that was at war with the authorities, with parents, the media, the moral guardians. Especially in America, rock & roll's clear relationship with R&B was the cause of concern; R&B had never been deemed respectable, mainly because it was black. To the American white mainstream, it was preferable that black music, like the black community as a whole, should stay segregated from the white world. Any music, including rock & roll – a white version of a black sound – which was giving profile or credence to black life, or promoting race mixing, was suspect; this was an era when the Harlem Globetrotters were denied entry to the NBA leagues because of the colour of their skin.

Whereas certain forms of music in the black community – notably so-called 'Negro spirituals' – were considered morally uplifting, other kinds of black music were deemed subversive. The blues, for example, was seen as a medium for railing against injustice, and the legacy of slavery and poverty, and these were uncomfortable messages for the white majority. In the case of rhythm and blues, the lyrics were thought to be inane and sexually suggestive; you didn't have to listen hard to find references to meat balls, king size men and big long sliding things (especially in 'Big Long Sliding Thing' by Dinah Washington). To the teenagers, this was precisely why the music appealed: the uncompromised lyrics, the rowdier big beats.

The big change came when some white disc jockeys began to play R&B to a wider, whiter audience. If some of its new listeners found the music immoral and inane, to many others it was irresistible. In May 1952 a record store in Los Angeles reported that forty per cent of its business was done with white customers, whereas only a few months earlier, the number of white customers was negligible. The music was also beginning to cross over because white artists were being influenced by R&B. Although R&B was gaining ground, it was primarily its lighter, white version – rock & roll – which opened the door, warmed up the market, acclimatised the listening public to the sounds. White acts were the most acceptable to the wider public; the first million-selling rock & roll song was Bill Haley's 1953 hit 'Crazy, Man, Crazy'. But even though the music had lost some of its rawness when it crossed over, it was still unconventional and still controversial. Even 'Heartbreak Hotel', with Elvis singing 'I feel so lonely, I could die', was deemed unAmerican in its sentiment. Anyone who wasn't optimistic, upbeat and feelgood was possibly Communist, let alone anyone betraying evidence that they'd been idling around listening to music made by coloured folks.

Once the music became available in the white community it became a white-hot issue. Fundamentalist church groups and white racists attempted to suppress 'Negro-style' music. The Alabama White Citizens Council called rock & roll 'a means of pulling the white man down to the level of the Negro. It is part of a plot to undermine the morals of the youth of our nation.' The handful of black singers who gained a white audience – like Nat 'King' Cole – were usually at the blander end of the market. But even then there was aggression; in 1956 in Birmingham, Alabama, threats by members of the White Citizens Council turned to violence when they attacked and beat Nat 'King' Cole during a concert.

Catholic religious organisations began to campaign against DJs who played suggestive material on radio or at record hops. The Catholic Youth Centre led calls to 'smash the records you possess which present a pagan culture and a pagan concept of life'. Dr Howard Hanson declared rock & roll 'acoustical pollution', and the product of a civilisation that had 'lost its sense of values'. In 1955 Peter Potter, a Los Angeles-based DJ and host of the TV show *Juke Box Jury*, hit out at rhythm and blues: 'All rhythm and blues records are dirty and as bad for kids as dope.'

R&B also faced obstacles from within the music industry. The major labels, the dominant music publishers (ASCAP) and major trade publications all resisted younger songwriters, independent labels and 'race' records; they were making all their money from white records. The increase in the use of recorded music, on radio and in dance halls, also led to objections; in the 1940s the Musicians Union saw the spread of recorded music in dance venues as a threat, and even tried to ban records played in the intervals between sets by live bands.

The music reached a growing audience through gigs, record hops, radio waves, films like *Rock Around the Clock* and television. After Elvis Presley sold a million and a half copies of 'Heartbreak Hotel', he started to appear on TV, where his onstage wriggling soon got him into trouble. In *Awopbopaloobop Awopbamboom*, Nik Cohn quotes the views of a Baptist minister in Des Moines: 'Elvis Presley is morally insane.'

In this climate of prejudice and disapproval, record hops also came under fire. In 1956 the Boston Licensing Board was one of the bodies that expressed doubts about rock & roll. The chairman said that rock & roll's 'exciting tempos could endanger the morals of our youth'. What's more, meeting en masse, late at night, at record hops was even more suspect: 'Teenagers have no business listening to disc jockeys at twelve o'clock at night. The way they're going, they'll have high blood pressure before they're twenty.'

In 1958 Alan Freed hit the headlines when trouble erupted during a show on his 'Big Beat' tour. There was a stand-off in the venue when the audience left their seats and began dancing in the aisles and police turned on the house lights to cool their enthusiasm. Outside the venue, fifteen people were assaulted or robbed, and rock & roll and Alan Freed took the blame. Freed was charged with inciting a riot; District Attorney Garret Byrne said he believed some disc jockeys put 'emotional TNT on their turntables'. A Catholic paper in Boston wrote, 'It is clear now that the disk jockey-ed dance is, in notable instances, a menace to life, limb, decency, and morals.'

Other musicians couldn't relate to rock & roll and were left behind by its energy and popularity. John Lewis of the Modern Jazz Quartet said that he considered rock & roll 'very poor quality musically', and claimed that he had no idea why kids liked it, or danced to it: 'the worst dancing I've ever seen'. British singer Frankie Vaughan said he thought Elvis was 'ridiculous; he just can't sing'. Crooners were especially dismissive. Frank Sinatra in 1957 said that rock & roll is 'the most brutal, ugly, desperate, vicious form of expression it has been my misfortune to hear'. Later in his career he duetted with Elvis and Bono.

DJs were considered pied pipers, with a powerful influence over their fans, and the opponents of rock & roll were the first to recognise the power of DJs as taste makers and role models. A judge in Cambridge, Massachusetts, commented that the 'leadership of the disc jockey had dangerously supplanted the leadership of the good elements in the community among these impressionable teenagers'.

Then big on jazz, the British music paper *Melody Maker* campaigned hard against rock & roll. Throughout the 1950s, columnist Steve Race kept banging on about rock & roll as a 'monstrous threat'. Unconventional music tastes suggested delinquency; Elvis Presley, Bill Haley, Jerry Lee Lewis remained controversial figures, and Jerry Lee Lewis didn't exactly help his reputation among the moral guardians when he married his thirteen-year-old cousin.

The Musicians Union maintained their support for live rather than recorded music, and attempted to develop ways to discourage DJs; even late in the 1950s the MU was calling records 'a grave threat' and 'an ever present menace'. In 1963 it campaigned with one of the most depressing slogans ever: 'Keep Music Live'. It seemed like a nostalgic, conservative organisation, clearly sympathetic to its traditional, older members (most of them trad jazz musicians), many of whom railed against the trend for 'gimmick-ridden rock & roll rubbish'. As an example of its less than evenhandedness, payment rates for beat group musicians set by the MU were less than those of traditional jazz bands. In 1971 the PPL – the copyright collection agency empowered to collect monies on behalf of musicians and performers – warned specifically against 'large quantities of soul records which presented particular problems in some types of discotheque use'.

Discotheques were the bane of the Musicians Union,

but they also faced the wrath of traditional rock musicians and fans. In the 1960s rock groups like the Beatles and the Rolling Stones took some flak for the length of their hair, sound levels at concerts, obscene LP sleeves, libertarian politics and drug references in lyrics. Each new generation of rock groups has gone that bit further to whip up controversy, and faced ritual denunciations by worried cultural commentators. But by the mid-1970s we also had disco. The most virulent discophobes were rock fans and rock bands.

Disco was an experience, a lifestyle, more than a genre of music. When Josh, in *The Last Days of Disco*, is dismissive of the mainstream froth and says, 'Disco was more and much better than that', it's an acknowledgement that it came to mean something to both its enthusiasts and its opponents. To Josh, I guess, it was about being lost in music, loving the nightlife, embracing a passion and excitement lacking in normal life. For disco devotees, it was liberation. Sister Sledge sang about being lost in music, and giving up the 9 to 5. In 'Lady Marmalade', Labelle address the soul sisters, and they go out looking for a man who can enter the colourful, carefree spirit of the night; they want to tear him away from his 9 to 5 and 'his grey flannel life'.

There was what Sarah Thornton calls 'a taste war' in the disco era, an extreme form of the tribalism of pop music; rock music and disco lined up in bitter opposition, many times more antagonistic than the beats and squares or the mods and rockers had been. The disco crowd weren't bothered, but the followers of the rock bands – progressive and punk – criticised the music for being formulaic, and the audience for being escapist. The audience was patronised and the DJ vilified. According to *Melody Maker* in 1975, the DJ was a 'parasite', 'a synthetic rock star with no musical ability'.

In the late 1970s dance music and rock music grew further apart when punk set itself against disco. This was the era in which Morrissey formulated most of his views about music; he looked to New York for inspiration, but to Patti Smith and the New York Dolls rather than Larry Levan. Morrissey's opposition to club culture survived deep into the 1980s with his calls to 'Hang the DJ'. *Melody Maker*'s opposition to dance music survived into the twenty-first century; when reviewing Midfield General's *Generalisation* LP, the *Melody Maker* reviewer had this to say: 'Don't worry readers, we hate these c**ts as much as you do . . . DJs and DJ f**kin' culture. The most loathsome development in contemporary music.' Less than six weeks after this anti-DJ rant, *Melody Maker* closed down.

The late 1970s witnessed the most notorious event of the anti-disco movement. In July 1979 Steve Dahl, a DJ on WLUP-FM, an all-rock station in Chicago, masterminded what was billed as a 'disco demolition rally' at Comiskey Park, home stadium of the Chicago White Sox baseball team. Fans of the team were admitted at a discount rate to a night featuring two games between the White Sox and the Detroit Tigers if they carried a disco record with them, and, during the interval between the two games, around 10,000 records were collected, placed in a container in the middle of the field and blown up. The crowd then invaded the field of play, set records on fire and chanted 'disco sucks'. The second game was postponed because of damage to the playing area.

Steve Dahl had earlier resigned from another station in the city when it switched to playing disco, and had a thing for scratching the needle across the grooves and then smashing up disco records live on air during his programmes. Dahl went on to attempt a national network of disco demolition rallies, and led groups in pickets and marches targeting local discotheques, demanding that they switch to rock music. He also organised the disruption of a concert by the Village People; marshmallows with 'Disco Sucks' written on them were thrown at the group.

The camp, glam impulses behind the upsurge in gay clubbing influenced the image of disco in the mid-1970s, so much so that disco was often perceived as the preserve of three constituencies – the black and gay communities, and working class women – all of whom were poorly represented in the upper echelons of rock criticism, the media and society at large. The Disco Sucks campaign was a white, macho reaction against gay liberation and black pride more than a reaction against platform shoes or drum machines. In England, in the same year as the Disco Sucks demo in America, far-right groups were also firmly set against disco. In 1979 *The Young Nationalist* – a youth-oriented publication from the British National Party – told its readers, 'Disco and its melting pot pseudo-philosophy must be fought or Britain's streets will be full of black-worshipping soul boys.'

Some of the great days of disco, in 1976 and 1977, coincided with punk, but the traditional versions of the history of popular music won't tell you that. The inveterate rock bias in the papers, magazines and academia has left much dancefloor history undocumented. The 1989 edition of the *Penguin Encyclopaedia of Popular Music* describes disco as 'a dance fad of the Seventies with a profound and unfortunate influence on popular music', and also laments the existence of anonymous 'disco hitmakers' and record producers using 'drum machines, synthesisers and other gimmicks at the expense of musical values'.

Discos worldwide were subject to political suppression. Neither Washington nor Moscow approved of disco music and nightclubs, though for apparently opposite reasons: the Western governments thought the discotheque explosion was part of a Communist plot to destabilise society, whereas in Communist Russia and China the authorities believed it to be a decadent Western capitalist conspiracy. In Russia, a pamphlet issued by a young Communist group complained that discos were 'full of empty and anti-artistic ideas', and suggested that attempts should be made to include a forum for discussion of serious issues at some point during a night's entertainment. In China in 1982 the government published a guide entitled 'How to Distinguish Decadent Music' (by its 'quivering' rhythms, naturally). They also came down hard on anyone attempting to circumvent rules about disco parties; a baker in Shanghai was jailed for fifteen days for charging admission to illegal dances in his home.

Disco music not only created moral panics but health scares, too. In 1981 scientists at the University of Ankara in Turkey published findings which claimed that extended exposure to loud music in discotheques 'causes homosexuality in mice and deafness in pigs', and that, by extension, the health of humans was under threat, especially those disco dancers who took up positions close to the amplification. The study, however, failed to explore all the implications of its own findings – notably why the sexual identity of the mice changed when they were bombarded with disco music but they didn't go deaf, and why the disco pigs went deaf, but somehow stayed straight.

Anti-disco prejudice occasionally came from unexpected sources. Reverend Jesse Jackson entered the fray in 1976 with demands to ban 'sexy songs' from the radio, concerned about the effect some disco music could have on the sexual morality of teenagers. He pointed to evidence from a survey of a thousand girls at a North

Hollywood high school which had found that ninety per cent of them had had sexual intercourse while listening to 'songs with suggestive lyrics and rhythms'. He was particularly fearful about the possible effects of KC & the Sunshine Band's hit song '(Shake Shake Shake) Shake Your Booty'.

The issues never really went away, and the political or sexual content of songs still caused broadcasters to ban them. American TV banned 'Disco Inferno' by the Trammps, and the BBC denied airplay to Donna Summer's 'Love to Love You Baby'. Disco music wasn't unfairly treated, however, with punk, heavy rock and gangsta rap all being targeted in subsequent years.

Morrissey found rap music 'offensive, artless and styleless', using terms that reflected both a moral and an aesthetic revulsion, but hip hop had more to fear from cliché and novelty acts diluting the music than from the rock traditionalists. 'Rapper's Delight' wasn't a novelty, but novelty records followed, including a rap song by breakfast TV puppet Roland Rat. Gangsta rap was embraced by the hip hop community in part because it went so far beyond the mainstream that it couldn't be neutered. And Morrissey's estrangement from club culture intensified in the 1980s with the arrival of acid house, when his trademark introspection, gloom and lyric-heavy songwriting looked increasingly old-fashioned.

Acid house had plenty of opponents in the music scene and among journalists. In the *Independent on Sunday* William Leith decried the 'deranged throb' of acid house, and Adam Sweeting's beliefs in the *Guardian*, that dance music all sounds the same, were typical of commentators who seemed to think that dance music was a passing fad, ignoring the fact that it had a history, and, it was to turn out, a hugely successful future.

Morrissey was going against the flow, which was

always his way; he knew that you define yourself by your choice of enemies. In the 1980s he was happy to offer strenuously negative opinions about Live Aid, Mrs Thatcher and Factory Records. You could never accuse him of jumping on bandwagons, with his steadfast refusal to accept any dance music, mainstream pop or computer-aided music. He shared the traditional rock view that through rock guitars and drums, music was somehow more authentic. When acid house arrived he was horrified: 'That two people can sit in their bedroom in Detroit with a little bit of machinery and come out with this huge wall of sound is sterility at its utmost. I want to see real people onstage, playing real instruments.'

The fear of new technology was key to discophobia in the 1980s. Certainly dance music producers had been among the first to use synthesisers and drum machines in the late 1970s, notably Giorgio Moroder, whose production skills on Donna Summer's 'Love to Love You Baby' marked the coming out of the computer as a dance music tool. The advances in dance music in the early 1980s, from electro through to techno, were also the products of a creative use of new technology which the technophobic rock music had avoided. As the 1980s ended, there was a backlash in rock music marked by a new format introduced by MTV: live music unplugged. Artists like Eric Clapton would perform without the use of technology, computers, drum machines, amplification and, of course, plugs.

Discophobia also took sustenance from an historic antipathy to black music among the traditionalists; from the jungle rhythms of jazz, the controversies about race records in the 1950s, the bitter opposition to soul music of the British National Party. The populace at large tended to accept or even embrace black music – from ragtime to Motown – but this only seemed to enrage opponents of black music even more. Morrissey used to complain that his exclusion from TV shows was nothing to do with the fact that he had a reputation for not turning up to them, or that the Smiths seldom sold enough records to get into the upper reaches of the charts, or that they never made videos. He was convinced there was a 'political' reason: 'there has been a hefty pushing of all these black artists and all this discofied nonsense into the Top Forty'.

The late 1980s and the rise of acid house was a victory for the forces of disco. Morrissey, ever contrary, when he left the Smiths and went solo seemed to be pursuing a rockabilly sound while the world moved on to fall in love with electronica. 'DJs and DJ f**kin culture' won.

In the late 1980s, and for a good few years afterwards, dance culture was subject to unsympathetic or sensationalist media coverage. In the media there's always a time-lag as the thirty year olds try to come to terms with what the teenagers are up to; or, in fact, until the teenagers are thirty-somethings themselves. To an audience used to gigs and more gigs, clubs were foreign territory. It was also a generational thing. On the left of the political spectrum, meanwhile, there was still a view that politically progressive music consisted of songs with an overt polemical message, not instrumental songs suffused with stolen break beats and weird bleeps.

The authorities are always suspicious of the young enjoying themselves, and it was this desire to control gatherings that lay at the heart of the Criminal Justice Bill which came into force on 13 July 1990, ostensibly to outlaw raves. By then, police and DJs had already been in conflict. Mike Pickering, a resident DJ at the Haçienda at the time, was served an injunction restricting him from travelling to one rave. DJ Rob Tissera had an even more wretched run-in with police. He was DJ-ing at 'Love

Decade' in a warehouse near Leeds which was stormed by police in riot gear. Tissera, to his eternal regret, got on the microphone and said, 'Listen, if you want to keep this party going, we need to barricade the doors and keep the bastards out!' In the end, it was the biggest mass arrest in British history; altogether 836 clubbers were arrested. Only seventeen people were charged, though, among them Rob Tissera whose outburst was caught on video. He was given a three-month prison sentence.

Ironically, by the time the Bill became law the culture had moved on. Events like 'Love Decade' weren't just being targeted by police but by drug dealers and organised gangs, and going legitimate was the best option for the scene. Mark Rodol from Ministry of Sound confirms that the club was launched in September 1991 to give customers a safe rave experience: 'We took those people who didn't want to stand in a muddy field, they didn't want their coat thrown on the floor, they didn't want to sit in that rave slush that you used to get on floors. I'd like to think that the Ministry is like a sort of civilised raving. We get letters from people saying it's really good not to be approached in every dark corner by some bloke offering them ecstasy and checking other people's twenty pound notes in the light to see if they're real.'

The media are more sympathetic to dance culture now, as people who were in those muddy fields, or under the balcony at the Haçienda, or on podiums around the country, are now in their thirties, and in a position to commission books or magazine articles that reflect club culture. Gaining mass media acceptance has some unfortunate results for dance culture, though, including endless programmes about kids havin' it large in Ibiza. But dance music is clearly a commercial success, and has to be taken seriously. Among the positive results of this is that now the dancefloor is in favour, dance music history is being rehabilitated. In his book *DJ Culture*, Ulf Poschardt invests the disco boom of the 1970s with political significance, describing it as 'a new strategy of resistance'. For Kodwo Eshun, in *More Brilliant Than the Sun*, 1970s disco is 'audibly where the twenty-first century begins'. So, at last, disco and funk, as well as house and hip hop, are getting their dues.

It's easy to get carried away, though, and some DJs are their own worst enemy, poor advertisements for clubland. In *DJ Culture*, Poschardt makes some grand claims about DJs as progressive cultural icons – they have 'turned their faces from the mainstream and conformity,' he says – but it's unwise to generalise too much about DJs. There are some embarrassing characters, with all kinds of ignoble motives for pursuing their profession – for the money, or to pick up women, or because they would have preferred to have been in a band but were too moody or not musical enough. There are many pioneers, of course, and non-conformists, but plenty of others who stick to the lowest common denominator; as in rock & roll, conformity is rife.

Then there's a devaluation in the idea of remixing; it's now almost a purely commercial act, less a canvas on which a DJ displays creativity than simply an attempt to tempt more record buyers. Armand van Helden believes remixing is now a scam; he should know, of course, having trousered many thousands of dollars remixing the likes of Tori Amos, CJ Bolland and the Sneaker Pimps. He's apparently disillusioned with it all now, though: 'Remixing is a marketing scam, period, just a way of marketing a record to a number of scenes. I've changed my philosophy on remixes and I'll tell you something. I don't really support them any more.'

Dance music is like any other form of cultural expression: over time, an innovation becomes a cliché. One reason why it's getting harder to generalise about DJs and clubs is that the variety is always increasing. For many DJs the onus is on new records on import or pre-release, but other DJs go backwards, rediscovering rare groove, Northern Soul or the golden age of disco. The activity and variety, though, is a sure sign that great rock gigs are rare, pub bands are dull, bars are too restrained; that there's a great thirst for going out dancing, whether to tech-house, lounge-core or a Smiths disco, whether at a 2,000-capacity London superclub or down the Manchester side streets at the Star & Garter.

It's gone midnight now, and there won't be many more people to come to the Smiths/Morrissey disco. Those that are here will stay until 2am. I ask Dave if he pays his mother wages for sitting and taking the money: 'Yeah, I do, but, I mean, she'd probably do it for free. I've never made much money, but then I'm never out of pocket.'

Have you ever had a big night, loads of people in and it's been bonanza time?

'No.'

I ask him to put me on the mailing list. I tell him I'll be back, and I did go back. The next time was Morrissey's birthday. Somewhere in Los Angeles, where he now lives, Morrissey was probably out with friends, but 200 of his most dedicated followers were in an upstairs room at the Star & Garter. Unfortunately there was no screen on the birthday night because some faulty wiring on Dave's slide projector blew the fuse when he plugged it in. The Star & Garter was full, but there were no birthday balloons. No cake. No candles. No disco biscuits.

CHAPTER 6

Leaving the Go-Go Girls at Home
the Northern Soul DJs

The entrance to the 100 Club on Oxford Street is an unassuming doorway stuck between a branch of Electronics Boutique and Vision Express. It's a Saturday night, late. Only a few hours earlier thousands of shoppers had crammed the pavements, but by 1am the street is quiet, aside from a few unlicensed taxis, night buses and the occasional noisy ambulance or police car. A few people have gathered in the doorway, hardly what you could call a queue, but that doesn't take long to change; within half an hour there's probably a hundred people waiting to get in.

They're not all middle-aged, but there aren't any teenagers. There are a few students, but the people in the queue are a wider selection of ages than in any club queue I've ever seen before, and shapes – wiry fellas in their forties queue alongside rotund beer addicts. None of the women have ordinary haircuts, and a few of the men are in sharp grey mod suits. Many are carrying holdalls or Gola or Lonsdale sports bags. The doors will open just before 2am and there'll be dancing until dawn. Everyone's happy now, greeting their friends pulling up in cars, joshing, harassing some of the DJs when they arrive with their boxes of seven-inch singles.

My journey down to the 100 Club from Manchester is

a reversal of the usual direction; the traffic has traditionally gone the other way, ever since communities of rare
soul fans developed in the North of England in the 1960s
in a club scene that's usually labelled 'Northern Soul'.
Northern didn't get its label until 1971, and the label,
then and now, hides a multitude of sounds and styles,
and tensions between purists and populists. The history
of Northern Soul goes back to the 1960s, and although
the scene reached a peak of popularity in the mid-1970s,
it's currently enjoying a big revival of interest.

The renewed fascination with Northern Soul is perhaps a result of the rise in the power and importance of
club culture – both commercially and creatively – through
the 1990s, unlocking interest in older dance music. Now
everybody is coming out about going out. In *Last Night
a DJ Saved My Life*, Bill Brewster and Frank Broughton
put Northern Soul in an historical context, not just as 'the
first rave culture' but also 'a vitally important step in the
creation of today's club culture and in the evolution of
the DJ'.

The 100 Club is just across the road from Wardour
Street, and many of the key clubs in the mod era are a few
hundred yards away. Those mod clubs formed the roots
of today's Northern Soul scene. To get here from where
Guy Stevens played R&B in the Scene in 1963 is a short
walk along Brewer Street and up Wardour Street.

But from 1963 to the present is a longer journey, a
journey through momentous, mostly derelict club venues
– Wigan Casino, the Twisted Wheel, Blackpool Mecca,
the Catacombs in Wolverhampton, the Golden Torch
near Stoke, Cleethorpes Pier – and a journey peopled by
collectors, record dealers, shady characters, music lovers,
night owls like those in the 100 Club queue, and a bunch
of DJs like Brian Rae, Soul Sam, Ian Levine and Richard
Searling.

Richard Searling hosts a weekly programme on Jazz FM in Manchester, playing a varied selection of retro and modern soul, and when he comes to do the guide of rare and classic soul nights in the North of England, the breadth of contemporary activity is amazing: Lowton Civic Hall, the Longfield Suite in Prestwich and Rossendale FC Social Club, venues in Bury, Failsworth, Stoke, Burnley, Sheffield, Salford. Every week there's news of reunions, one-offs and anniversaries, weekenders, all-nighters, monthlies.

Run by Ady Croasdell, the monthly all-nighters at the 100 Club were established more than twenty years ago. In 1979, with some friends, he launched the 6T's soul nights in London at various venues, including the Starlight Room in West Hampstead and the Last Chance on Oxford Street. The all-nighters started in the basement of the 100 Club in 1980.

Once the doors open the queue moves slowly down into the basement, a room set out with cheap canteen-style tables and chairs, apart from a long dancefloor in the middle. There are two bars, but only the one on the right is open; the bar at the other end is closed, and in front of the shutters trestle tables have been set up and record dealers have set their boxes up on them. By 2.30am the twin poles of clubland are neatly represented: the drinkers are at one end of the room, the record dealers at the other.

At three in the morning people are still coming in and the dancefloor is beginning to fill, but there's still quite a lot of wandering about, getting drinks in, sifting through the dealers' boxes, picking up flyers. The most brightly lit part of the club is the DJ area on the stage. Posters on the walls advertise the club's past glories, the 100 Club's jazz history especially. It opened in 1942 as a music venue hosting live swing bands, but in the early 1960s the building was split between a jazz club upstairs and a soul club downstairs as the young Soho bohemians switched their allegiance from bebop to other black music from America: soul and blues and R&B.

In 1963 and 1964, parallel to London's soul and R&B clubs there was a well-established scene in the North of England peopled by various maverick characters clutching their Chuck Berry LPs, frequenting coffee bars, scoffing at lightweights like Cliff Richard and Tommy Steele, and namechecking blues heroes like Sonny Boy Williamson. In Manchester a club called the Twisted Wheel opened on 26 Brazennose Street in March 1963 with no licensed bar and only very basic decor. It was founded by Roger Eagle, and took over a venue that had formerly been a beatnik hangout known as the Left Wing club.

Manchester at that time was clued-up about pop music, but in 1963 and 1964 Roger Eagle, playing records by Sam & Dave or the Impressions, marked the Wheel out as very different from clubs like the Oasis or the Jungfrau then championing the British beat groups that had emerged in the wake of the Beatles. Roger was one of the connoisseurs, unimpressed by the mainstream. Martin Barnfather, who would later DJ as Soul Sam, sums up the views of the soul and R&B fans at that time: 'The scene in Britain was saturated with Merseybeat and that was a real turn-off for me because it all sounded the same and I wanted to get into something different.'

Roger Eagle wasn't just the resident DJ at the Twisted Wheel; he booked the bands and organised the publicity as well. In his booking policy he exercised amazing quality control, in the early years at Brazennose Street treating his customers to gigs by the likes of John Lee Hooker, Screamin' Jay Hawkins, Champion Jack Dupree and the Spencer Davis Group. To comply with licensing regulations, the Wheel ran a membership scheme; within a year of opening, the 300-capacity club had a membership of 14,000.

In 1963 Roger lived in Oxfordshire and would travel up to Manchester on his motorbike every weekend, although he later moved North permanently. He also edited the fanzine 'R&B Scene' which described itself as 'Britain's Leading Rhythm and Blues magazine' and sold for a shilling. The magazine had a clear preference for contemporary black R&B, raw blues and the Sue label, both the US version and the London-based Sue run by Guy Stevens.

As noted earlier, Guy Stevens and Roger Eagle became friends. Stevens had realised the importance of DJs as aficionados and taste makers from his own experience, and began to send records on the Sue label up to Roger Eagle in Manchester; he knew he was an ally. Roger Eagle was renowned for his varied playlist, blending the new soul sounds with blues and R&B, and later, bluebeat from Jamaica. The taste and vision of Roger Eagle gave the Twisted Wheel a position at the cutting edge of club music, up there with the Marquee, the Flamingo and the Scene. He was an evangelist, and this cuts to the heart of the motivation behind all great DJs: a desire to share songs. A key skill is obviously not just to drop the familiar, popular, well-known songs at the right part of the night, but the ability to pick the right new releases, track down the more obscure tunes and newest imports, get hold of next month's big tune this month; you gather this pile, this tinder, together, then you work the records, beat them all together until they ignite. Result, you hope, disco inferno.

Roger Eagle never went for the easy option in his genre bending, though. He would play what he thought were the most relevant releases as they came out, and mix them with his chosen classics without trying to label them or follow any fad. He distanced himself from 'mod' movement, for instance. It could have been the time when he cashed in, but that's exactly what put him off the scene; if you could hear the record at every club in town, you wouldn't hear it at the Wheel.

Roger Eagle didn't just react against music becoming more compartmentalised, he also feared dance fans were becoming too pre-occupied with looking right, falling into line, conforming to fashion. In the April 1965 issue of his fanzine he praised the Esquire Club in Sheffield. 'Here's one club where the "mod" influence has not ruined the appreciation of R&B,' he wrote.

In 1965 the Twisted Wheel moved from Brazennose Street across town to 6 Whitworth Street. In the manner of clubbing cognoscenti through all eras, many of Roger Eagle's fans are still adamant that the nights at the original venue were never surpassed, despite the fact that many more lives would go on to be changed by the intensity and popularity of the Wheel in its Whitworth Street site, and through the work there of DJs like Les Cockell, Rob Bellars, Phil Saxe and Brian Rae.

Brian Rae had grown up in Cheshire in the village of Little Lea where his father ran a sub post office. Now he lives in Colwyn Bay, surrounded by records, videos and boxed sets. He has folders full of cuttings, and he'll gab for hours about the old days, how he eventually got a spot DJ-ing at both the Twisted Wheel and Wigan Casino, and then moved on to work in promotions and at record companies. Now, nearly sixty years old, he still DJs once a week or more, playing Northern Soul and R&B to audiences in Blackburn, Manchester, Wigan – wherever.

Brian Rae talks of the inspiration of Roger Eagle, but he was first turned on to soul through the mod scene in London and nights out at the Scene and the Flamingo.

Brian Rae has never been a media star, but he was still one of the first DJs to find a way into the business. His story is typical of a generation of DJs, with a background in both the mod scene in Soho and the soul scene up North in the 1970s, and he's one of a number of early mods who give the impression that they did their share of pills in the 1960s and have never gone to bed since.

Aged sixteen, Brian won a scholarship to college in London to learn the retail trade, hoping one day to become a member of the Grocers' Institute. He studied for a year and got his diploma, and then stayed on a year in London, eventually settling in a flat with some other lads in Powis Terrace near Portobello Road, and living a lifestyle that revolved around going to see bands, clubbing and hanging around in record shops. He begins to tell me about his life in London at the beginning of the 1960s: 'At that time Portobello Road was full of record shops, and that was great for me because I'd already been buying black music, the Coasters, Little Richard and a few other bits and bobs, and in Portobello Road there must have been eleven or twelve record shops.'

Despite his qualifications, he hadn't enough practical experience to get a good job in grocers' shops or supermarkets, so he took a job at John Lines, a wallpaper and paint wholesalers on Tottenham Court Road. At John Lines, the guy in the desk behind him was Chris Lorimer, a young lad from Leeds who knew his way around the clubs, took him down to the Flamingo for the first time, and partnered him on various forays around the nitespots of London. In August 1965, when the Small Faces released 'Whatcha Gonna Do About It?', Brian Rae saw them play at a club called the Cellar. As ever, he was relying on word of mouth or rumours, and a lot of his better nights out were accidents, when he'd stumble across some club or other. He admits that he's not able to recall exactly where the Cellar was or what the inside of the Flamingo or the Scene looked like, and he's not sure why: 'Maybe it's down to chemical abuse or I'd never really clocked it.'

Brian had a passion for coffee bars, and rhythm and blues. He also had a certain amount of musical knowledge, and was a proficient piano player. His father was the organist at the local church back home, and in his visits up North Brian occasionally used to stand in for him, but this arrangement came to an abrupt halt later in the 1960s when Brian arrived at the church one Saturday morning after having been up all night at the Wheel. He sat at the organ and played 'When A Man Loves a Woman' and was sacked.

In his defence, I tell him he picked a very spiritual song to play.

'Of course it's spiritual, it sounded brilliant,' he says, 'but the old fella had to take over and I got crucified for that.'

If soul music hadn't made inroads into the lives of the congregations of churches in Cheshire, word was certainly spreading elsewhere, thanks to *Ready Steady Go*, Radio Caroline and the emergence of Motown. Brian Rae recalls the attractions of the Motown sound. 'It was earthy and it had a wide appeal because it was just the best dance music,' he says, contrasting it to less hip sounds in the hit parade. 'Billy J Kramer and stuff that was in the charts was too thin or it didn't have a constant dance beat, but with Motown you could keep the dancefloor going. It was the base of all club music.'

Rumours of the thrills to be had at the Twisted Wheel were now circulating widely. Brian Rae – back down in London – remembers getting a letter from a girlfriend of his writing to say she'd been going to the Cavern in Liverpool but that someone had recommended the Twisted Wheel in Manchester. She'd taken a trip over there and heard a record called 'Harlem Shuffle' and wanted Brian to track it down and buy it for her. The next time he went North he went to the Wheel. Brian Rae can't recall the date, but whenever it was, Solomon Burke was on.

Soon Brian had moved back up North for good and taken a job at Lockers, the metal fabricators in Warrington, befriending two girls who ran the printing department from a separate building. They were big music fans, and in their building they had a record player, stacks of records and a radio, usually tuned to Radio Caroline. He remembers he used to find an excuse to leave the office, along with another lad, just so he could be in the printing department and catch a scrap of a record like 'Open the Door To Your Heart' by Darrell Banks.

Brian Rae travelled to the Wheel from Warrington, which is midway between Manchester and Liverpool. He remembers people waiting eight deep all along the platform at Warrington Central station on a Saturday night and getting on the last train into Manchester or Liverpool, such was the pull of clubs like the Cavern, the Wheel, the Oasis, the Birdcage, the Stax Club or the Jigsaw.

He also recalls watching Roger Eagle DJ-ing at the Twisted Wheel: 'He had two Garrard decks with a Bakelite arm and metal turntables, brown. He had a little thirty-watt amp to run the entire club and little ten-inch speakers through all the rooms. He had a Reslo ribbon microphone which is one of the worst microphones ever invented.'

What was wrong with them?

'They were terrible things. You used to talk and then all of a sudden you'd get nothing because the condensation off your breath was breaking the ribbon inside. The same used to happen for bands like the Beatles. They would just pack in.'

And if that happened your set was ruined?

'Yes, so what we used to do was unscrew the top and replace the broken ribbon with some silver paper from out of a cigarette packet. That would get it working again, just enough to get through the night probably.'

When Guy Stevens played at the Scene no-one bothered him, and, similarly, to the pilled-up regulars who piled into the Twisted Wheel, DJ Roger Eagle was anonymous, but Brian was drawn to him: 'At the Wheel I was one of those guys that I've suffered with and no doubt you've suffered with who come to the club to check out what you play and they ask you about records and you can see them scribbling in their notebooks, writing it all down, or at least memorising the names.'

As the records were spinning, Brian's head would be going round and round trying to read what was written on the label. He wasn't conducting himself in a cool way but he was certainly gaining a musical education. 'By standing there and taking it all in I'm sure I was building up a knowledge of what was being played,' he says.

Unlike other DJs at the time, Roger would go hours without saying anything on the microphone, and just develop a flow by the way he programmed the records, building a night, then taking the tempo down, then building the night up again. The technical side looked after itself, according to Brian: 'You just got on with what you'd got. It was not about technical expertise, because there was no technology to speak of.'

Roger Eagle's name was unknown, not because he wasn't a great DJ but because there was no media to spread that kind of information. His club had a great reputation built almost entirely on word of mouth and advertisements in the *Manchester Evening News*. He was very influential, though, and not just in the way he put quality into the music scene in Manchester, but through 'breaking' promo records and imports, picking tunes, playing them and building demand. Also, just as hearing Sasha play inspired DJs like Steve Lawler and Anne Savage, so Roger Eagle inspired people to start DJ-ing, including Brian Rae. Brian's first experiences DJ-ing weren't at temples of good taste like the Twisted Wheel, but at concert halls like Northwich Memorial Hall, playing records from the back of the stage in the intervals between groups. The Memorial Hall was run by Lewis Buckley, who also controlled other venues in the North West, including Southport Floral Hall and Warrington Co-op Hall, and Brian Rae was soon working at all of them.

DJ-ing was a new thing and the equipment provided wasn't up to much: just a single deck that loaded ten discs at a time and dropped them onto the turntable. Brian was sat behind a trestle table, being very formal and announcing each record on the microphone, saying, 'Ladies and gentlemen, this is the Beatles,' and then playing the record and trying to gauge it right, time it right, so the records dropped correctly and the intro fitted. It was all very primitive, he says. 'I was talking to this rave disc jockey type fella in Keele the other day and he couldn't imagine a day when disc jockeys were operating without twin decks. I tried to explain, he couldn't believe it.'

He continued to DJ during live gigs, but his first disc-only night was at the Blue Candle Club, a YWCA establishment in Warrington where he did a disco twice a week; it was just Brian and his records, one deck, and more technical headaches. Every time he tried to link up another deck he got loads of hum, so he asked an engineer from the local radio shop to twiddle about, fix a condenser and attach some volume controls. He was finally DJ-ing with two decks, without a hum. He got paid thirty bob a night.

Eventually, through persistence and trial and error, he had his twin decks, and more gigs started coming in. Looking back now he admits that another important factor in the surge in demand for his services was that he'd started to employ two girls dancing with him on-stage – his very own go-go girls. One of them was a girl from the printing department at the metal fabricators in Warrington; the other girl was one of her mates. He helped them to synchronise their routines, and with their choreographed spins and back flips they were a cut above the competition: 'I got some good gigs, and I was making a name for myself for having these girls.'

They were good?

'Not only were they good, Dave, but they had these short skirts on and tassels in all the right places.'

Along with the go-go girls, he did very well, at weddings, 21sts, clubs and halls, and continued to work at Lewis Buckley's venues which, as the 1960s progressed, would lead to him sharing the bill with the Small Faces, the Walker Brothers and Pink Floyd.

But Brian was still hankering after an opportunity to make his name as a DJ on the specialist soul scene; the big gigs with the go-go girls weren't satisfying his soul roots. He understood and valued the difference between the Twisted Wheel regulars and the average mod, let alone the average record buyer: 'In those days we reckoned we were years ahead of the average record buyer, even the average mod. We were as "in" as an "in" crowd could be, with our own music, and fashion, and way of life.'

You were like a tribe?

'Definitely. We were separate from everyone else.'

The purist soul fans would travel for miles to hear the right records, the cult records, finding their way to places way off the beaten track, a long way from Carnaby Street and the media front-line; the Cavern in Burnley or the

Bird Trap in Brierfield, for example. Somewhere else with a huge reputation was the fantastically-named Plebeians Jazz Club in Upper George Yard in Halifax, just off George Square, known as Plebs by the dozens of dance fans who journeyed there from all over the North to hear DJ 'King' Arthur mix rarities like Chubby Checker's 'At the Discotheque' with classics like Lee Dorsey's 'Ride Your Pony', hard-to-get versions of hit records, and big emotional anthems like James & Bobby Purify's 'Let Love Come Between Us'.

Elsewhere in Yorkshire, Peter Stringfellow, a young DJ and promoter who would later become something of an embarrassment to the nightclub world, was running a night called 'The USA Import & Classic Soul Show' at a small venue called the Tin Chicken in Castleford. From there he moved to the King Mojo in Sheffield where, although his playlist included great records like 'Wade in the Water' and 'Rescue Me', he remained a few steps back from the cutting edge; his was a mission to entertain, not to change minds. If a record wasn't working and the regulars had stopped dancing, Stringfellow would take it off halfway through and never play it again.

This was in stark contrast to the attitude of other DJs who inherited Roger Eagle's thirst for obscure discoveries. A record like 'Ain't Nothing But a House Party' by the Showstoppers, for example, would be massive at Plebs in Halifax until it charted. Then no-one wanted to hear it again. A tradition and rivalry developed among DJs determined to 'break' records and gain kudos in the scene for their reputation for picking obscurities and turning them into dancefloor hits.

In 1967 when psychedelia arrived, the soul scene looked to have died. Chasing the dollars, after the 1967 Summer of Love, Stringfellow renamed the Mojo 'the Beautiful Mojo' and had it decked out with flowers. But the new era marked the birth of Northern Soul, when clubbers in the North of England rejected psychedelia and maintained their passion for sharp, soulful sounds. The Northern Soul fans were keeping the faith, believing that the power of soul music was too big to be ditched on the whim of the fashion-hungry media and the record-buying public.

Club crowds in the North had become hooked on the Motown sound, demanding uptempo beat-driven stompers and rejecting slower syncopated or blues-oriented sounds. There was also growing awareness of other small labels and forgotten artists, many of them trying to capture the Motown sound, sometimes ending up with poor quality recordings, but more often making raw, passionate records that had probably only stayed obscure because of inadequate distribution or promotion. The obscurities and commercial failures – this was the reservoir of music Northern Soul fed upon over the next decades.

Brian Rae got a job DJ-ing at the Wheel in 1967. By this time, his mentor, Roger Eagle, had moved on to the Blue Note (later still he moved on to the Stax Club on Fountain Street). Restless, and refusing to be categorised, Roger Eagle was disillusioned by the domination of the beat-driven soul sound which undermined his determination to play a broad range of black sounds. The amount of drugs around in the mainstream mod scene also dismayed him. The big pill of the era was the black bomber, Durophet (black capsules stamped with the name of the manufacturer, Riker), and in the Wheel in the late 1960s, you could get eight for a pound. They were being gobbled like sweets, and casualties were common at the club. Later, looking back on his Wheel days, Roger Eagle told Ian Levine, 'I got very, very fed up having to call ambulances.'

Brian Rae had hung out in the DJ booth, played the odd record here and there, so it was not uncharted territory for him, but he remembers being called in for an audition on a Tuesday night presided over by DJ Ray Teret. The Wheel was no place for commercial fripperies; the go-go girls stayed in Warrington.

Brian already had a regular DJ-ing gig at Sheffield University earning him twenty pounds an evening. For his spots at the Wheel he accepted just two pounds; for this he also agreed to the owner's demand that he should help sweep up at 8 o'clock when the all-nighter finished. Brian Rae started playing there every week and developed a routine; after putting away the dustpan and brush he'd go off to the toilets at Piccadilly Station for a wash and a change of clothes and then get down to the Stax Club. He began to play sets there on Sunday mornings after Roger Eagle, and sometimes he'd still be DJ-ing at midday, until he'd finally get the train back to Warrington.

It was worth doing the gig for a couple of quid for many reasons, not least the amount of credibility being a Wheel DJ gave Brian Rae. Association with the venue opened doors for him: 'I did a regular gig in Warrington on a Sunday at the Co-op Hall which was packed, basically on the strength of me doing the Wheel. This is 1967, '68. Locally it would be advertised as "Brian Rae Presents . . ." and they'd put on Eddie Floyd, or William Bell.'

For Brian, finding the right records to play wasn't problematic because the Wheel had an in-house collection – made up of records supplied by Barry Ancill's record shop on Blackfriars Street – which Brian would augment with his own tunes. Brian wasn't as choosy in what he played as Roger Eagle had been. 'One of Roger's big records was "Poverty" by Bobby Bland and it took me years to get a copy,' says Brian.

Every week at the Wheel the ceiling leaked when it rained, and the club overheated in the summer; neither the licensing authorities nor the style gurus of our era would have been overly impressed. On the face of it, the Wheel was no more than several rooms of gloom, but late on Saturday night it would be transformed. Regulars would arrive with holdalls containing a spare set of clothes in case the Manchester rain, the leaking toilets or their body sweat ruined what they were wearing. Girls would carry vanity cases, lads would smell of Brut. The queue would stretch round the corner an hour before the doors opened.

The main part of the club was in the basement. Near the entrance, on the ground floor, was a cloakroom, a drinks bar and the toilets, as well as a small area with some benches along the wall where you could sit and take a breather, but music from the basement was relayed up through speakers. From the bottom of the stairs, the stage was on the right and on the far left was the DJ area. Most of the basement was painted red, white and black, the room broken up into a series of alcoves, each containing speakers.

The DJ area was one of the only areas brightly lit, and the DJ cage was surrounded by spokes and wheel frames (the decor of the club, such as it was, was based on a wheel motif). The Wheel's record library was stored behind the decks, but was stolen sometime during the Christmas break in 1968. There was a stage for live acts which included the Ronettes, Bo Diddley, Lee Dorsey and Jamo Thomas. Jimi Hendrix turned up one January night in 1967 after his gig at the New Century Hall and watched a set by the Spellbinders. It was virtually dark in some parts of the club; 'Naturally such scarcity of illumination tends to have a widening effect on the pupils of the eyes,' wrote Dave Godin in 1971.

There were plenty of drugs around at the Wheel. Steve Higginson remembers riding over to Manchester on his scooter from Liverpool, and claims that the travelling crowd at the Wheel tended to be the most hardened music lovers, the local Mancs the most hardened pill poppers. Driven on by chemicals, the crowd were not always into DJs who veered from the tried and trusted, as Brian Phillips, one of the Wheel's DJs who started playing in 1969, told David Nowell in *Too Darn Soulful*: 'There was always a certain element who unless the stuff was fast and furious they used to pull at the wheels like wild animals. They wanted the same old stuff all the time. It was hard work sometimes. You had to drop your new stuff in once a week and hope that it would take off.'

Rob Bellars also joined the line-up at the Wheel in 1969. He discovered 'You're Gonna Make Me Love You' by Sandi Sheldon on the Okeh label and Jackie Lee's 'Darkest Days' on an ABC promo. At first, people didn't dance to 'Darkest Days', but Rob persisted. No-one else knew how to get hold of the record and it became such a cult item that Bellars actually sold it at the end of an evening for £25.

Collectors were playing an important part in the scene now that certain rare records were becoming dancefloor favourites. Brian Rae would buy 'doubles', and if he built up demand by playing one copy of the record he would sell the other, like Guy Stevens did. The tradition of cover ups took hold, too; Rob Bellars is said to have been the first DJ to do this, covering up the labels of the records to keep the titles and his sources secret.

Some DJs benefited from the work of collectors. Ian Levine grew up in Blackpool and started collecting soul records in 1968. He was lucky enough to go on holidays to the USA with his parents, where he would trawl local record shops for singles. After these, and subsequent visits, he had an enviable collection. He began hanging out with the DJs at the Wheel, occasionally taking a precious record to them for an airing. He'd picked up Rose Batiste's 'Hit & Run' on Revilot on one trip, and handed it over to Les Cockell. It was an instant classic and Cockell practically fell to the floor in amazement.

American imports became easier to get hold of around 1969, so DJs at the Wheel like Les Cockell began to concentrate a little more on older, more obscure tunes, rather than new releases. Brian Rae left the Wheel in September 1970, and even sold some of his records. Colin Curtis bought a demo copy of Moses Smith's 'Girl Across the Street' from him for £40. Collectors pounced, according to Brian: 'I used to come home from the pub and find people sitting on the wall outside my house waiting to buy stuff from me.'

In 1971 the Wheel closed, cueing the anguished cry of another generation of dance music fans ready to declare that things were never going to be so good again. The more clued-up ex-Wheel customers went to the Mecca in Blackpool (not an all-nighter), and, from 1972, the Golden Torch in Tunstall, Stoke on Trent, was the place to be seen.

The Torch had been open for seven years as a pop music venue where bands played and disco-only nights were hosted by a DJ called Barmy Barry, a gag merchant, a big fan of Mr Savile's. In fact, Jimmy Savile played there as a guest DJ, as did Peter Stringfellow. In March 1972, though, owner Chris Burton was persuaded to give Northern Soul all-nighters a go. For him it was a big departure from providing a live band and a madcap DJ, but it turned out to be a great success, especially in the short term. The DJs on the first Northern night were Keith Minshull and Colin Curtis. They DJ-ed from 8.30pm to 8.30am, and took home £10 each.

Guest DJs were brought in from other big clubs at the time, including Martyn Ellis from the Pendulum in Manchester, and Chris Burton's experience of booking bands helped the Torch secure the services of an astonishing selection of groups during 1972 and 1973. Back then you could have walked down the back streets of Tunstall and paid £1 to see Junior Walker, the Drifters, Sam & Dave or the Stylistics.

Apart from the problems caused by more than a thousand people trying to get into a club that only held half that number, built halfway down a residential street, drug use at the Torch also attracted the attention of the police, who took to stopping cars on roads leading to the venue and searching the occupants. Other DJs had been drafted in, including Tony Jebb who was poached from Blackpool Mecca, but Minshull and Curtis moved on and the club closed soon after. Colin Curtis remembers it like this: 'I don't think the drug taking was out of control in relation to what went on at Wigan Casino and today's ecstasy scene. People were doing the drugs because they cared about the music and wanted to stay awake. However, we didn't need all the negative stuff that was going down at the Torch. It was depressing and we decided to move on.'

Like all great nights, the Torch left a legacy. Dave Evison was a regular at the club and would go on to play a part at Wigan Casino and afterwards. His own career as a DJ took inspiration from what he heard Minshull and Curtis play there. But the Torch was bulldozed, and Evison, like others, was left with his memories; among them an occasion when a girl with heavily lacquered hair asked him for a light and he obliged with a match, but unfortunately set her hair on fire. Thinking as quickly as he was able, he doused her by pouring a pint of beer over her head.

After the closure of the Wheel, the Blackpool Mecca

became a favoured venue, and its popularity increased when the Torch also closed. The Mecca was a huge venue with a room upstairs – the Highland Room – available for functions. Ian Levine knew the DJs there and supplied DJ Tony Jebb with rare records. He also helped get Les Cockell a job with Tony Jebb, but various other permutations were tried until finally Blackpool Mecca's two main residents were Colin Curtis and Ian Levine; the collector had become a DJ. Curtis and Levine were to preside over the Mecca's most famed years, the years when it pulled more than a thousand regulars a week and went head to head with Wigan Casino.

Wigan Casino opened its doors as an all-nighter venue on 23 September 1973, running from 2am until 8am, with Russ Winstanley at the helm, and was an instant success, pulling in hundreds of young clubbers. The Casino closed in 1981 to make way for a civic centre that Wigan Council planned to build on the site (they never did). After the closure, the building was destroyed by fire, but long before then the Casino had become the quintessential Northern Soul venue, somehow maintaining a mystique as well as popularity, showcasing great music and famous Northern Soul fashions (32-inch wide baggies, vests or bowling shirts covered with badges).

Customers travelled from Scotland, the North of England and the Midlands for a night out at the Casino. Eventually, the Casino gained a second room playing oldies. The heat was sometimes unbearable, the dancing incredible, the regulars obsessive. In 1977 the American music magazine *Billboard* designated the Casino the best disco in the world (ahead of Studio 54).

In the main room the DJs were high on the stage, and Russ soon gained a reputation for being a lot more populist than the Mecca DJs. He also recruited Richard Searling in 1974. Born in Bolton, Richard secured a job at

Global Records in Manchester and began DJ-ing at the Pendulum, then became the resident at Va-Va's, an all-nighter in Bolton. When Richard took the job at Va-Va's he got paid £8 for seven hours, 1am to 8am, a useful addition to his earnings at Global Records. He was also not the last DJ to find that working in a record shop was ideal for a DJ – being surrounded by music and getting first pick of any new stock.

One of his jobs at Global was to go to the USA. Over in the States there were warehouses full of boxes of unsold records, and Richard would be sent over there to find demo versions and undiscovered gems, and pick up records for a few cents that were collectors items back home. On one occasion he came across a dusty copy of 'Tainted Love' by Gloria Jones which at the time wasn't just obscure, it was unknown. He popped it into his bag with all the others and gave it a spin a few weeks later at Va-Va's. 'Tainted Love', of course, went on to become a huge record on the Northern scene, and, covered by Soft Cell in 1981, went to the top of the charts.

Va-Va's soon closed, but by this time he had guested at the Casino a number of times, played monthly, and then weekly from March 1974. When he got his slot at the Casino it felt like a big deal: 'I made my debut in January 1974. It had already been up and running for four months.'

And it was already big.

'Yeah.'

And how much did you get paid when you started there?

'I don't know, probably twenty quid, twenty-five quid.'

Richard worked at the Casino, DJ-ing in partnership with Russ Winstanley, and also behind the counter at Russ's record shop in Wigan. On the decks, Russ was open-minded and populist, while Richard was more of a collector and a purist. But the Casino was big and the dancefloor needed to be filled, and as every DJ knows, it's easier to empty one than fill one. Richard: 'Russ played some records that I wouldn't have, but they were popular, and it would be hard to criticise him for playing stuff that got people through the doors of the club.'

And the pop stuff may have been a useful way in to the scene for people.

'I suppose so, yes. They would become interested and go on to discover more things, better things.'

From February 1975, for just over a year, the Pier at Cleethorpes hosted an all-nighter, promoted by Mary Chapman. In the sleevenotes to the compilation *The Cleethorpes Story*, she writes, 'Our DJs' musical policy was not only the envy of every other club in its day, but the most varied ever attempted on the Northern scene up to that time.'

Among the DJs at Cleethorpes Pier were Eddie Antemes, Soul Sam, Ginger Taylor and John Vincent. Soul Sam was living in North Wales in the mid-1960s, teaching English and History at a school in Wrexham. As well as trips down to London, he would go over to Manchester, though not to all-nighters at the Wheel, but events at evening clubs. 'I was never an all-nighter person,' he says. 'I've never taken drugs – that sort of thing in the scene didn't appeal to me at all, but the music did, and I used to go to clubs, in Manchester, until about 2 o'clock and I heard early Tamla Motown, Stateside, stuff like that.'

He also used to read *Record Mirror*, and if reviewer James Hamilton talked about a soulful, tuneful, good dance track, Sam would buy it purely on his recommendation; that's how he got most of the rare Motown releases, plus things like the Incredibles and the

Invitations, and the American Poets on the London label. As his collection grew, through 1965 and 1967, he began to be asked to DJ: 'People in the Wrexham area were begging me to DJ because I had the records.'

He had the right records, and, having stood in front of his English and History classes, had no fear of getting on the microphone, but the technical aspect of DJ-ing intimidated him: 'I've always had a great fear of technology, and the reason it took me two years to do it was not because I didn't have the records but because I didn't have the nerve to use the equipment! Like today, put me in front of a computer and I see stars almost. I am totally untechnical. It took me longer than it should have done, really, but my hands and brain don't really work well together!'

Even though DJ-ing then wasn't about mixing, it was enough for Sam that he had to cue the records, press the right button and make announcements all at the same time. In 1968 he tried to overcome his nervousness and began working with somebody who had the equipment and the know-how. Sam would choose the records and announce them, and his partner would put them on. By 1969 he'd got his own equipment and finally had the confidence to start DJ-ing in a club: 'I did a club in Wrexham called Peppers which was playing all soul, plus new releases. We used to play "Stoned Love", those sorts of things, but pre-release. By the time "Stoned Love" got a UK release, we were on to the next one; a bit like the import scene has been ever since.'

Did you find it easy to think about what was needed to fill a dancefloor?

'I found it easy. I've always been able to judge what would go on the dancefloor, but whether I've always been prepared to play it, that's another matter.'

Through word of mouth he got various other gigs

round Wrexham and then the upstairs room at Whitchurch Civic Hall on a Saturday night, which attracted punters like Colin Curtis before the Torch. He was asked to do Stoke Top Rank: 'It was all very political at the time, and I don't think I was far off from being at Blackpool Mecca, let's put it like that, but there was pressure from a certain source and I ended up at the Top Rank with Keith Minshull who was the big Torch DJ. It was then, whenever Wigan was starting, that I got approached by Russ to do the Casino, and I turned it down.'

So you turned down a residency at Wigan Casino?

'I turned it down for two reasons. I wasn't into staying up all night to DJ and doing all-nighters. And the other was economic: I was getting paid twice as much at the Top Rank as I was offered at the Casino.'

The Top Rank was packed every night, but within a few weeks the head office decided to turn the building into a bingo hall. Ginger Taylor and Eddie Antemes were already at Cleethorpes and they asked him to join them, and suddenly he was there, doing his all-nighter thing. Cleethorpes did well, commercially and in terms of credibility. Soul Sam:

In my personal opinion – speaking as somebody who went to Cleethorpes and later went to Wigan – I preferred Cleethorpes. I preferred it because I found that there was less pop stuff played there, but then Cleethorpes was probably at its height before the big boom of 1976. It also had a bunch of DJs who weren't so well known, and I was playing mainly Sixties stuff, but there were other DJs like John Manship and Ian Dewhirst who came in playing the more soulful Seventies stuff.

Most other clubs found that credibility and commercial success were two very different things. In terms of taking the music to new audiences, Wigan Casino was huge. You might hear a record first at Blackpool or

Cleethorpes, but sustained play at Wigan made it a hit. Russ and Richard would have meetings each week to decide on which records to push, but musical differences often put a strain on the partnership. Richard tended to be more purist – but not always.

All DJs must have a few tunes that make them cringe in hindsight, but there's a lot of rewriting of history that goes on. There's not much wrong with the records Richard played at the Casino, not when you consider I've heard Mr Scruff playing 'Love Cats', Mike Pickering playing Erasure and Paul Oakenfold playing Mandy Smith; not when you bear in mind Terry Farley remixed The Farm, and one of Pete Tong's floorfillers in the old days was 'Tiger Feet' by Mud (I made that last one up).

Even the most consistent, cool DJ has a rush of blood, a lapse of taste. Recently I asked Graeme Park to cast his mind back over his two decades of DJ-ing:

> I don't really listen to old tapes but my wife, Jen, has a habit of digging them out, usually at five o'clock in the morning when we're sat round the kitchen table pouring another drink and talking complete nonsense, and she'll pull out some tape from the Haçienda in 1989 and we put it on and for a while it'll be 'Check these tunes out!' and then there'll be one and it'll be 'What's that, what is it?' and I won't even recognise it and it'll be really awful. There's plenty of records you only play once!

When Northern Soul went overground, thanks to the quality of the music and the profile of Wigan Casino, a few lowest common denominator records began to appear in the mainstream charts: Wayne Gibson's 'Under My Thumb', or 'Footsee' by Wigan's Chosen Few. Records were released which plumbed depths of tack no Northern DJ would support. In June 1975, just as disco would spawn a novelty hit by Cookie Monster and rap inspire hit singles by Roland Rat, so Northern Soul suffered the indignity of being the subject of a song by The Goodies: 'Black Pudding Bertha (the Queen of Northern Soul)'.

In any high profile club, the politics and relationships between everyone involved can become strained and degenerate into a scrum of backstabbing and jostling for credit. The heated debates between Richard and Russ continued, and the pair were rumoured not to have spoken to each other during the last two years of Wigan Casino. In 1978 Richard stopped working at Russ's shop. Richard is only too well aware of the notoriety his bust-up with Russ has gained, and seems weary of the subject: 'Of course there's rivalry in the music. You want to play the best records you can. If there isn't the rivalry there, you might as well pack it in.'

Ian Levine claimed that Blackpool Mecca was more innovative than Wigan, and certainly the Mecca playlist incorporated new records, and, more importantly, softer sounds, disco-tinged tracks and singles not reliant on the instant buzz of the big Motown stomping beat. Levine himself broke the rare 1973 release 'It Really Hurts Me Girl' by the Carstairs, and then championed the brilliant 'Turn the Beat Around' by Vicki Sue Robinson, one of the first records to capture the energy of disco.

To the Northern Soul faithful, this embrace of new 1970s sounds was a dilution of the scene's rare soul roots, but Levine was unrepentant about his evangelism for the contemporary, and began a studio career by producing 'Reaching for the Beat' by the Exciters, which charted in February 1975. His trips to America began to include visits to gay discos in New York and they further inspired him. He also began to get into the remix business, having picked up on the work of DJs like Tom Moulton. Through 1977 and 1978 he and Colin Curtis steered the Highland Room into an even more contemporary space, with Curtis playing jazz funk and Levine doing disco. At the

Mecca in that era you'd hear the likes of Crown Heights Affair, Sylvester and Brass Construction.

Over in Wigan, Russ Winstanley had banned Levine's productions, and steered well away from the disco sound. The conflicts and controversies were creating a volatile atmosphere. Richard was threatened when he played Gary Lewis & the Playboys' 'My Heart's Symphony' at a gig in Blackburn. He recalls it like it was yesterday: 'It was some inebriated yob who ironically wanted me to play a record by Carol Douglas instead, which was probably just as far from the essence of Northern as the Gary Lewis one. I think the record he wanted was "A Hurricane is Coming Tonight".'

Why was it such an issue?

'It was all a part of the Wigan Casino, Blackpool Mecca rivalry and he was obviously on the other side, as it were, but he got pretty het up about it and I remember Ginger Taylor came to my rescue that night. There wasn't much difference in the soul content of either of them, they were both ludicrous records.'

You played the odd ludicrous record?

'Yeah, being honest. I played that Gary Lewis record and Bobby Goldsboro's "Too Many People" but it didn't seem wrong at the time and there wasn't that much furore, but in retrospect you look back and it's easy to judge, but at the time they worked. Gary Lewis was actually quite a big hit as a result of getting played at the Casino, so as evidence of the importance of the club and its impact, I was quite proud about it actually.'

The proliferation of drugs at Wigan Casino contributed to the heady atmosphere; at various times different drugs were the rage, including Riker's black bombers, Filon, Duramin (a time release capsule which meant that instead of one big kick and a slow drain, you had periodic highs) and Dexadrine (small yellow dexies). Dealers would get their supplies either through raids on chemists' shops or obtain their own homemade versions. Late in the 1970s there were plentiful supplies of homemade amphetamine sulphate and backstreet versions of dexies.

In 1998 the 'Gatecrasher' kids started covering themselves with Mitsubishi logos, but in Wigan Casino twenty years earlier you would occasionally see kids with Riker or SKF (for Smith, Kline & French) tattoos or badges. As drug use continued to expand on the Northern scene, there's some evidence that although many pill users never suffered any long-term effects, others began to take barbiturates to take the edge off the Monday/Tuesday comedown.

Soul Sam managed to avoid all this, the way the surge of interest in the scene in 1976 seemed to lead people to latch onto the drugs rather than the music: 'You could tell when people were on it, I suppose. Basically I turned a blind eye to it. But people who didn't know me automatically assumed I was on it because I used to do so many gigs – in the Bank Holiday weekends in 1976, 1977 I would do seven bookings between the Friday and the Monday. I would probably do a thousand miles in the weekend and arrive back at school on the Tuesday morning absolutely knackered, but I hadn't had anything.'

Teaching English and History at school; was it difficult to go from the world of the all-nighters back to school?

'I must admit, I would coast through those Mondays and Tuesdays and just hope the kids were quiet and we could get on and work quietly and just get through it.'

Richard Searling knows the drugs and the music have become attached but he's a music man: 'I can only speak from personal experience on that, Dave, and it's always been the music for me. I've never got too close to the drug side of it, but at the Casino we'd have the drug squad arriving, and drug busts were a regular worry.'

The presence of police in the Casino was one thing, but the arrival of camera crews from Granada TV proved to be even more controversial as far as the regulars were concerned. They filmed a documentary on Northern and once it was broadcast there were more gawpers than dancers in the club; the original secret scene had gone public.

A couple of years before the Casino closed in 1981, the Levine/Curtis partnership at Blackpool Mecca had split amicably. Levine headed south, spinning hi-energy at London club Heaven, and produced the million-selling anthem 'High Energy' by Evelyn Thomas and Take That's first hits. He came back to Northern Soul at the end of the 1990s, making the phenomenal video *The Strange World of Northern Soul* in 1999. Colin Curtis, meanwhile, continued to DJ on the all-dayer and weekender circuit, including major nights at Rafters and the Ritz in Manchester. He gave up his full-time DJ-ing career in 1987, but still plays out.

Interest in Northern Soul went into decline at the beginning of the 1980s and gigs temporarily dried up for Brian Rae. Roger Eagle had long since given up on the Northern Soul fraternity, who were even more boxed-in and constrained in their music policy than the mods. He'd managed Eric's club in Liverpool in the punk era and then the International in Manchester. He died in 1999. When Brian Rae talks about Roger Eagle's views on Northern Soul he gets his present and past tenses mixed, like he's still not quite convinced Roger Eagle has gone: 'He had a following at that time but he was never a fan of what became known as the Northern Soul scene because he thinks they were too off their heads to take in anything good. He wasn't being nasty about it, but he didn't like the way they followed one genre of music and that's it and they've no width in what they liked.'

Brian has his own views on why interest in Northern Soul dipped in the early 1980s: 'Northern disappeared up its own backside. At that point it was like if it wasn't from Detroit it wasn't worth playing, but everything from Detroit wasn't worth playing, was it? In the end they were playing crap from Detroit and ignoring stuff from Memphis, Chicago, New Orleans or wherever else.'

The fact that the 100 Club all-nighters started just as the scene in the North went into recession makes the night's longevity all the more impressive. The playlist contains records that Roger Eagle might have played at the first Wheel (Bobby Bland), or Guy Stevens might have championed at the Scene (the Impressions). It's almost exclusively 1960s soul, nothing modern and no rhythm and blues.

A less intimate club in the North of England, the Ritz in Manchester, is another venue where the survival, even the prosperity of the rare soul scene is obvious. The Ritz is an old-fashioned venue with a big red curtain behind the stage, a great dancefloor, a balcony and plenty of bars. Like the 100 Club, it also has a potent history: in the 1940s the Northern Dance Orchestra was based there; in the 1960s Jimmy Savile, in a gold suit, ran Sunday night gigs there; New Order, Was (not Was), Morcheeba and Primal Scream have all played there. In Northern Soul history it's remembered for a series of great all-dayers organised by Neil Rushton and the Heart of England Soul Club in the late 1970s.

Richard Searling restarted Northern Soul events at the Ritz in December 1993. For some commentators on the scene, the events are too big – like a superclub – and too compromised compared to the intimate and purist nights held elsewhere. I ask Richard if he gets tired of the controversies, or whether the scene is less volatile now:

No, I think more volatile now than they were. I think people have got their agendas now, and you've got the R&B crew who don't particularly like the Northern Soul old school and vice versa. You've got the guys who don't think any modern should get played, but it certainly does now and it's one of the main reasons the scene has grown; the playlists aren't as narrow as they used to be. No, the politics are worse than ever, and not helped by certain fanzines who seem unappreciative of the work that goes into promoting gigs and getting a thousand people through the doors. It takes more than a few mentions on the radio, it takes a lot of doing.

You feel targeted?

'To an extent, but it doesn't get me down, it fires me up.'

Outside the Ritz on an Easter Bank Holiday Sunday the queue goes up the road, past the phone box, to the traffic lights. Cars are filling the adjacent NCP car park. At midnight mini-cabs drop more people off outside the club. There's a steady hum of expectation. It's very different from the usual Ritz crowd, but very similar to the 100 Club crowd: friendly, mostly in their thirties and mid-forties. In the queue and in the club a favourite topic of conversation is where people have travelled from. You ask them and they'll tell you: Ormskirk, Carlisle, Burnley, Leeds, Bedfordshire.

Inside the club I josh Richard, having heard him admitting that the other night he'd had so much to drink he'd kissed the other DJ: 'It happens very rarely, Dave. The fact that I did it is the least concerning thing; the fact that I can't remember doing it is more worrying!'

The DJs talk between records. Some keep the chat short and sweet, just giving the name of the last track and the name of the next, maybe with a bit of an embellishment – 'This is one of the best records ever to come out of Philadelphia – the Volcanoes', or 'Next up, a big sound from the Twisted Wheel days' – but a few of them get into a more extended ramble. Dave Evison ends his set with 'I'm still looking for a lift for next weekend. I'm going down to Hampshire, so if anyone can give me a lift down there, please come up and see me. It'll be a good night. Thanks.'

Richard's busy in the DJ box, putting up a small sign giving the rundown of which DJ is playing when; each DJ gets half an hour or an hour. Ginger Taylor does a set and plays 'I'm Coming Home in the Morning' by Lou Pride, one of the records of the night. The DJs switch over, like a relay, picking up the baton, the way the spirit of the music has been passed from venue to venue, DJ to DJ, over the last forty years.

Sometimes the audience claps at the end of the record, during the pause and the DJ's announcements. Soul Sam is up soon. Richard is scurrying between the front desk and the DJ box. I have a look at the list of DJs. At the bottom of the sheet he's underlined this sentence: To Be No Spaces on the Dancefloor. I ask Richard why he needed to remind the DJs of this: 'Because we want to make it as much like the Casino as possible.'

Brian Rae arrives and people in the crowd say hello to him, but when I ask him if he knows them he tells me that he sees a lot of regular faces on the circuit without ever knowing names. Someone else shakes his hand. It's now three o'clock in the morning and I'm talking to a man who's only a year or so off being sixty. I look round the Ritz; in our heads we're all still eighteen. At half past four Brian Rae will take his turn on the decks, just before the sun rises. I ask him when he's going to get a proper job and he laughs.

Soul Sam has just begun his set, and there's a pause after his first record which doesn't end. Then, on the mic, Sam makes a frantic announcement: 'The deck is playing up ... The deck is definitely playing up!' More than twenty years on from his nervous first nights with a Dansette, Soul Sam is still suffering technical traumas, but he battles on and the music comes alive again. The speaker pops, there's a click from the disc, the seven-inch spins and the dancefloor fills.

CHAPTER 7

Music is the Key:
the Southport Soul Weekender

In tracing the roots of today's massive club culture and the status of the superstar DJs, as well as acknowledging the importance of the Northern Soul scene, there are other hidden histories; among them, the story of black music in London in the 1980s – the days of rare groove and warehouse parties, and the rise of Trevor Nelson, Norman Jay and Soul II Soul – and the story of soul weekenders at off-season holiday camps at Caister, Prestatyn and Southport.

Founded and promoted by an affable and music-loving Geordie called Alex Lowes, the Southport Weekender started at a caravan park in Berwick-on-Tweed in 1987 and then moved to Blackpool for two events, finally settling in Southport in 1989. Over ten years later, the £99 ticket for the Southport Soul Weekender includes accommodation in one of the on-site chalets at the Pontins holiday camp where the event is held, but I'm staying at the Scarisbrick Hotel in town; someone told me it's where the industry stay. I had hoped to bump into legendary New York DJs in the lounge bar, but the place was full of wedding party guests and golfers. I escape the hotel, take a taxi, and five minutes later arrive outside Pontins, the chill wind from the Irish Sea blowing November rain in my face. Just up ahead are the main gates of the camp.

Three and a half thousand people have already bought tickets for the event, and over the next forty-eight hours something like eighty DJs will be playing to the crowds. I'll be surrounded by DJs, spoilt for choice.

The Southport Soul Weekender always features a well-picked selection of DJs representing various scenes and eras, with regulars including Trevor Nelson, Norman Jay and Bob Jones, the Dreem Teem and Freddy Fresh. Many of Southport's DJs have been playing there for years and have gone from relative obscurity to high profile jobs at Radio One – Danny Rampling and Gilles Peterson, for example – but the range of DJs at the weekender extends well beyond the big names, embracing younger DJs and plenty of veterans. The event has its roots in the soul scene of the 1970s and 1980s, among those clubbing generations who maintained a devotion to music from black America, the true believers who kept the soul flame alive.

Soul fans were, in effect, part of a secret society. A network had developed, as had a habit of travelling to events. Like ravers who clogged up motorway service stations in 1988 and 1989, the 1970s soul fans travelled out of necessity, following the crowd, searching for the right parties, the one-offs, the best DJs. Soul fans were generally in a minority in their home towns, and few venues regularly played soul music, so the culture revolved instead around organised regional or national clubs with membership. The clubs had membership numbers running into the thousands, which helped publicise events but also solved a practical problem: all-nighters and events in unlicensing premises could by-pass stringent licensing legislation if they were held by organisations with membership schemes.

All through the 1970s and into the 1980s, and all over Britain, promoters ran hundreds of events through the soul clubs, from Whitchurch in Shropshire to Kettering in Northamptonshire, from the Yate Centre in Bristol to the Cat's Whiskers in Leeds. Twenty-five years later, the network is international, and people travel to Southport for the Soul Weekender from Amsterdam, South Africa, America, France, Germany, Holland, as well as from Aberdeen, London and the Midlands.

Many of the monthlies, one-offs, all-nighters and weekenders were held in locations off the beaten track, rather than in city centre dance halls. In May 1974, for example, the West Midlands Soul Club organised a soul cruise, taking a boat from Worcester to Droitwich. A few months later, a soul train journeyed from Crewe to Stoke, Wolverhampton and Birmingham and ended at Reading Top Rank; DJs on board that day included Richard Searling and Soul Sam. Occasionally the promoters of these soul extravaganzas get too ambitious; the following autumn a trip for soul heads to Majorca collapsed when the tour company went bankrupt.

All this activity in the mid-1970s went comparatively unreported – compared to the booming punk scene, and compared also to the hype of the dance music industry today – but was encouraged by a specialist, small scale soul and funk press, which included magazines like *Black Music*, *Blues & Soul*, *Black Echoes*, and fanzines like 'Shout' and 'Hot Buttered Soul'. The radio waves had opened up, and by 1975 many local BBC and commercial stations were finding room for DJs who played soul and funk, like Greg Edwards on Capital Radio, Robbie Vincent on Radio London, Terry Lennaine on Radio Merseyside. At the same time, the Emperor Rosko on Radio One would be playing Sly & the Family Stone, the O-Jays and Esther Phillips. Soon other radio DJs found themselves with influential soul programmes: Andy Peebles on Piccadilly Radio (Manchester) and Mark Jones on Radio

City (Liverpool). Out in the clubs, in addition to the DJ-only nights, there were quality live bands charting and touring who appealed directly to dancefloor devotees: the Fatback Band, BT Express, Kool & the Gang.

The soul fans of the 1970s and 1980s weren't united, though. The Northern Soul fans preferred hard, fast soul made in the past, the era directly before psychedelia. As the 1970s progressed other dance music fans embraced the waves of funk and disco. Throughout the 1970s and 1980s, there were constant conflicts between progressive and conventional DJs, and all through those decades the difference between North and South hardened; generally, down South the soul scene was less retro, more funk-oriented, with fewer mod drugs.

In the South of England in the 1970s one of the highest profile DJs was Chris Hill. He started DJ-ing in the late 1960s playing R&B, and then established himself on the Essex club circuit, first at a small club in Orsett and then at the Goldmine at Canvey Island. In the mid-1970s the Goldmine was legendary as a popular party venue playing soul. Hill wasn't too precious about the music he played, and encouraged fun and party games at the Goldmine, in contrast to the tendency of more purist soul nights. He would run theme nights and customers would arrive dressed as characters from a Monty Python sketch or the TV series *Happy Days*.

Nevertheless, Chris Hill had a good instinct for picking records that would pull a commercial crowd towards soul and funk. In the years just prior to the *Saturday Night Fever* boom, his playlists were a fair reflection of the beginnings of disco. In 1975, for example, one of his big tunes was 'Fly Robin Fly' by Silver Convention, a Euro dance record that helped define the disco era. At the peak of Goldmine's popularity, Chris moved on to the Lacy Lady in Ilford. The Lacy Lady attracted a wide variety of clubbers and press interest, with its diet of be bop, disco, jazz funk and modern soul.

Buoyed by the success of the Lacy Lady, and along with DJs Chris Brown and Tom Holland, and later Robbie Vincent, Froggy, Greg Edwards and Sean French, Chris Hill launched soul all-dayers at the Reading Top Rank Suite, and massive events in Purley and Alexandra Palace. The same bunch of DJs were integral to the Caister Soul Weekender which started in March 1979. According to DJ Dr Bob Jones, the idea was originated by Robbie Vincent with half an eye on the all-nighter scene up North. Holiday camps had already hosted themed breaks – for 1950s revivalists and old teddy boys, for example – and, aware of this, Robbie Vincent believed a weekender bringing together the soul boys would work. The soul clubs in the South were small and dispersed – from the Rio in Didcot and Deejay's in Chelmsford to the Gold-mine at Canvey Island and Flicks in Dartford – and the weekenders became a great meeting place, as Dr Bob recalls: 'Initially it was the music that brought everybody together, the fact that they'd all been attending these little clubs and now they could meet together.'

In the second half of the 1970s various attempts were made to bring the Northern Soul devotees and the Southern soul crew together; among them, an all-dayer at the Top Rank in Reading in 1977 which put Brian Rae DJ-ing in one room and Chris Hill in the other. Nights at venues like the Top of the World in Stafford and the Birmingham Locarno tried to do the same. Some clubs tried to bring various scenes under one roof: at Bar-barellas in Birmingham in 1979 you could watch live punk and new wave bands – the Clash, Generation X, Iggy Pop – playing in one room, or sneak down the corridor and listen to a DJ playing the likes of the Real Thing and Earth, Wind & Fire in another. Pips in Manchester had several rooms, each playing a different kind of music. If you walked through them all you'd hear 'Tears of a Clown' one minute, David Bowie's 'Suffragette City' the next. Some DJs would try to fuse various scenes in their set – Jay Strongman playing rockabilly and funk, for instance. It was an era of proliferating club fashions; from spats to trainers, from zoot suits to new romantics ruffs and Bowie pegs.

In London in 1980, George Power, DJ-ing at Crackers on Wardour Street, resurrected the idea of Friday lunchtime sessions; then and most weekend nights he would fill the venue with bright young soul boys paying 50p in. Norman Jay was a big fan of George Power: 'He was totally on the button, understood what black kids were about. He became a legend. In the eyes of us inner city kids, George Power was more relevant than any Chris Hill or Robbie Vincent. After discovering George Power, they didn't mean that much to us. They weren't as cutting edge, or as up to the minute.'

The music and mixing innovations Froggy had witnessed in America were being picked up by other DJs; promotional material advertising Steve Walsh's night at J Arthurs in Catford promised 'New York style mixing'. As well as the older soul DJs, another, young bunch of DJs were making their way through the scene, and, in recognition of their contribution, by 1980 they were being invited to join the Caister set-up. This crew included DJs like Jeff Young, Dr Bob Jones, Mick Clarke and Pete Tong.

Pete Tong was a drummer in a rock band when he was fifteen, but then, at a school disco, he decided a career change was necessary: 'I saw the DJ there and thought that'd be a much better thing to do. It just looked like a sexy job.' Soon he would start hanging out in soul clubs and watching DJs like Froggy mixing. He got his own mobile set-up, and by 1980 Tong was playing various venues in Kent, like Woodvilles in Gravesend, King's Lodge in West Kingsdown, and getting gigs at Caister, watching rooms full of people getting down to 'Oops Upside Your Head'.

In the North, the Northern Soul scene appeared to be fading away by 1978, and the progressive jazz funk playlists pursued by Colin Curtis and John Grant at Rafters in Manchester took hold. Alex Lowes reckons it was the music played at Rafters that most influenced him. Back in those days, though, there was nobody catering for soul in the North-East so Alex began to put on his own events at clubs like Macmillans in Yarm and Buddy's in Gretna Green: 'At Macmillans we used to get a thousand people every Sunday night from all over the place, as far as Manchester and everywhere, you know. It was like anything goes in those days, hip hop, soul, and it was just starting out with the house scene.'

In the early days of the Southport Weekender it was easier to secure live bands, but now the focus is on DJs. For Alex Lowes the basic philosophy behind Southport was originally his love of soul, but now he's moving on, following interests and enthusiasm for garage, jazz, r&b. In recent years Southport has featured live PAs by the likes of Shola Ama, Jody Watley, Craig David and TQ, but mostly the event relies on DJs; DJs getting paid a lot more than they ever used to get. 'That's right,' Alex says, laughing, 'I never got paid anything like what I'm paying some of them now, bloody hell!'

The British soul scene in the 1980s had its own network, its big DJ names, and a network of magazines and radio shows. The soul scene had energy and, even before Southport, events and DJs, but it also had some shortcomings. Dr Bob Jones was witnessing a deterioration in the atmosphere at Caister: 'The weekender was degenerating. It got so commercial at one point that they were taking out adverts in the *Sun*. The main hall changed from being music lovers to a load of piss-artists. We were just turning up, playing, holding our hands out for money and then going home. It got to the point where we didn't want this any more.'

Dr Bob reckons it was at this point that Alex Lowes and Nicky Holloway began planning revitalised versions of the Caister Weekender at other holiday camps: 'There was certainly a demand for places to go, but for punters who wanted a weekend away without all that crazy foam and beer.'

In the mid-1980s there was also a perception that the West End clubs and the established soul and funk scene were white dominated. On one occasion, for instance, Trevor Nelson and his black friends were advised not to go to the Goldmine. Norman Jay was refused entry to the Lacy Lady on his 21st birthday. 'You never forget things like that,' he says. 'That was the climate at the time. The doors were quite openly racist in those days. Now, to an extent they probably still are, but in a covert way. Then it was blatant. I can remember there was no queue, and I could hear black records being played in there.'

Which is the irony of it, I suppose.

'Yeah, in that part of Essex which is very white they thought five or six black lads together, no chance.'

The black community had always valued music and had established ways of making their own entertainment, keeping alive their music through sound systems. The network of neighbourhood and family-run sound systems in major British cities like London, Birmingham and Manchester formed a real counter-culture. The sound systems would play house parties, halls or venues, often in competition against other sounds. Sound systems began to carry with them a sense of history, operated by old family members, or passed on to the youngsters. Through working with sound systems young DJs understood the responsibility of entertaining, and the DJ's role as a focus for a community. Norman Jay's first experiences as a DJ were with his brother's sound system.

I met up with Norman Jay a few weeks before Southport. I was on his trail, wanting to hear something of his life story, knowing he could shed light on some of the more overlooked parts of British music history. He met me at Euston Station in his 4x4 and we drove over to Ladbroke Grove, swapping stories en route. He was telling me about a trip he'd made to Namibia in Southern Africa, funded by the British Council, which included trips to the townships:

In my arrogant British way I thought I was doing them a favour bringing my records over, like I was planting a flag there. But they're divorced from all our club culture and all our music. For me it was a humbling experience. They had their own thing going, their own music, their own culture, and I realised I was wrong to think they wanted or needed what I had. At the first gig, after fifteen minutes I packed my records away in the box, and asked one of them to take over. I told him I'd watch and listen. I realised I was the one who was there to learn.

We stopped off at the Coins Bar & Grill in Ladbroke Grove, the neighbourhood he grew up in. It's an area that's changed a great deal in the last thirty years. He tells me how two or three families used to live in each of the big terraced houses in the early 1970s, and how, later in the decade, many were squats. More recently, most of the streets have been gentrified, tidied up; look through the windows and you'll see all the latest colour schemes and home decor trends. Norman knows his history.

That he's managed to stay high profile and credible for over two decades is a testament to his ability to manage his career, to be aware, fluid, open, personable. He

gets on with most people. This is what I think, but
Norman doesn't sell himself as hard as that. He's more
modest, unaffected by his status, carrying his CV lightly,
those major achievements, that global success, DJ-ing
gigs at private parties for Prince, Mick Jagger, Lenny
Henry.

His story begins a long way from any kind of show-
business razzmatazz, but not a long way from music.
Growing up, he heard pop music incessantly and was
soon a fan, exploring: 'I used to buy reggae at first; ska,
bluebeat. And I always liked other sorts of black music
but I didn't know it was called soul. I always liked Stevie
Wonder, Marvin Gaye. Obviously Aretha. My mum and
dad always bought records. You become exposed to those
songs early on and they just become an essential part of
your childhood.'

He used to shop at Contempo on Hanway Street,
buying Chairmen of the Board records, stuff on Stax, and
he read magazines like *Blues & Soul*, devouring the music,
the ideas, the life. One of the first records to make a major
impact on him was the Isaac Hayes classic 'Theme from
Shaft': 'I played that record to death. I discovered the
feeling you got when you heard a record that drove you
mad. That rush. That feeling.'

His brother Joey had helped build and run the
Tribulation sound system, and Norman was a part of it,
too. The most important event of the year for the sound
systems was Notting Hill Carnival. 'In the beginning
Carnival was the only place black DJs could play,' Norman
remembers. 'We did occasional house parties or late night
blues but nothing of any significance. But when we came
to Carnival it was the one chance we got, for two days
in the year when you could show that you had a system
that was worthy, and secondly that you could play music
better than anybody else. As a black DJ you weren't being

hired to play in clubs, that was an unwritten rule. The only time you got to show your taste and your skills and your knowledge would be Carnival, so I'd play a ten-hour set every day.'

So how were you aware of that unwritten rule?

'You looked around you and that's just how things were at the time. I know, I was the first black DJ to get any mainstream white music media recognition. Prior to that we didn't exist, but we did, and we had been making a valuable contribution to UK club culture for years, but it's only now, in recent times, that the wrong is finally being put right.'

And that respect thing was important to you?

'I wasn't in it at the beginning for a respect thing; as long as what I'm doing is right, then I don't really care what the media are saying, because my judges are my peers who pay the money to hear me play, who turn up in the rain, who talk to me, and I listen to their gripes.'

They changed the name of the sound system to Good Times, and got away from the competitive culture of Jamaican soundclashes ('Sometimes,' says Norman, 'the competitiveness breeds violence'). Good Times was the first system to move from reggae and make a conscious decision to incorporate funk, soul and disco. By moving on from reggae-only playlists, they had broken with convention, says Norman: 'We rewrote the rulebook. I need to be stimulated. I need to be challenged that way. It's all too safe and too cosy and after a while the complacency does set in.'

West Row has been the Good Times site since 1991 when the system moved from Cambridge Gardens. Away from the main part of the Carnival and insulated from any heavy vibes, appealing to a varied crowd and a preponderance of girls, the Good Times sound system has a reputation for playing celebratory sounds of funk, house, soul and disco. 'We play populist stuff but it's quality stuff at the same time, and its rooted in black music. So it's about entertainment, and the vibe appeals to girls which is good because girls keep the mood up, light, not moody.'

Sitting talking at the Coins Bar & Grill, Norman and I get into a discussion about 'Yellow', one of my nights in Manchester that Norman came up to play at. I told him about one of our strategies when 'Yellow' started in 1992. At the time, most high profile clubs were playing serious, grim, progressive house, but three of us – myself, Jason Boardman and Elliot Eastwick – wanted a different vibe altogether. One of the key things we did in the first few weeks was to say that every time we played a record and girls wandered off the dancefloor and boys got onto the dancefloor, we would make a point of not playing the record again. As time went on, other records emerged that got the girls going: Cheryl Lynn's 'Got to be Real', Patrice Rushen's 'Forget Me Nots', and anything by the Young Disciples. We continued to pick records that seemed to have that special something: Tina Moore's 'Never Gonna Let You Go', TQ's 'West Side'. As a tactic, and as a method of ensuring a successful night, it worked; the night lasted seven years, until 1999, and only finished because we got too busy to do it every week.

When you're doing a regular night, a residency, you can pull in the kind of crowd you want by what you play. You realise the effect certain kinds of records can have. You maybe don't want to go too populist, but you also don't want to be too dogmatic. If you want a big night and longevity then you have to look further than throwing on the obvious music. Good DJs are keyed in to the crowd, neither leading nor following. They realise that DJ-ing is about communication, two way, between the DJ and the audience. The DJs who develop the keenest sense of what a crowd should hear are usually the ones who promote nights. It focuses the mind, running a night, promoting. Norman Jay has done his fair share of promoting – when he ran 'Shake & Fingerpop', for example, with Femi Fem and Marco Nelson (they went on to become part of the Young Disciples).

'Shake & Fingerpop' was one of the nights that earned Norman Jay his reputation for rediscovering old music. He did this not for any retro reason, but because the music seemed relevant to him. Norman was a black Londoner, living in the early years of Mrs Thatcher's government. He felt his community under pressure and was unmoved by the smoochy soul that was around at the time. He ignored the likes of Alexander O'Neal and went looking for music that reflected his life: 'I was black British, here, going nowhere basically. I didn't have any music which was really me, not here or in America, and I got tired of those sugary soulful I-love-you albums. I wanted music with attitude. I wanted music that was gritty, raw, and I started playing some of my old records. I always do that; if new's not happening I'll play an old record.'

The records Norman dug out from the past he dubbed 'rare groove': 'I went back to a lot of music out of black America in the Sixties. At the time you had civil rights, Muhammad Ali, James Brown, and America was giving me pride in being black that I hadn't ever got here. It was dance music but it was social commentary as well, songs with a message.'

The height of rare groove was 1987, the era of 'Shake & Fingerpop' and 'Family Funktion', events held on Saturdays, anywhere and everywhere, in warehouses or halls: 'We were a self-contained unit, we had DJs, we had sound systems, rudimentary lighting, our own generator. Completely mobile. We could go in somewhere and an hour later the party would begin. And this was way before acid

house. I did my first warehouse party in 1983, and it had
been slowly building up.'

There was no big hype surrounding what they were
doing:

> The club media wasn't like it is now, so we were able to grow
> organically, purely by word of mouth. People would go there
> because it was a living experience, not because it was something
> you could read about in some magazine two months afterwards. I
> used to get people in clubland who used to wonder how Norman
> Jay gets two thousand people; how's he doing it? There were no
> adverts in *Blues & Soul*, nothing on the radio. Well, you know, the
> street network is a great thing, especially in a big city.

One of the people he was working with at this time
was Jules O'Riordan. Back then Jules was studying law,
and occasionally his legal background helped give some
legitimacy to the warehouse parties; hence Norman gave
him the nickname Judge Jules. He worked on 'Family
Funktion', and, together with Norman Jay, did about
thirty warehouse parties. 'I was very much at the right
place at the right time,' Jules remembered later. 'I suppose I had a bit of business panache, if that's what you
could describe kicking down the door to a warehouse or
going to an estate agent, borrowing the keys and copying
them.'

By this time Norman Jay was also deeply involved
with Kiss FM. He had begun to realise the power of the
DJ: 'You can use your power in the media to great effect.
I realised doing those kind of interviews reached new
people, outside the people who already knew about it.
The whole point of making something massive is winning
new fans and not playing to the converted; what's the
point?'

Kiss is now a mainstream station, one of a number of
broadcasters – including Galaxy and Radio One – that

give hours of airplay to dance music. It wasn't like this until the mid-1990s; that's why the ILR soul DJs in the 1970s are remembered so fondly – fifteen years ago, dance music could only be heard on specialist shows or on pirate radio stations.

Kiss started as a pirate radio station. Like sound systems, the pirates had become another favoured means of presenting black music, and a positive way of dealing with the apparent marginalisation of black DJs. 'I was quite politicised in those days,' remembers Norman. 'We saw it like this: we were the generation of black British who would no longer be ripped off and there were other voices who are now massive who were saying the same thing – Jazzie B, Trevor Nelson.'

These characters were beginning to have profile and influence. Jazzie B's Soul II Soul hosted Sunday night sessions at the Africa Centre in Covent Garden in 1987, and when they came to make the tracks that would form the *Club Classics vol. 1* LP, their music was a brilliant mix of reggae basslines, hip hop beats, soulful vocals and positive messages. Soul II Soul, in this period, were reflecting and shaping a subculture for a new generation of black British youth.

Trevor Nelson was also contributing to this positivity. He used to run the Madhatter Sound System parties and worked on Soul II Soul nights, playing rare groove and hip hop alongside Jazzie B, and guests like Nellee Hooper and Norman Jay. He also did the weekender circuit, especially events organised by Nicky Holloway. Once Trevor Nelson drove all the way to a weekender at Prestatyn in Wales to play to 5,000 people, got lost on the way, finally arrived, opened the boot of his car and realised he'd left all his records at home. There were pirate radio stations all over inner London, and sound systems moving into hip hop like TNT, Beatfreak and Heatwave. This activity meant that the late 1980s were not just about acid and ecstasy.

The growth of Kiss is part of the same story, and an important reflection of multi-culturalism. Norman Jay feels that up until Kiss, radio stations weren't giving black DJs opportunities: 'The whole point of it was what we wanted was a chance, equal opportunities, no special favours.'

So you didn't react in a bitter way about being shut out?

'No, I wasn't going to get bitter and twisted about it. It was a powerful motivation for me to do my own thing because sooner or later – and I still live by this adage – if you keep doing what you're doing, if it's right then sooner or later they will cross the street to see what you're doing.'

Kiss became massive, with DJs like Trevor Nelson and Danny Rampling on board, and Norman's show, the Original Rare Groove Show, every Saturday evening, became the flagship show for the station. He had helped to recruit all the DJs from the different scenes to reflect the diverse cultures in London – hip hop, reggae, soul: 'I know that's all idealistic nonsense because in the long term the honeymoon won't last, but I knew for a short while we could have a utopian situation.'

The growth of Kiss had a momentum of its own, until a soul boy who was working in the City at the time, and had money and legal contacts, gave them a proposal which would make them legal. It was an opportunity that Norman believed the station had to take: 'We had great media support, and public support because what we were doing was genuinely good. No other pirate radio station had even dreamed of being able to take it to another level.'

Norman hosted the very first show on the new non-pirate Kiss on 1 September 1990. The station now had greater reach and influence, and at last the music was getting recognition, but in becoming legal things had changed. 'Everyone had self-interest at heart and the whole ideal on which it was founded was lost, but I knew that. I knew then, even as I was talking on the radio in that first programme, I knew that it was the beginning of the end.'

Three years later changes began to occur at the station in the wake of the takeover by EMAP, and Norman was only too aware that he could become a victim: 'I didn't want to wait until the night of the long knives. It had been bought by a huge corporate group and I was already under the impression that things were going to change quickly, radically. I was looking after myself, just like EMAP were looking after themselves.'

Norman Jay loves London, and when he talks about how Kiss drew on the strength of London you can sense his idealism again: 'Capital cities attract people from all over who come to realise their dreams and their creative aspirations or contribute to making something brilliant. It doesn't work with the input of just one particular type of people, it's a melting pot, and if you harness that creative energy nothing in the world can beat that down.'

Music can be a positive force, but utopian ideals conflict with the real world, and good intentions can get dashed. Various factors have worked against his perception of a creative city and a multi-cultural music community, not just the corporatisation of Kiss. As another example, he tells me about one night at the Fridge in Brixton. It was 1986 or 1987 and Jay Strongman had just left after he'd been doing Friday nights for years. Norman was at the height of his rare groove fame and was offered the slot. Wary of going south of the river to Brixton, he agreed that he would do it for a month as a trial: 'The second night there were some raggas in there, real South London, worst types in there, and they were shouting at me to change the music and I just ignored them, as I do.'

A few minutes later he was DJ-ing when a full can of beer thrown from the crowd just missed him: 'I thought, surely it can't be black geezers chucking things at a black DJ – that's not heard of. But it was. Then they threw another can, and it hit a doorman standing next to me, and cut the guy's mouth and there was blood everywhere, on my jacket, and the decks, and I got on the microphone and said, "Fuck all of you, I'm out of here." Then the guys wouldn't let me out of the DJ box and it took eight security to get me out and into a taxi, and I never went back.'

One positive factor in this era was the erosion of the North/South divide. Colin Curtis was a DJ who deserves special credit for his work in the mid-1970s onwards, playing records to audiences in all regions, from Bournemouth to Blackpool – one of the great 'radical progressives', according to Norman. There are still regional differences in what people like, but the guest DJ circuit of the early 1990s has helped break down parochialism among clubbers. So too the rise in dance music on networked radio. Club culture is global now, and magazines, compilations, the Internet and gigs abroad mean that Norman Jay can take his musical vision around the world.

The other positive in the late 1980s was the evolution of black music, which encouraged Norman to move on from his rare groove roots. In 1988 he started 'High on Hope' with promoter Patrick Lilley on Thursdays at Dingwalls, after having spent much of the summer hanging out with Judge Jules and Justin Berkman in New York, sharing a flat off Christopher Street in West Village, ten minutes' walk from Paradise Garage. Norman Jay also had family in Brooklyn and South Bronx. They heard DJs like Larry Levan, immersing themselves in the New York version of house: 'This was at a time when rare groove was all the rage in London, everything retro, and I loved

that and I love old music but I love new music and when I
went there I realised that was the direction I had to go in.
I'd been going to the clubs, listening to the likes of Larry
Levan, and my driving ambition was to come back and do
that kind of thing in England.'

Norman had championed the whole retro rare groove
thing, and although he was aware of the way the spirit of
New York clubs was, in part, a reinterpretation of the
funky sounds and raw attitudes, many of his original
followers resented the inclusion of more contemporary
records at 'High on Hope': 'I was facing a certain amount
of hostility from my hardcore funk and rare groove
fans who accused me of selling out playing house, but
that didn't bother me because I'm quite thick skinned.
Anyway, by that time we had nine hundred people every
week at "High on Hope", and it was underground then, it
wasn't getting reported in the press, nothing, just by word
of mouth.'

Norman was the first person to bring Tony Humphries
into the country, and he brought over the likes of Louie
Vega and David Morales. Those days were more innocent
in a way, the calculations weren't solely about money.
'Exactly. It was a fan thing,' says Norman. 'I was a fan of
the music.'

A few years on, when the guest circuit had taken off,
with the Americans especially in favour, you got the feeling that some promoters and club owners were paying
the big names whatever they wanted in an attempt to buy
credibility. For them, running a club involved little more
than looking up names in *Mixmag* and trying to get on a
bandwagon. On the other hand, when Norman booked
him to play, Tony Humphries wasn't all the rage: 'Of
course not, no. Look, when I put on Tony Humphries he
didn't even have a passport and he'd never been out of
America before and most of them hadn't. I put bands on

like Blaze. The whole plot for me was to illustrate the links between soulful house music and original old disco.'

The period from the height of rare groove in 1987 to the end of the decade saw big changes in clubland as acid house and ecstasy boomed. The bpms speeded up, to the dismay of the funkateers. The soul boy weekender scene had been lager-led and the new music and the new club drugs suddenly made the weekender scene look dull. Trevor Nelson, looking back, says that 'house music broke the scene up'.

DJs and clubbers in London at the time confirm that people opposed the changes and were hostile to house. Soon, other London clubs like 'Shoom' and 'Spectrum' would help bring a focus to the acid house scene in Britain, but in some venues people were booing DJs who played house music. Norman Jay delights in the continual revolutions in dance music, the thirst for new things, the way the best DJs are always looking to keep things fresh, even though acid house put the rare groove scene on the back foot: 'It was meant to be. I'm glad I was around in those times doing what I was doing because I really saw myself as the generation that was a link between the whole 1970s holier-than-thou soul thing with the dance renaissance.'

Instead of blocking his ears to the new records, Norman was enjoying himself: 'I travelled, I bought new records, I discovered new forms of dance music outside my old Al Green records and Chi Lites records. I realised I liked electro, and hip hop, and I liked house music.'

You have to be aware of the changes, absorb them: 'and you have to remember that not everyone gets onto something the same time you do. I hold my hand up; sometimes I'm onto something too early for my own good and it takes people months, years to catch up, and at other times I'm the last to get the plot, but that's cool.

It's not about having it first or having it last; when I get hold of something you know I like it, because I don't care if it's being caned by everybody else or not. I'm there to do a job; I'm a public servant.'

How far would you go to serve the public. I mean, would you play a record you don't like?

'No, because there's so much choice out there now, there's always one example of a genre that I like. I can play the odd techno record or the odd garage record because I like it. That's the only criterion you need.'

It's about programming. Programming is something DJs don't talk about much because, unlike technical skills, it's not a part of a DJ's armoury that can be passed on. You can't practise it in private like you can mixing; it comes through experience and trial and error. It's about what choices to make, the order of the tunes, how to take a night through its various phases; it's about playing to a crowd. If you're crossing the genres, you have to know how to sew all the elements together. 'Yes, it's all about programming,' says Norman. 'In time, if DJs want to have any kind of lifespan they'll realise that's what you have to do.'

In the early 1990s he was hosting 'High on Hope' with occasional big guests and playing a contemporary house sound, but he also did a night at the Bass Clef during the same period, playing funk, seven-inch singles to a smaller, purist crowd. His nights at the Bass Clef were out of the media spotlight – 'undercover' he calls it – and he'd get 200 people in, the right 200 for him.

He'd championed rare groove in the 1980s, and emerged the other side, a decade and a half later, with a great record collection, a wealth of experience and a desire to mix the old with the new, to illustrate where the new records get their inspiration from, or their samples, and the way the spirit of the old records lives on in the new. But he's not going to push music down people's throats. He's a pragmatist: 'All music is connected, but I've found that the younger the audience, the less interested they are in that so I never preach it. Older DJs make the mistake of saying that it's not as good as it used to be, and always harking back, but I know when I was sixteen I wasn't interested in looking back; I wanted what's happening now.'

That's why he's such an important part of Southport. Like the event, he's a soul specialist with an open mind. And that's why I'm in the rain in Southport, a few weeks later, to hear him play. I pick up a ticket from the production office portacabin and follow everyone else splashing through the puddles to the reception area. The building is alive with the buzz of expectation. There are more queues, people chattering and laughing, groups of four, five or more waiting to register and picking up keys to their chalets. I'm cold, but already impressed; the queues are moving, the vibe is good.

The music at the Southport Soul Weekender is in five different rooms, four of them in the main building. The rooms are programmed slightly differently, so, for example, you get the housier stuff in one room (the Powerhouse) and the r&b and hip hop in another room (the FunkBase). As you walk into the main building you see the reception area on the right, a supermarket on the left, arcades, and a café down a corridor on the right. I stand around trying to imagine what Pontins is like on a normal busy summer's day: full of kids, I suppose, and ice cream, and teenagers dodging in and out of the arcades looking for ways to escape their parents.

Recently, perhaps spurred on by the success of Southport, other organisations, like Bugged Out, have begun to reinvent the weekender scene, and Ded Beat hosted a weekender in Great Yarmouth in the spring of 2001.

Dance music festivals became part of the clubland calendar in 1998, notably Homelands in Wiltshire and Creamfields near Liverpool. These events each attract around 30,000 people, so they're bigger than the Southport Soul Weekender, but they're also younger (the Southport Weekender crowd is a little bit older than the festival crowd; more like twenty-three or twenty-four instead of eighteen or nineteen). You also don't get an r&b room at any of them, and Southport is probably stronger on the American house and garage scene. They're outdoors with massive marquees, whereas Southport is held in an indoor complex, so even if it rains you don't get mud on your trainers. If you can't hear r&b at Homelands, then at Southport, with its soul bias, there's no chance of finding a room playing heavy techno or pop trance.

On the first night of Southport a priority is to pick up a free programme of events which details the onstage times and areas for the dozens of DJs. I bump into a few people from Manchester, and browse a stall selling merchandise. Then, suddenly, there's Norman Jay. He had a gig booked at Liverpool John Moores University the night before but it got cancelled at the very last minute and he was already on his way there with a hotel in Liverpool booked: 'It's worked out OK because the drive up to Southport from London on a Friday is like a ten-hour nightmare, so I spent the night in Liverpool and got up bright and early, properly rested, and spent the day in Liverpool eating and shopping and stuff and then had a leisurely late afternoon drive up to Southport.'

He's come with four mates – Andy, Ricky, Kelly and Wayne – and he's staying at the same family-run b&b he always stays in every time he plays at the Southport Weekender. He's almost part of the furniture at Pontins, having played at almost all of them, and there's been more than twenty-five. Back in London he'd told me that

Southport was always a good gig for him, with one reservation: he thought it had been through a phase in the early to mid-1990s when it wasn't keeping up with the pace of change in clubland. 'I didn't want to go there and just play my old records all the time because where I come from, Chuck D has as much relevance as Marvin Gaye.'

We're standing near reception, with Norman Jay being hailed by old mates, and a few new ones too, and me realising that every time I go out anywhere with him I never get more than a few sentences out of him without being interrupted. But Southport did move on in the mid-1990s: 'It had to move with the times, Dave. That's why for a couple of years I didn't do it, and Alex thought I was being belligerent, and maybe I was.'

I wander off to the FunkBase, my first port of call. It's only 9.30 and DJ Swerve is on the wheels of steel, cursed with playing an early set; the doors were opened just a couple of hours ago, and there are still hundreds of people yet to even register, hundreds more in their chalets getting changed. The FunkBase isn't very full, but the line-up for later is looking good. I'm introduced to Kelvin Brown who DJs in Manchester at 'Eyes Down' at Dry Bar, and we fall into an easy, funny, DJ-to-DJ conversation. That's the thing about DJs: even if you've never met before, you can lock straight onto the shared language. What do you play? Where do you play? What's it like?

I talk to Kelvin some more and listen to Swerve. Doing a warm-up set can be soul destroying, playing to just a few people when you know that later on some other DJs are going to play to a massive crowd. When there's hardly anyone there you're tempted to be self-indulgent, and make no effort to reach out to the crowd, but DJ Swerve is doing well, moving in a populist direction, putting a smile on everyone's face. He plays some Beverley Knight, keeping it light, then Tony Touch's 'He's the Greatest DJ'.

To the left of the stage three stalls are set up selling records, and digging in among the boxes looking for old disco is Marc Rowlands, who DJs and writes reviews, among other things. He wanders with me and Kelvin through the Powerhouse to get to Connoisseurs Corner. The Powerhouse is the main room, basically little more than a huge gym, with a stage at one end and lights, big video screens and a huge mirrorball at the back. Simon Dunmore is playing Defected, Azuli, Subliminal, disco-influenced records, punchy, clean-cut versions of the kind of sound pioneered by the likes of DJ Sneak in 1995 and Etienne De Crecy in 1997. In Connoisseurs Corner Andy Davies is playing 'The Bottle'.

Connoisseurs Corner, where Norman will be playing later, is heavily red in its decor, with big red love hearts on the back wall and red drapes hanging from the ceiling. It's in the corner of the main room and holds maybe 300 people. The door just next to the DJ stage keeps swinging open, and when it does music from the main room leaks through. There's no air conditioning, and behind the small bar there's a VIP room but it's not open yet.

Back in the Powerhouse, Boris Dlugosch takes over at 11pm and it gets a bit more abstract. He uses effects, taking out the treble or the mid-range, flanging, distorting the sound. It's becoming more prevalent in DJ-ing, the way the effects buttons have started coming into play, and, in part, is due to a new generation of mixers coming on the market which have effects facilities built in. Kelvin tells me he heard Joe Clausell at 'Electric Chair' in Manchester moving from spiritual house to the O'Jays, Bob Marley and Mos Def, giving every record a new twist, tweaking the effects like his life depended on it. Like all technology, it needs to be in the right hands. Give some

DJs an effects button or two and you get a mess. In the hands of Danny Tenaglia it's masterful. Boris Dlugosch is just into a bit of distortion and it's sounding good.

Marc tells me he's not sure he's going to enjoy all the rooms and thinks he'll find somewhere playing slow music, and just stay there. At the moment he rates Connoisseurs Corner and we go back in there just as DJ Terry Jones starts talking on the mic. He's been playing jazz funk, but getting a lacklustre response, so he gets on the mic. 'This is Southport, not a fucking funeral parlour!' he barks. A few people are taken aback. 'What's he blaming us for?' I ask Marc. 'After all, it's his job to get our feet moving.'

'This is Teddy Pendergrass,' announces Terry, and a few people cheer; he plays 'The More I Get, the More I Want'. The crowd seem to be warming up now, and there are some great dancers among the older folk in Connoisseurs Corner. A few tracks later Terry has turned the situation round; he's beaming with happiness and the room is full. He ends his set with Loleatta Holloway singing 'Runaway'.

Norman Jay takes over, gets on the microphone, thanks Terry and introduces himself. There are two TV cameras tracking him, one in front of the staging, and one behind Norman, right up against his shoulder. He plays Patti Jo's 'Make Me Believe In You', and 'Spread Love' by Al Hudson. He's having some problems with the sound, and he takes it uptempo quite quickly. After a while at Southport, unless you're wedded to the DJs in a certain room, you start to worry you're going to miss out on something and you wander. I notice the VIP room is open, so I check it out, and reach the bar just after Joey Negro. He's there with Johnnie van Heldreich. Last time I played with Johnnie some guy walked into the DJ box and started messing with the crossfader when I'd turned my back; Johnnie tells me he's hassled DJs a few times since then and he's now banned from the club.

Back in Connoisseurs Corner, the crowd are still grooving to Norman Jay. There's none of that sweaty pogo-ing of a Fatboy Slim or Paul van Dyk crowd; this is gentler, more mellow, more subtle dancing, real moves. Another DJ walks past us and Marc says, 'Is that who I think it is?' I nod. 'I hate him,' says Marc. 'He gets more DJ-ing work than me and the music he plays is shit.' This shocks me a little and I realise that I'm comparatively liberal in my attitudes to other DJs, more easy-going than many; deep down, you suspect, many DJs seethe with resentment. They'll be nice to each other's faces, polite in public, but put some DJs in a room and you will see this: DJs like wary wild dogs, circling round and round, watchful. They know it's a very competitive world, and it's kill or be killed.

Danny Rampling is about to take over in the Powerhouse, so I go out there. There's a lot of sponsorship around, which is hard to ignore. There's a huge Marlboro banner prominently displayed behind the DJ on the main stage. The production values in the Powerhouse are high, the sound is good, the room is still full, but before Rampling takes to the decks there's a PA by Brian Chambers of the Cleptomoaniacs. He's only doing two or three songs, if that, but it's too poppy for me, so I take refuge back in Norman's room. He's just finishing his set, and the crowd has thinned out a little. Marc tells me, 'He was playing stuff nobody knew – good stuff, fast – but no-one knew it.'

Away from the DJs, out near reception, I meet Lisa from Wallasey. She's complaining that the FunkBase is too full. It's her first Southport. She tells me she's having a good time: 'I knew I would because everyone had said the music was good and there's always a big crowd. I've heard all sorts of things people get up to in the chalets.'

So you're telling me Southport has a bit of a reputation for lots of shagging opportunities?

'Yeah, but that's going out, know what I mean?'

People here seem well into their music, don't they?

'Yeah, but the whole thing as well, the atmosphere, the crowd.'

Do you go to any festivals?

'Creamfields.'

And Ibiza?

'Yeah. We all went over. It's too expensive but we met this guy who works in the clubs and we got into "Cream" and that was great. We had a mad week.'

Which clubs?

'All over, "Cream" most weeks.'

Southport is just up the road from Liverpool, but you get a crowd from all over: Birmingham, Chester, Wales, Scotland and overseas. There's a big contingent up from London, especially the UK garage crew. I meet a group of girls from Kent who are studying at colleges all over the country. Olivia (studying in Lincoln) and Thea (in Bangor) have both been to Southport before and they've persuaded their friends to join them. They're having something to eat. I tell Thea my two Bangor facts: it's got the highest suicide rate in Britain, and it's where Sasha first DJ-ed. They all look at me as if to say, are those two things connected? 'Those things are not connected,' I tell them.

Olivia is a big music fan. She's looking forward to hearing Trevor Nelson, Joey Negro and the Dreem Teem, she says. She reads *Touch* and *Blues & Soul*, likes going out to the Hanover Grand, but feels a bit cut off in Lincoln. 'Is there much of an r&b scene in Lincoln?' I ask, already fairly sure what the answer will be.

'No,' she says, 'not at all, but you get some clubs

coming to play there and that's the highlight of the year.'

How do you survive?

'I just stay in and listen to the radio.'

It's nearly one o'clock in the morning and time for François Kevorkian's set in the building next door. There are only about ten people in there when I arrive ten minutes before he's due to play, but Kevorkian is out front, having his photograph taken by some customers. He's polite, answering questions in his accent (New York with a bit of French). He seems nervous, anxious, possibly because of the lack of a crowd. He disappears, returns ten minutes later and the room has filled. He starts with Jimi Hendrix's 'Rainy Day, Dream Away'. Heads nod. It's a four-hour set and I decide to come back later. I don't, but my intentions were good.

In the FunkBase, DJ Jazzy Jeff is playing to a huge crowd. Apparently Samuel L. Jackson is in the crowd somewhere. I start looking out for him, but it's hard even getting a few yards inside the door. Jazzy Jeff cuts up some Dr Dre. The FunkBase is the hottest room, with a great atmosphere, but there's no room to move.

Later I bump into Mike from Cheadle. He's a veteran of these events: 'Every time I'm here I always experience something new and there's always an add-on every time, either new rooms or new types of music or genre coming through. As you go through the years you tend to find each room becomes more fashionable – it doesn't always stay in fashion, because other rooms then take over – and I mean r&b is big this year because of the Dreem Teem and the Ayia Napa thing. It's interesting just to see how things go in cycles.'

Years ago Mike had been to Caister: 'It was all about jazz funk. And you had DJs like Chris Hill, Robbie Vincent. I remember even at those early events people like Pete Tong and Jeff Young were appearing. And I remember going to some events on the south coast at Bournemouth when Gilles Peterson was starting out his career.'

So you've been coming to these events for twenty years?

'Yeah, what I like about them is the camaraderie of all the people who are there. For me, if you like football then I suppose the peak of your season would be getting to the Cup Final and going to Wembley with your team, so for me going to a weekender twice a year is like going to Wembley.'

I'm pleasantly surprised how young the crowd is. Younger than me. Younger than Mike, too, as I point out to him. He's happy with that: 'Well, I think that the Caister event still attracts an original crowd, so you get a larger proportion of thirty somethings and forty somethings in that crowd. If you look at Southport, the crowd is young which means new people are coming into the scene and that's good. But there are still the same faces around if you know where to look. And that's good as well. People travel long distances to be here and you still see the same heads twice a year.'

And what's your highlight so far?

'Norman Jay. It thinned out a bit near the end but you tend to find that because people have got the programme and they'll jump from place to place. They set out an itinerary and then cram in as much of each room as they can. In Norman's room, the more surprising thing was all the lads that were in there, singing along to girlie anthems, because normally you get the females singing along to those kind of songs. So it was different, very enjoyable.'

Mike's a big fan of Dr Bob Jones, who'll be playing later in the weekend. He also says he's been coming to South-port long enough to get to know Alex and to make sure he gets a guest ticket. Mike introduces me to his friend who's offered to let Mike sleep in his chalet: number 616.

Meanwhile Norman Jay has a four-hour wait until his next set, in the Powerhouse. He wasn't put off by the cameras, he told me. 'It used to be a bit off-putting, but in the last year or so I've had so many cameras on me while I've been DJ-ing – it sounds a bit pretentious saying that, but it's true – and so it doesn't faze me any more. It used to, but I've got used to it.'

You don't think they expect you to spin on your head, or do some turntable tricks?

'I don't know, but there's not a lot you can film when you film DJs, just some guy putting on records or CDs and in between he might be picking his nose, and there isn't a lot else happening; unless you're a deck maestro and you can play up to cameras and mess with the crossfader and all your knobs and switches, you're not really doing anything. There is some action, I suppose; if I'm enjoying myself, which I invariably am, then at least I'm dancing a bit and smiling and interacting with the people in front of me in the crowd.'

Do you get tired playing a late set?

'No, because I run on adrenalin and I'm so used to doing that. I'm a bit of a night-owl anyway and the later it gets the more alive I become, especially at Southport if the atmosphere's happening, and it usually is at that time in the morning.'

I know you don't do drugs, but with all the long nights, the travel, the late gigs, maybe you should.

'No, I'm unique in that sense and I'm really used to it, it's no hassle. I'm used to being awake eighteen, twenty hours without sleep.'

Most of the time between sets he spends being interviewed by dot.com TV crews doing Internet TV clips: 'It goes with the territory but you get pulled a bit pillar to post,' he told me later. 'And I was getting harassed by people who mean well, you know, chancers and other associated people and people from record companies telling me they'd sent me a record three weeks ago and saying "What did you think of it?" and, to tell the truth, I end up just switching off.'

He's seen dance culture grow, and he doesn't think the status of DJs will diminish: 'Not in the foreseeable. I don't even think it's reached its logical conclusion yet. It's on an upward curve. It will eventually fall flat but I don't foresee that in our DJ lifetimes. It will only get bigger and DJs will reap even more rewards as DJs are able to become self-contained entities; they can present, they can remix, they can make music, they can play on the radio, they can tour, they can entertain huge crowds.

'I'm using "entertain" loosely here!' he adds, laughing. 'It's all the image. You don't have to be good, you only have to be popular. Kids nowadays have had it dumbed out of them. They're not interested in whether you're good but whether you're popular; you have to understand that and you either deal with it on those terms or you get out of it.'

He knows the world he works in has gone from being a community activity to a corporate one, but takes a pragmatic view: 'When I was younger there wasn't a DJ culture. I'm part of it now, but that doesn't mean I can't see through it. The only talent a lot of DJs have is that they convince everybody that they're fantastic.'

I can't stop here talking to Norman all night without getting some sleep soon, so I make my way back to the golfers' hotel. Norman finally gets some sleep on Saturday morning at half past eight. By one o'clock he's up and by half past one he's checked out. After a visit back to Pontins he's on his travels again, to a gig in Coalville in Leicestershire on Saturday night, and, after a two and a half hour car journey, he finishes up at the Cross in London in the early hours of Sunday morning.

Passion in Coalville has two rooms: a bigger room where the likes of Judge Jules and Paul van Dyk play, and a funkier room where Norman Jay gets to play. He loves it there: 'I can't believe a small town in the middle of nowhere draws crowds like that. You get there at nine o'clock and there's a couple of thousand people queueing outside and you get in and it's already full. It's not really ravey, it's just a young crowd, trance kids and regulars. It's a big night out.'

By the time he gets to the Cross he's running on energy. He leaves there about six and finally gets to bed at eight. He sees his kids as much as he can, usually in the week. It's all about time management. When he's at home he's at home. He likes to have a lot of quality time at home in the week, playing football with his boys on Sundays.

Meanwhile, I catch up with events in chalet 616. Mike had stayed over there on the Friday night. 'Not as cold as it has been in the past. I mean, I used to go before they put the double-glazing in the place so you'd go some Novembers and it would be really freezing and you couldn't find the token for the electricity. The chalets are quite warm actually and there were about six or seven people in there. Yeah, it's basic but that adds to the fun of it really.'

So, I ask cheekily, was there much shagging?

'Yeah, there was. In our chalet there were two people who never came out of the bedroom all weekend.'

They missed Danny Rampling?

'Yes.'

Dr Bob?

'They were in there the whole weekend. My friend who had that chalet said that they just locked themselves in there. They didn't see a single DJ.'

On Saturday night, Mike was still at Pontins, but he

didn't go to chalet 616, he slept in his car. In April he'll be back. Before then, Norman Jay has got more travelling to do, a part of the job he enjoys; he loves playing in New York, and the annual Vibes on a Summer Day Festival in Sydney is another highlight of his year.

He'll be on a world tour all through November and into December, starting in Milan, then Istanbul, Sydney, Melbourne, Singapore, Hong Kong, Manila, Tai Pei, Cape Town and finishing in Bombay. He'll have played back rooms, big rooms and parties, done radio shows, maybe a few celebrity events, but in April and November he'll also be in Southport again, at Pontins, trailed by cameras, greeting friends, dodging through the rain to the warmth of the packed crowds.

CHAPTER 8

Looking for the Perfect Beat
the DMC Technics World DJ Championships

'm talking with DJ As-If in Manchester, just six weeks before the first stage of DMC's Technics World DJ Championships. There are regional heats in cities around the world; she'll be entering the Birmingham heat, and hopes to get through to the UK Final, then – who knows – on to the World Final featuring the best DJs in the world, or, rather, the best 'turntablists'; these championships are for DJs versed in turntable trickery and hip hop techniques, intent on demonstrating their scratching, cutting and mixing ability.

The competition is not about filling a dancefloor, but creating a collage of sounds and beats. The term 'turntablism' was coined in 1995 by DJ Babu of the Beat Junkies. As Babu told Christo Macias, 'My definition of a turntablist is a person who uses the turntables not to play music, but to manipulate sound and create music.'

There'll be other heats around Britain, at Bristol's Café Blue, the Subterania in London, Edinburgh's Liquid Rooms, Planet K in Manchester and the Zap in Brighton. Each DJ has a six-minute set to show off his or her technical skill with the decks, mixer, crossfader. DJ As-If is one of the few women who enter these championships. Her real name is Leanne, and I'm telling her my plan – to follow the competition from the heats to the World Final. I tell her I'll be in Birmingham, cheering her on. She tells me she won't win. I tell her to have faith.

The roots of turntablism go back to the early years of hip hop, the 1970s, and the work of DJs like Kool Herc, Grand Wizard Theodore and Grandmaster Flash. Back in 1973, New York DJ Kool Herc (a.k.a. Clive Campbell) began using two turntables and two copies of identical records to isolate and loop disco and funk breaks. He also took what he'd seen around his original home in Jamaica – a selector playing instrumental reggae tunes which reggae vocalists would 'toast' over – and encouraged MCs to rap over the chopped up and reassembled funky breaks. Hip hop is now a huge international scene, but the basic DJ set-up – two turntables and a microphone – remains the heart of the culture.

Other pioneers built on these innovations, including Grand Wizard Theodore who was the very first DJ to scratch. He wasn't doing block parties or dance halls at the time, he was a young fourteen year old, messing about on his decks at home, just cueing a record when his mother started banging on the door. He stopped the record simply by putting his hand on it and stopping it from spinning round on the turntable: 'I felt myself moving the record back and forth and forth and back while she was talking to me, because I wanted to keep that same groove I was on. I was talking to her and I was listening to the record and I said to myself "Hey this sounds really good!" so I kept practising it, and it became a scratch.'

Kool Herc and Grand Wizard Theodore may have been the pioneers but it was Grandmaster Flash who took DJ trickery overground. Grandmaster Flash, born Joseph Sadler in 1957, grew up in South Bronx listening to a variety of music, from Frank Sinatra to Aretha Franklin. He also pursued an interest in electronics, and studied the subject at High School. He took up DJ-ing in 1974, inspired by Kool Herc, but, importantly, he was the first DJ to get his work to a wider audience: 'The Adventures of Grandmaster Flash on the Wheels Of Steel'.

Other pioneering New York DJs included Afrika Bambaataa, Marley Marl, Grandmixer DST and Jam Master Jay from Run DMC. In Philadelphia, DJs Cash Money and Jazzy Jeff emerged, and the music made waves in Los Angeles, Miami, San Francisco, Canada and Europe, always evolving. It's also the one genre of DJ-ing in which you're guaranteed to get some strange names: DJ Toast, DJ What and DJ Rectangle.

There's always been a competitive edge to turntablism. Out in the clubs, community centres and sports halls that hosted the parties featuring the first hip hop DJs, 'battles' were popular: head to head clashes between sound systems. In 1977, DJs like Grandmaster Flash and Afrika Bambaataa were battling at local venues and even in the parks, although at first the battles mostly revolved around who had the loudest system, the biggest bassbins and the bigger crowd. Then the DJs started incorporating tricks and skills on the decks to show off their prowess, helping to generate more and more outlandish moves.

It's hard to describe how revolutionary this kind of DJ-ing was at the time, not just because the raw music and street attitudes were so different to the personality DJs on the radio and the jokers in the clubs, and not just because of the showmanship and skill levels on display. It was also the way it clearly opened up new possibilities. One of the phrases you still hear about hip hop – 'hip hop is the new rock & roll' – avoids the more challenging and perhaps more accurate definition: hip hop is the end of rock & roll. The foundations of rock & roll – songwriters, bands, musicianship, verses and choruses – are threatened by DJs, dancefloors, breaks and samplers. For this reason, 'Adventures on the Wheels of Steel' has been described as a revolutionary moment in the history of music. But it was so different to everything else around at the time that Flash says, 'I didn't think anyone was going to get it.'

As hip hop began to filter into Britain, we witnessed the slow death of the personality jock, but, in the interim, there were some nights when both eras clashed. In February 1980 the Sugarhill Gang came to the UK, the first big hip hop act to play in Britain, and they were booked to play at discotheques around the country. At an all-dayer in Nottingham, the Sugarhill Gang rocked the house with their hit song 'Rapper's Delight', cutting up old disco and shaking the dancefloor with funky, rolling basslines. The compère on that day at Nottingham Palais was a Radio Trent DJ called Dale Winton.

When hip hop emerged from the underground through worldwide hit records like 'The Message' and 'Rapper's Delight', the turntablist origins of the culture were obscured, and the element that got most attention was the rapper. Out in the wider, whiter world, the voice and message of the rapper was something to get a handle on. Since then, hip hop heroes have been rap stars. This shift has obscured the origins of hip hop music as instrumental collages devised and created by DJs and their breaks.

But DJ-ing never disappeared; in fact, turntable trickery became more refined and defined, with different kinds of scratches, and techniques using the mixer to bend the pitch or take out the bass or the treble (again something originated by the Jamaican sound system operators), and beat juggling (an advanced form of what the Bronx DJs were doing cutting between breaks).

The showmanship and technical prowess of the hip hop pioneers had begun to make an impact on British DJs like Froggy, Greg Wilson, Chad Jackson. To harness and encourage the new wave of DJ-ing, DMC – the Dance Mix Club – was set up by Tony Prince, a singer songwriter in the early 1960s. He'd moved on by 1964 and become a DJ, going out on the road live for Radio Luxemburg. He started DMC in 1983, convinced that mixing was going to be the new skill for DJs rather than chat, and that a rise in the status of DJs was imminent. DMC started out as a mixture of a trade union, an agency, a record pool, an information point and a commercial enterprise. The organisation distributed an early version of *Mixmag* magazine and remix records – for club play and available only to their members – including tracks by Michael Jackson, Shalamar, New Order.

DMC held a convention in 1985, and, using the annual DJ battles hosted by the New Music Seminar in New York as their model, launched their DJ Championship in the following year. The first one was won by Chad Jackson; it was this victory which stirred the interest of a *Blue Peter* researcher and led to his appearance on kids' TV. The following year he went on to win the World Championship at the Albert Hall, and through most of 1987 and 1988 toured the world.

In the evolution of turntablism, and the story of DMC, these were very early days. When Chad Jackson entered the UK Mixing Championship he didn't even possess a pair of Technics and used to practise on a normal disco double deck system with belt drive turntables, and therefore with no vari-speed facility. He'd do what all the old school DJs would do – he'd keep a bpm book: 'I kept a bpm book for years and years and that's how I'd get over that, just by choosing records with the same bpm. The mixing was a matter of the good old quick finger job. But that honed your skills really well. You learn your craft the hard way.'

Hip hop DJs made a further breakthrough in the mid-1980s with their association with some of the big acts then emerging: Run DMC's DJ Jam Master Jay and Public Enemy's Terminator X were two DJs who were making a conspicuous contribution to the music, and the live shows. Another big name in this era was Red Alert, who'd been a colleague of Afrika Bambaataa's and made his name with his work on radio; he went on to DJ with KRS-One.

Hip hop history is packed with unknowns and big names. In the explosion of interest in hip hop, the music went in many different directions, with some artists favouring party rocking sounds, others heavy social comment, some choosing funky music, others dark beats, but in hip hop the history is never forgotten; the old skool, as it's called, is venerated, with its legendary figures, American and British.

In 1989 Cutmaster Swift won the World Championship. He now compères events in the DMC Technics World Championship, and features in the En4cers, one of the UK's leading turntablist teams (along with Pogo and Biznizz). The En4cers entered a new category in 1999 – the DMC Team Championships – which was won by another British team, the Scratch Perverts (Tony Vegas, Primecuts, Mr Thing and First Rate). The Allies – featuring DJ Craze (from Miami) – were second in the inaugural event, Scratch Action Hiro (France) third. The En4cers' chances disappeared during their routine when Biznizz snapped his crossfader.

That victory for the Scratch Perverts back in the 1999 Team Championships upset the form book; DJ Craze was the winner of the Individual Championships, and the audience at the finals in New York fully expected Americans to triumph in the team event as well. The Scratch Perverts had dominated in the UK, though; the team provided the 1999 UK winner Tony Vegas and the 1998 winner Primecuts.

1998 was also the year DJ As-If became the first ever female competitor to win through to the UK DMC Final, cutting up records like 'Fight the Power' and dropping the big favourite, Run DMC's 'Peter Piper'. Since then, she's not managed to build on that breakthrough, but her attitude continues to represent the spirit and dedication of turntablism.

In Manchester, telling me she doesn't think she'll get far in the competition, Leanne is just being realistic about her chances. That's not to say she doesn't take it seriously; she tells me she practises on the decks around three hours a day, more when competition time approaches. She has a day job as the hip hop specialist at Dance 2 Records in Brighton. She has a degree in Musical Technology, is a member of the Fat City Allstars, and turntable team Surgical Cuts.

In the beginning she was living at home in Essex and she hooked up with a group of lads who were into music and going out to clubs: 'When I started listening to music at home I was listening to electro, early house, right across the board. I wasn't really sure what I was into myself so I was buying all sorts of things, but when I was going to clubs the big thing at the time was the rave scene, so I heard a lot of early hardcore.'

She was journeying to clubs around Essex, but also to Brighton and to a club called Stearns in Worthing. In 1992 she would be listening to early breakbeat stuff, the whole mixture. Among the DJs, she liked Lenny D, who used to play mad techno sets, and hardcore DJs like Ratty: 'To be honest, though, I wasn't following the DJs as such. It was just about the music; it was about the music that they were playing.'

She was only about sixteen at the time; a couple of the

lads were DJs and she was into the whole club thing. From clubbing and listening to DJs she was inspired to get a pair of decks: 'I bought a really naff pair of belt drive decks and set them up in my bedroom at home. I had them rigged up through a stack system with these two crap little speakers, and I had about ten records and I kept on with those until I started getting somewhere and started getting that vinyl addiction thing, and it went on from there. I've got a big collection of records because I was buying all sorts of music. Now I just buy hip hop and breaks.'

Most DJs start off by going to clubs and then want to do it themselves, but a lot of people go to clubs and never get that urge; something tipped her towards deciding not to just be a punter forever: 'Maybe it stems from right back from my youth when my dad was always heavily into music and he had a band which he went around pubs with and when I was really little I used to go round with him and watch him on the stage. I think it was pushed on me, in a way.'

The idea of getting involved?

'Yeah, exactly, to get involved rather than to stand back and watch.'

The first time she got on the decks in public was at a club night called 'Eurobeat' at Turnmills in London. She played a techno set, secured after she had chatted to the promoter on the phone a few times and sent him some charts. She got paid fifty pounds, and DJ-ed under the name Witchy – as in broomsticks and black cats, she explains. 'Witchy was my nickname from school. I had long hair and it was all wild and people nicknamed me that.'

She was playing techno sets with an electro influence, but she maintained her interest in hardcore, playing underground parties: 'We had a wide range of friends from all over the country, because we were hooked onto the whole underground Spiral Tribe circuit. It was never really that difficult for me to get work, but there was also stuff that I really had to work hard for. And sometimes that was more satisfying in a way, the stuff that didn't just land in your lap.'

On the hip hop scene there aren't many famous female DJs: Spinderella is one, DJ Pam The Funkstress another, and the Philadelphia radio jock Lady B is a legendary figure on the Philly old skool hip hop scene. Young women starting out need to be assertive and maybe more determined than young lads, reckons Leanne. Even before you have to get on the phone and hustle, just going into a record shop can be a brave first move: 'I think I bought my first record in Blackmarket, which was quite a daunting experience for someone of my age and my sex in a record shop full of guys.'

The sound of Dusty Springfield nearly drowns out what she has to say. I push the tape recorder nearer to her. 'People always say I talk too quietly. I always have to speak up loudly,' she says.

Leanne finds it hard to be assertive, but knows you have to be to get good gigs. She also displays determination in her willingness to do head to head DJ battles as well as competitions. She'd been down in Maidstone battling: 'It was ninety-second rounds, and you had to battle your opponent and diss your opponent and all that sort of stuff.'

Just by using decks?

'Just by using the turntables and your expression, and that was really good, but my practice routine before that was just knowing my stuff back to front.'

She gives me a rundown of some of the techniques turntablists use in competitions, apart from scratching, back-spinning and mixing: 'chopping' (using the

crossfader to switch in and out of the scratch, thus chopping the sound into segments), rapid-fire scratching
('chirping'), as well as the 'hydroplane', 'the flare' and
'the crab' (one of Q-Bert's favourite manoeuvres). She
tells me how you can get sounds by scribbling (vibrating
the needle on the record) and beat juggling.

Very few house or techno DJs have these techniques
in their armoury, but when Leanne was starting out she
wanted to go beyond traditional beatmixing: 'The mixing
thing at the start was a great novelty, working it all out,
finding out what worked and what records went with
what. Then when you get competent at that it becomes a
little less interesting. What happened was a couple of
people were staying with us, including this guy from
Australia and he was an old skool hip hop guy, and he
started cutting up on my turntables and I was inspired.
When he started doing that it gave me a whole new buzz.'

I tell her I have been invited to be on the judging panel
for the heat at Planet K in Manchester and ask her what
she thinks are the key things the judges are looking for: 'I
think that the thing that stands out the most is your confidence. Initially though it's your skills. Everything has got
to sound right. It's your presence on the decks. You can
see it in a DJ when the confidence oozes out of them and
it's usually those DJs who are the most successful.'

And the music?

'Obviously. A lot of people say it's the funk, the
funkiness of what you're doing; a lot of people are really
technical but they don't get anywhere because the way it
comes across live is too much for people to take in all at
once, so the funk works, you have to make it funky. Those
things are the most important.'

The Manchester heat is a few weeks before Birmingham. When I get there, it's clear, and good to see, that the
crowd in Manchester for the DMC heat includes a higher

proportion of women than three or four years before.
I'm introduced to one of the other judges, Peter Parker
from Fingathing. Peter Parker wasn't as moody as I had
expected; in among a sea of khaki, he was wearing a white
Kangol beret and a big blue shirt covered with large white
flower prints. He looked dashing.

Pete Roberts took us all backstage to give us our
guidelines. Pete was telling me that it's all supposed to be
fun, but admits there can be needle: 'Of course sometimes it gets too serious, but it doesn't happen often with
the DJs, it has to be said. Generally they support each
other and respect each other. We used to do a rap contest
and people would be dissing each other. Like, about ten
years ago we did a rap competition in Bristol and that was
bad; it got far, far too serious.'

I had the impression that the turntablist thing had
been undergoing something of a renaissance over the last
three or four years.

'Yeah. There was a lull in interest when it got dirty,
nasty in America, and interest dropped away, but now it's
picked up again. Swift, Pogo, Biznizz, work at this six or
seven hours a day, and they're great role models for what
we do.'

Hip hop has had to mutate to survive. When gangster
rap and glam videos became the norm, others in the hip
hop community looked to a return to basics, the music,
the DJ – the positive elements in hip hop culture before
the violence and the materialism took hold. It's part of
a recognition, perhaps, that hip hop has lost its way,
rappers saying nothing new or creative; that most of the
innovation is in the music, on the production side.

In 1994, DMC didn't stage a championship because
the interest and excitement seemed to be waning, but
the culture wasn't dying. Hip hop – the DJ-ing, MC-ing,
breaking and graffiti – was born in New York City in the

1970s, but it was the turn of America's West Coast, particularly the Bay Area – home to the Invisibl Skratch Piklz (Q-Bert, Disk and Shortkut), Peanut Butter Wolf and DJ Shadow – to influence the next wave of turntablism. The *Return Of The DJ* compilations put out by San Francisco's pioneering Bomb Hip Hop Records in 1995 and 1997 featuring the likes of Q-Bert, Shortkut, Mix Master Mike, Peanut Butter Wolf, Beat Junkies, Rob Swift, Roc Raida and Kid Koala (each of them contributing a five-minute mix) became a new blueprint for turntablism. DJs also began to get a higher profile in new bands, like DJ Cut Chemist in Jurassic 5. In 1995, after just a year's break, DMC resumed the competitions.

Meanwhile, Pete Roberts is addressing all the assembled judges, giving us clipboards and drinks, explaining the marking system, and asking us not to be swayed by the crowd: 'They might be cheering for the big record that they recognise, and not necessarily the technical skill. Or they might be cheering because the DJ is their mate.'

DMC has accepted twenty-seven competitors in Manchester. Each of them has a three-minute set in the afternoon, the eliminator. The top ten competitors then go forward to do a six-minute set in the evening. They take the stage in reverse order to the standings in the afternoon, so, in theory, the last DJ on the night is the favourite.

As well as Peter Parker, the other judges include Mark One, DJ Pogo (who won the UK final in 1997) and DJ Biznizz from the En4cers, Mr Scruff, Darren Laws (from Grand Central) and Anders (from Basement DJ supplies). We introduce ourselves on the microphone. DJ Pogo has been warming up the crowd, dropping some more old skool tracks, records from DJ Cheese and early stars of the championships (Cheese won the first DJ Championship in 1985). Now Pogo joins the rest of the judging panel, and takes the microphone and plugs his website: djpogo.com.

The DJ who starts proceedings needs a lot of bottle, even though the crowd seem pretty supportive; the honour goes to DJ Camille. He uses a lot of wordplay in his set, cutting up records to bring out snatches of words, most of them well-worn phrases like 'Listen up' and 'Put the needle on the record'. With one minute to go, Pete jumps up and waves an upright finger at him. It's not an offensive gesture, as it turns out; it just means he's got one minute to go. Pete is very strict on timing.

Others follow: Trick Daddy, No Sweat. Three competitors so far, but none of them has stood out. All the turntablists put the decks side on; they scribble away at the crossfader like kids colouring in pictures. Over the six minutes the sets sometimes descend into a mess, but, in theory, six minutes gives you just enough time to build, take it up, switchback, drop, finale. It's all quick, noisy, soon over; like a computer game.

It's also soon clear that the DJs either tend to keep the music funky but leave out the tricks, or DJ technically brilliantly but lose the soul of the music. I'm hoping one will manage to be technically spot-on but funky, too. Sam DuPres nearly gets there; he's very musical and creative but there's possibly not enough traditional cutting and scratching moves.

DJ Technique hammers the vari-speed, and the gains, distorting the sound; Yo 1 survives six minutes, which is better than the previous year when he had major technical troubles. It's bad when the equipment lets you down. As fellow judge Mr Scruff told me, 'Six months' work can go down the pan.'

Fast T played for less than six minutes, but in the time he gives himself he makes some well-executed moves and uses some original breaks. DJ Woody is buoyed up by a local following and works the mixer and decks with very fast fingers. DJ Bunty has travelled down from Edinburgh and executes a very clean set that oozes with showmanship. He wins.

The judges put forward a top three, and the competitors are given points for each placing they receive from the panel. The top two go through to the UK Final, and the first three win other prizes, too: a jacket, decks, mixer or headphones. I mark my one, two, three as Bunty, Woody and Sam DuPres. Bunty goes through to the final with Woody, but when the other judges' marks are added up it's Yo 1 who's third. He seems upset by that, and stomps off without collecting the headphones he's won. Just before I leave, DMC's Nick Darby grabs me and asks me to judge the Birmingham heat, too.

I meet up with Leanne again just five days before Birmingham. Over the last week or so she's been busy with the Aboriginals and that's distracted her preparation for the DMC event. Her six-minute set isn't yet together as one routine, but all the parts are perfected and she knows what records she's using. Anything goes among turntablists; most of them use old skool breaks, but then you get DJ Slyce cutting up Michael Jackson, and Pone from France scratching the Spice Girls.

One of the records she'll be using is an old Tim Dog track which she knows the audience will recognise. She's also got a couple of scratch routines and some wordplay. Once the routine is arranged, it's about practising, practising, endlessly. 'It's just a matter of doing it over and over until you can do it in your sleep,' she says.

How easy is it to change your mind?

'When you're into scratching in the routine it's fairly freestyle, but you need to know where everything goes, get your records right, but there are a lot of other things riding on it, like the quality of the equipment, but if you've worked hard enough it's usually fine. The more you know what you're doing, the less likely anything will go wrong.'

Do you use headphones?

'I won't at the DMC. I'll use them before to cue up the first two records on the decks before I get the nod and everything but I won't use them once the routine starts. I use headphones a lot at home and when I'm DJ-ing out, but battle-wise I don't. Some people use those little ones that just fit in the ear but I feel that's a bit off-putting.'

Body tricks and props have become part of the championship and can provide a strong visual element, helping to hype up the crowd or sway the judges; DJ David from Germany, who won the Individual title twice, in 1990 and 1991, did a handstand on one of the turntables in 1990. In the Individual 1999 DMC/Technics World Championship Final, DJ Mek in New York attacked his technics with an eight-inch kitchen knife. Leanne wishes the gimmicks from the old days had gone: 'I never really liked that sort of thing. It's good for amusement, but it isn't anything to do with turntablism. I like Roc Raida, the DJ from the X-Men, who does lots of body checks, going all round and doing the crossfader with his back and all that sort of stuff and he pulls it off, but when you start getting out props and stuff it turns it into a bit of a circus.'

When the Sunday of the Birmingham heat dawns Leanne leaves her flat in Hove at eight in the morning for the drive up from Brighton with Ben (Leanne's 'other half', as she calls him) and their friend Jim from Surgical Cuts. Ben, DJ-ing under the name Blood One, is also competing. The eliminators are due to start at 10.30am, but after their car breaks down, they arrive late, at just after 1pm. Fortunately, their names still haven't been called.

Leanne and Ben could have entered the heats in

Brighton, but Birmingham was first, and, in any case, forty-six people had entered in Brighton which wasn't much help to anybody. When I catch up with them in Birmingham I tell them that I always thought Brighton was like that – one of those places full of kids in wide trousers with decks in their bedsits. Leanne laughs. Jim explains, 'Brighton is very cliquey; at hip hop nights you get one clique or another but they don't really mix.'

Circo, the venue for the Birmingham heat, is just down the road from Miss Moneypenny's Bar. Circo is busy, although it's not a big venue; there are perhaps 150 people there. Most have their coats on even though it's a warm night; a big baggy brown coat, trainers and a hat looks like the informal dress code. The crowd is mixed in age, though, from older teenagers to hip hop veterans in their late thirties. There are a number of young and not so young black kids, and a few women. Everyone has been drinking for hours.

Thirty-two people turned up for the eliminators. Nine are selected to go through to the evening, and one of them is Leanne; that's the good news. The bad news is that she was ninth to be selected, so not only did the day-time judges not put her among the frontrunners, but she will have the dubious honour of starting off the proceedings in the evening. Ben, Blood One, is also through. One of the final nine, though, Fast T, didn't stay on, maybe not rating his chances, although he'd impressed me in Manchester.

An hour to go and Leanne is beginning to feel the pressure of all the work, the long drive, the hanging around. 'I'm just looking forward to it being over,' she says. She's trying to find something positive to say about being first on: 'You can get your set over with, you're not hanging around,' is about all she can come up with. And then we hang around some more; the eliminators finished a couple of hours ago, and the main competition is yet to start. I go outside for some fresh air.

I'm a bit bored of waiting. I was told it would start at six o'clock, but being a judge again, I was encouraged to come at five, just to be on the safe side. I got there at 5.30, only to be told it will start at seven. In fact, it's just been announced that it will get started at 7.30. I'm learning that this is 'hip hop time'; it goes slower and runs later than straight time. I can't help thinking there's an irony to this. I remember Public Enemy's Flavor Flav who used to wear a big clock round his neck to symbolise the Public Enemy wake-up call. 'Do you know what time it is?' he used to chant. That was his big message: take a look around you and look what's going on in the real world.

Leanne is drinking orange juice. Ben is drinking half a Guinness. I offer him another, but he's pacing himself; he'll have another one later. Us judges are perched up high, on a balcony to the left of the stage. Cutmaster Swift is giving away t-shirts again, and anyone who wants one has to justify why. 'Because I'm the tallest man in the room,' says one character. He's certainly pretty tall and so gets his prize.

I talk to Nikki who's sitting at the next table with her friend. She tells me she's just wandered in, having been out all night and all day, but she's not impressed. She loves the old days. This has been the theme of a thousand conversations I've had for the last ten years or more: the good old rave days. 'Things aren't as good now,' says Nikki. 'The clubs are full of babies. The drugs aren't so good as they used to be. The kids don't even know what they're missing. I was telling these kids the other day about Doves; that was the best ecstasy you could ever have, weren't they? They didn't even know what I was talking about.'

The world of the turntablists doesn't impress her, but,

even though she's a devoted clubber, neither does the rise of the superstar house DJs. Tonight, she's just looking for somewhere to have a drink: 'I don't go for the DJ or the club, I just go for the music. Not in Brum, though. There's nothing. Miss Moneypenny's isn't much really. And Baker's is supposed to be the big club, isn't it? But if I go clubbing I go to the Emporium in Leicester or to Stoke.'

Do you go to 'Golden' in Stoke?

'I don't know. Is that what it's called? I don't know. I don't usually even know what town I'm in I'm that wrecked.'

Nikki and her crew go out all the time, and they know how to enjoy themselves. 'If you don't feel ill on a Monday then something's not right,' she says.

So you don't follow DJs?

'No, but I've been up to "Cream" in Liverpool. You see it on the telly so I just had to go up and see it. I love Seb Fontaine. He's number one.'

I tell her about the night I discovered the fridge at 'Cream', and she introduces me to her friend Michelle. Michelle wants to marry Judge Jules. I tell her he's married already but she knew that. She knows that his wife makes records, too. 'Angelic she's called, isn't she?' says Michelle. 'Well, she's only doing that because she's his wife. That could be me.'

Nikki then remembers one of her best nights out ever. It was when Boy George DJ-ed at the Hummingbird, a club that's now closed down. Her favourite club at the moment, now she thinks about it, is in Wolverhampton: 'I tell you where we go, we go to the Light Bar in Wolverhampton. It's on till two, and it's got a courtyard and you get in there at twelve and it's empty but then it gets packed and it's wicked. Michelle, what's the Light Bar like?'

'Wicked,' says Michelle.

The competition is about to start, so I go to the judging area on the balcony. Pogo has been playing his Big Daddy Kane records again, and the heat, the drink and the early start for some of the DJs is beginning to take its toll. Plenty of people are unsteady on their feet, and DJ Go from the Mixologists is asleep at the side of the stage. It's been a long day.

Leanne is the first on, and she's already cued up the first records on the turntables, but Cutmaster Swift asks her to hold on while the judges introduce themselves, and he passes the microphone down the line. Pogo plugs his website, djpogo.com

Leanne, naturally, looks a bit nervous, and I'm nervous for her. As the first records spin, the music doesn't seem loud enough to me and that's making it hard for her to grab the attention of the crowd and the judges. But soon the music begins to cut through, and halfway through the set she gets funky, cutting up two copies of Aim's 'Ain't Got Time to Waste', and going into some fast scratching. It's record on, record off, and by the time she's relaxed, it's time to finish. 'Well done, my dear,' says Swift. Leanne fans herself with a record. Outside Circo three or four by-standers have their faces pressed against the window; they're trying to work out what all that was about. The crowd cheer Leanne, and the judges make notes on their clipboards. I sense she's done OK, but it's unlikely she'll make it through to the final.

DJ Quest is up next, with a casual style, perhaps a bit too casual; the second bit of the routine seems to unravel, and he takes a good two or three minutes to get it together. Next up is Funk Freaker who has lots of local support; he makes loads of great noises and seems highly confident. Then he does a bit of body work and his friends down the front start whooping. One of his most vocal supporters is the tall man with the new t-shirt.

Payback is about to start when he realises he's forgotten one of his records, so he burrows quickly into his pile and pulls the missing record out. His start doesn't quite work out, but he gets back into the groove quickly, although his baseball cap is the wrong way round and I'm tempted to mark him down for that. He was followed by Ben, Blood One, who's more frantic than some, plenty of scratching and lots of wordplay.

Go was the one who had fallen asleep earlier on, but now he's recovered and really is ready, at last, to go. During his first minute the music rumbles and grumbles, but he turns it around, funks it up, and gets some dynamism into the set in the last minute or so. There's a punter on the front row wearing a fawn-coloured beanie hat and he's drunk, looking for cash in his pockets, but getting his hands confused. He's swaying, perplexed, and I find my eyes wandering to him, worrying that he might fall into the decks, imagining the moment.

There are handshakes from the other DJs sitting on the stairs behind the stage when each competitor finishes, and I'm struck by the camaraderie of the occasion. Cutmaster Swift is good, keeping the crowd cheerful with incessant chatter during the changeovers, lobbing slipmats into the crowd. He's been encouraging the DJs, and using his MC-ing as a platform for talking about the history of hip hop. It's clear that he's a big believer in the younger devotees learning about the roots of the genre. He talks about the old skool. He namechecks DJ Cheese, who won the World Final in 1986.

The final few take to the stage. DJ Skully opens with a few bars from Young MC's 'Know How', and then into a snippet of 'Tom's Diner', then he takes two balls out of his pocket and juggles with them. This doesn't seem to quite have the wow factor he'd obviously hoped for. The last competitor, Mike L, follows, and he's very confident, performs a tight routine and impresses the judges.

My first three are Mike L, then Funk Freaker, then Blood One. I wonder to myself what I would have done if Leanne had been one of the main contenders for a top three place; would I have gone out of my way to give her a good score? The DMC competition is bedevilled with accusations of favouritism, and as everybody in the world of turntablism seems to know everybody else, maybe a certain amount of distortion is inevitable, but in the end, as it turned out, it was clear that it just didn't happen on the night for Leanne. She's not arguing with the judges: 'Mike L was a cool customer, and that counts for a lot.'

Leanne seems tired and hot, but although she's not happy with her performance, she's not upset: 'There was obviously a disadvantage going first, although someone has to do it. I felt like I was warming up for the others.'

We continue to analyse the evening. Ben is pleased with how well he's done. Jim says he heard some DJs talking at the bar. 'I don't get it,' one said. 'They put on a good part of the record and then they fuck it up.'

There's a delay as Nick and Pete add up the scores, and the three DJs from the En4cers team perform. When the results are announced, and the result calculated from the votes of the judging panel, the first three chosen by the judges match my top three. The top two, Mike L and Funk Freaker, will go through to the final in London.

Funk Freaker is the most surprised. His real name is Stuart Barber, but he's been Funk Freaker for five years now. He lives in Tamworth, on the outskirts of Birmingham, and has a crew called Ill Skills which also includes Payback. This is the third year he's entered the DMC, and although he's always got through the eliminators in the daytime, this is the first time he's gone on to the UK Final. I feel like a sports announcer tackling a boxer who's just stepped out of the ring, but Stuart has never done an interview before. How do you feel? I ask him. 'I'm chuffed to bits, mate.'

After the eliminators you were graded sixth, but ended up second; how did you turn it round?

'Three minutes is a hell of a short time. There's not a lot you can do in three minutes, but the six-minute set was clean, it flowed.'

I got the top three dead right.

'Well, I got it wrong! I didn't have myself in it! I thought Skully would have been in the top three.'

Did you think having your supporters club helped?

'Maybe, maybe not. It's down to the judges at the end of the day.'

Will you keep the same routine for the final?

'I'm going to change a few little things, but it's basically going to be the same. I'm sick of it to tell you the truth! I've done it that many times, I want to do a new one for next year.'

Will you be nervous?

'Nerves play a big part. I'm nervous anyway, and you look out into the crowd and all you can see is heads everywhere and the judges looking at you; it's a lot of pressure. The first year I entered I went down to the Thekla in Bristol and it was nerve-racking. It was a nightmare.'

Who do you think will win the UK Final?

'Plus One might win, I think. But you never know, do you?'

Leanne, Ben and Jim are off back down to Brighton. There's a queue in the gents' toilet, and as I stand there someone says, 'You're the tallest man in the room.'

Am I?

'Yes, mate,' he says, insistently. 'Yes, mate, you're definitely taller than the tallest man.'

The Birmingham qualifiers have a month to prepare

for the UK Final at the Shepherd's Bush Empire in London, which takes place on a Saturday night in July. Even though it's warm, the crowd, as usual, is in coats and hats. The previous year the Individual title was won by Tony Vegas, and he's come back to be one of the judges. Other judges for the UK Final include Fusion and Tee Max (from MTV BASE), Shortee Blitz, DJ 279 from Choice FM, Primecuts (Scratch Pervert), DJ Yoda, and Biznizz and Pogo. When the microphone is passed round the judging panel Pogo again plugs his website, djpogo.com

Before the UK Final there's no eliminator in the afternoon; it's just straight on with the main event, although before the doors open the finalists are invited to warm up on some of the practice decks set up backstage. Yo-1 goes on first, pulling off some fast and accurate beat chopping. Daz reads a book while DJ-ing which makes me laugh; writing one would be more impressive.

Funk Freaker does well, certainly holding his own in this exalted company. Mike L incorporates some heavy basslines and some dub reggae, and the two DJs who qualified through the Bristol heat – DJ Tang and Madcut – also look good. Woody and Bunty from the Manchester heat take very different approaches to turntablism: Woody performs a very technical and combative set, whereas Bunty puts the emphasis more on the funkiness than being too technical.

Mr Thing is twelfth up to the platform. He fills his set with familiar hooks and keeps the beats funky rather than using any obscure breaks or hectic trickery, and gets a fantastic response from the crowd. This puts the pressure on Plus One; he's on last and is probably the favourite to win. He's very technical, clean and confident, but he doesn't seem to have quite done enough. Sure enough, when the votes are counted, Mr Thing wins, followed by Plus One, with Madcut third. Mr Thing is well pleased, but Plus One isn't. He was second the year before, too. 'It's getting better and better – structurally it was right, but mentally I lost it,' he says afterwards.

I also catch hold of Funk Freaker and ask him what he thinks of the final result. He shrugs his shoulders: 'They definitely went for the right one. It was a clean set. It wasn't really technical, do you know what I mean – so you couldn't understand it – but it just sounded good. But Plus One was trying to do too much.'

Stuart isn't too disheartened by his own performance. He's enjoyed himself and his friends had a good day out; even though the venue was busy, he could see them cheering him when he was on the stage. I ask him if the tallest man is having fun. 'Yeah,' he replies. 'He's got lashed. It's a long day.'

There's a lot of hanging around.

'Yeah, waiting about.'

Drinking time for the tallest man.

'Correct.'

The UK Final isn't the last night out for the turntablist crowd. Everyone's now looking forward to the World Final. It's a big event for the hip hop fans, and getting bigger; the Royal Albert Hall, Wembley Arena, the Parc d'Exposition in Paris and the Hammerstein Ballroom in New York have been among the venues for the World Final in previous years. The clear escalation of interest in turntablism over the last three or four years has mirrored the sale of SL1200s, the increase in magazines and websites and the globalisation of dance music. There's a second generation of turntablists, many of them almost young enough to be the children of the early stars like Grandmaster Flash.

The DMC World Finals are always surrounded by some story or other. The 1999 Final in New York occurred the weekend Hurricane Floyd hit the city. DMC America and DMC UK were expecting around seventy DJs from twenty-six countries, with DJs being flown in from around the world, but due to the weather the Dutch party were diverted to Milwaukee, the Germans were sent to Maine and the Australian posse were left in Los Angeles. On the night before the final seven inches of rain fell on New York, and the event looked like being blown away, but blue skies prevailed and the show survived. That was the year the Scratch Perverts unexpectedly won the Team event and Craze won the Individual title for the second year in succession. In 2000 the final was set to take place in the Skyscape arena at the the Millennium Dome in Greenwich.

Travelling out from central London, taking the underground to North Greenwich station, I'm soon at the steps leading to the entrance of the Dome. I'm wearing a cream bomber jacket in another sea of khaki, muted shades of grey, woolly hats, logos and baseball caps. The audience is young, in clusters of three or four, mostly lads, mostly white.

The Dome itself is on the left as the crowd walk towards the Skyscape arena. The Skyscape is filled with the kinds of colours designed to express technology and the future: aircraft grey and metallic decor, green and purple lights. There are TV screens everywhere (the Skyscape is sponsored by Sky TV). Inside, the arena is spectacular, with a deep stage and a high ceiling, standing room in the front for a few hundred, banks of seating at the back. There are backdrops on the walls carrying the logos of the sponsors: Rawkus, Technics, Ortofon. At the very back of the stage there's a fifty-foot TV screen, and, to the side, suspended banks of heavyweight speakers.

The DMC World Finals take place over a weekend and fall into three categories. On the Saturday it's DMC's Team Championship and the Battle for World

Supremacy. The Allies, down to a duo – Craze and A-Trak – this time gain sweet revenge for the defeat in New York by beating the Scratch Perverts in the Team Championship. On the Sunday it's time for the Individual final, with twenty-two countries represented. The talking point today is whether Craze will win his third victory in a row. The only other character in recent years to match Craze's domination is San Francisco's Q-Bert who has won three world titles – once as a solo DJ and twice with his crew, the legendary Invisibl Skratch Piklz.

The competition was expected to start at 6.30, but this is hip hop time, and when I arrive at 6.55 there's still not much happening. I'm standing down at the front, having been ushered there. I can't work out if I'm honoured to be in the standing area or not. I have a wrist band on. 'Keep that on all night,' the security guy had said.

By 7.15 there's music pumping out of the speakers, warming the crowd up, but no-one's dancing; it's not that sort of event. The seats are filling up. Down in the standing area a group of girls arrive, standing out not just because the vast majority of the audience are men, but because they're wearing light-coloured clothes, including two in white pedal pushers and white Adidas trainers. The music gets louder and many in the crowd are nodding their heads now; a few are blowing whistles. To my left, a group of people start taking photographs of each other. Half a dozen sets of decks are set up, and press photographers and TV cameras are crowded on either side of the stage, jostling for a good view.

Finally an announcement is made: the competition will start at 7.30pm. The announcer also tells the audience that smoking is not allowed in the auditorium; smoke can set the fire alarms off and cut off the electricity. Anyone wishing to smoke is requested to smoke in the bar. Someone plays Marley Marl. I have a wander. Leanne has been sitting up at the back on the seats, quite near the bar. A few of her friends are having a furtive smoke. She's upset that you can't take drinks from the bar into the auditorium: 'We've been sending the boys out one at a time and they're coming back with four bottles hiding in their trousers.' Now I realise one of the benefits of the huge trousers everybody seems to be wearing.

At 7.50 Tony Prince and Cutmaster Swift take the stage and begin explaining the schedule for the evening, running down a list of the DJs, including DJs from Germany, New Zealand, Japan, Holland, Noize from Denmark, DJ Pone and Dexter from Australia, and DJ Craze. We've come a long way from those heats in Manchester and Birmingham. This is the big one. They introduce the judges. I've been here before; any minute now DJ Pogo will plug his website. Unbelievably, he doesn't.

The Skyscape is full. MTV Base and CNN have set up their cameras, and the Webcast, courtesy of i-gig.com, has begun. Cutmaster Swift throws some DMC t-shirts and slipmats into the audience, and introduces one of the guests for the night, the legendary DJ Jazzy Jay. The two of them talk about how scratching and mixing started, and run down the story of the old skool pioneers. Cutmaster Swift says Jazzy Jay was a big influence on him: 'He turned my negative energy into something positive.' Jazzy Jay goes to the decks and twenty or so cameras point towards him. He's going to do a demonstration mix before the finalists begin. All eyes in the building are watching him and the decks, just a few square feet of lighted stage.

Jazzy Jay cuts, spins back and scratches, at one point dragging the needle across the record while still keeping the music flowing and funky. As a marker for the rest of the evening it's immense. Swift skips up to him again and Jazzy Jay tells his story; how he began DJ-ing before twelve-inch singles, digging out the breaks from old seven-inch singles. He tells the crowd to keep the faith: 'Hip hop is a culture made of lots of different things – attitude, the way we carry ourselves, and most of all the DJs. Without the DJs there would be no story.'

Swift introduces Grand Wizard Theodore, who also turns in a fabulous demonstration mix, pared-down rather than hectic, including a cut into the '900 Number', heavy big beats and extreme crossfader action. The crowd watch, delighted, mesmerised, as Theodore turns noise into notes.

Tony Prince and Swift are joined by DJ Cash Money, the other MC for the evening. Backstage, the gladiators of the groove are shuffling about, still shaking hands, still showing respect, but battle is about to commence. DJs from all around the globe have gone through hundreds of days and nights of disciplined practice; now it all comes down to this: two decks and a bag of vinyl. Later, Cash Money proffers this advice on how to get on in the world of turntablism: 'Give up the girls, give up food, give up everything!!'

DJ Hanger from Japan looks like a rock star but performs well, although all his records seem pitched way up. The Malaysian plays havoc with the crossfader, the New Zealander does a funky set. Dexter opens up the music references by including Jimi Hendrix and the Beatles in among the dope beats. Craze is last up. The judges on either side of the stage watch as he keeps it tight, makes it look easy, gets heads nodding and performs all his tricks to perfection. His position as favourite is justified.

As I leave, and walk outside, the air around the Dome smells of fast food. On sale in the Skyscape entrance is more DMC and Technics merchandise, and a selection of videos; you can get videos of competitions going back a few years, and for £15 a beginner's video entitled 'Do You

Wanna Be a DJ'. Outside it's desperately modern, all steel, grey, and banks of TVs, but inside it's like something primitive is going on, everyone gathered to watch people trying to tease something out of nothing, rubbing at records, scratching bits of plastic together in the hope they'll catch fire.

The world of turntablism is evolving. For the younger DJs it has a tendency to be overtechnical, serious and too wrapped up in certain records, certain styles and certain bpms, all west coast, indie, but when Grandmaster Flash got together a set he'd be using all kinds of tracks. Mr Scruff: 'I used to get loads of complaints from people saying "This isn't hip hop", so I'd say "What did hip hop DJs play before 1979?"'

Turntablism, the DMC competition, can seem like a Grade 7 piano exam, or an ice-skating performance, or a guitar solo from a young prodigy; technically, DJs can be outstanding, but that's not enough. You can be immensely skilled on a saxophone and not be John Coltrane. On the other hand, Treva Whateva was telling me about when he saw DJ Spinna play live: 'He's the perfect party DJ, he can cut and scratch but he can also rock a crowd on any equipment. He just turns up with a box of records and people get into it. He chops the records perfectly, scratches stuff in. That's what a good DJ is, a good hip hop DJ, or a good DJ generally; it's technical and it's emotional, isn't it?'

When it all comes together, it's astounding, when the trickery and the ability to fill a dancefloor are working in tandem. You don't get this at the DMC Championship because of the nature of the sets, but the top DJs can take the techniques and use them in a club environment. Craze sometimes does a long set, and he goes up and down the bpms, can do a fifteen-second juggle without losing the floor.

As the profile of turntablism rises, so does the in-fighting. DMC gets criticised for cashing in on hip hop DJ culture; DJs seem to have a love/hate relationship with the organisation. Rob Swift acknowledges its help in giving exposure to turntablists – DMC has undeniably raised the profile of hip hop DJs and provided a platform for talented DJs – but still it grates. 'You win a battle and probably get a cheap plastic jacket and some slipmats. While the person organising the battle is walkin' away with twenty Gs in his pocket, plus the video tape sales.'

Rival organisations like the International Turntablism Federation (ITF) claim to be able to offer a better environment for DJ battles. Leanne went to the first ITF event in Britain, in a dirty old warehouse in Birmingham with rain coming through the roof, and it was, she says, very disorganised. She admits the ITF is gaining a good profile but remains sceptical: 'The ITF battle has become quite prestigious, but one of the other problems with the ITF is that they categorise things. So you go into the beat juggling section the judges don't mark you for wordplay, even though doing wordplay well is very difficult.'

At the DMC Technics World Championship Final there are five TV crews on stage, fifty-two photographers and 130 journalists. The costs for staging the event, including local heats around the world, the various National Finals, the World Finals, advertising, travel, flights and hotel costs for the World Finalists, the parties and the prizes, is probably something like five million dollars. DMC invest in turntablism as well as reap rewards. As Tony Prince says, 'If DMC has been guilty of anything it is in taking a new art form, expanding its possibilities and placing it on a platform for the world to see!'

Funk Freaker isn't getting any financial reward from competing, so when I spoke to him again several months after the World Finals, I thought he might have a downer on DMC, but he had only positive things to say: 'They probably do make money out of it, but they've got to put the event on, haven't they? The only thing is it's always running late. Apart from that, it's really good.'

Funk Freaker enjoys the challenge and the camaraderie. Every Friday night his team gather their turntables together and work on team routines. Stuart also practises individually every night. During the day he works in a warehouse. 'It's shit but it pays a wage. I've got to get the money, you know what I mean? There's not enough gigs in Tamworth, there's nothing happening here.'

I meet up with As-If nearly a year after the Dome, with the 2001 competition looming. When I get to Dance 2 Records she's just about to lock up for the day. She's been pondering whether to get involved in promoting a night at the Zap. She's done nights before, including a Friday night called 'Five Elements' that started at the BN1 and then moved on to Cuba. With her friend Tracey (DJ Tyra), they set up four decks and people got up and jammed, and they also put some lino on the floor to encourage some b-boys to come down. They were busy some Fridays, like when the Scratch Perverts played, but they couldn't sustain much consistency, although the lino worked: 'We had a lot of break dancers. Some nights we had more break dancers than actual clubbers.'

She's unsure whether to get into promoting again, despite the offers. She helps out other people doing nights, and has a few residencies, including a monthly at 'Counter Culture' in Brighton at the Ocean Rooms which gets queues round the block. Sometimes she hardly uses any tricks or technical stuff when she's playing in a club, to a dancefloor rather than in an exhibition; sometimes she uses a lot: 'It depends on the way I'm feeling and what the crowd is like. Sometimes it might be the kind of crowd who just want to get into the music and dance, or they might be leaning along the side of the DJ booth waiting for me to do something. You're there to please the people who've paid to get in so you've got to gauge what kind of set they want.'

Leanne tells me she's going to enter all the competitions this year, including the DMC, and starting with DJ Pogo's Battle Royal event. Her team, Surgical Cuts, have got a new recruit called Ian. She's been practising every spare hour. 'I'm definitely doing the DMC, yeah, torturing myself again!'

Later we go to Concorde 2 and see Mr Scruff who's brought his eighty kilos of records down to Brighton from Stockport. While we wait outside in the guest list queue two people mistake me for a bouncer and one of them asks me for a pass out. Inside it's phenomenally busy, girls down near the front, drinking at the back. Tonight Mr Scruff is playing a five-and-a-half-hour set. He plays some dope beats, then into 'Turn Off the Lights' by Frank DeJojo and Jimmy Jones' 'Do What Comes Natural'. He plays 'Singalong' by his friend Treva Whateva. A girl passes Mr Scruff a piece of paper with 'Chicken in a Box' written on it, the name of his first single. His night is called 'Keep It Unreal'; he's out there bringing wit and variety to bear on hip hop traditions. The crowd seem to be loving it.

I'm staying in Brighton at a hotel called the Pelirocco. It's got themed rooms, including a mod room (influenced by *Quadrophenia*) and a room in honour of local label Skint. I'm in the hip hop room which has a big graffiti piece on the wall designed by Petro, one of the people who work at a night called 'Worm Jam'.

Hip hop is big business, a world culture. No-one owns it or controls it. It's not a New York thing any more. It spans the obsessive technical trickery of turntablism to rocking Friday nights at Concorde 2; from Mek to Go; from Funk Freaker to Dr Dre; from Tamworth to LA; from house parties in the Bronx to a bedroom in a Brighton hotel. To be honest, I'm a bit disappointed by the hip hop room: the graffiti is pink, indigo and green, which doesn't come across as very hardcore, and I'm sure they could have taken the theme further – more graffiti on the ceiling, a crossfader in the bathroom so you can mix between the hot and cold tap. But there's a dollar sign on the bed cover, and dollar bills on the lampshade.

Not the Big Market
Vogueing with Lottie at 'Shindig'

Some DJs turn up to a club with their records no more than ten minutes before they're due to play; the decks are set up, banners, mirrorballs and drapes fill the club, and there's a crowd listening to the warm-up DJ, waiting for the big name to arrive. Maybe the big name is playing in another club first and maybe there's somewhere to go to afterwards, another club, another cheque. All the publicity, the setting up and the organisation has been done by the club owner, or, more likely, the promoter.

Successful promoters develop an instinct for what a crowd wants, and book the DJs and programme the night accordingly. People like Ricky McGowan, Darren Hughes, Geoff Oakes, James Baillie, Charlie Chester, Jon Hill and Henry Blunt put a lot of energy and creativity into clubland. They make things happen.

In theory, a DJ is ideally placed to be a promoter; DJs have to understand and read a crowd, and they're likely to have strong opinions on music, but many of them are too flakey, or too busy, or just not interested enough in the mechanics of how a night works. But a number of promoters have had spells as DJs – Alex Lowes and James Barton, for example – and a lot of nights are run by DJs themselves, just as Norman Jay ran 'Shake & Fingerpop', and Ady Croasdell hosts his night at the 100 Club.

These are the DJs with more at stake in the night than the DJs who just turn up and play. For a DJ to take on all the extra responsibilities of a promoter, it's more of a headache, but the rewards are worth it. Doing the big gigs and travelling is fun, but there's no deeper enjoyment than originating and developing your own night, working with a team, filling a club on your own terms and through your own work. You can't guarantee to break even, but there's no third party to share any profits, so a DJ/promoter can also benefit financially if things go well.

Nevertheless, few DJs start their own night just hoping to make a quick buck; instead, it's a way to play what you want, follow your vision, and maybe kickstart or maintain your career. It's a gamble, of course, and sometimes the night dies a death. Friends say they'll support you, but they don't. The local *Mixmag* writer says he'll profile your night but then stops returning your calls. It takes courage to put your head above the parapet, but sometimes the night takes off, pays off, makes you a living.

In Manchester, nights promoted by the resident DJs are among the best clubs the city offers: 'Spellbound', 'Sub Tub', 'Eyes Down', and two of the most well-established nights in the country, 'Tangled' and 'Electric Chair'.

'Tangled' was founded by Terry Pointon and Phil Morse, massive clubgoers, inspired by nights like 'Freedom', who drifted into running clubs rather than via any formal career plan. In 1994 they'd been DJ-ing at parties in houses for a while, and decided to try a 'Tangled' night at the Dominion Hotel bar. This was the first of many venues, including the Underground at UMIST, the Attic, the Boardwalk and finally the Phoenix, their home since 1997. They've had problems in the past, including violent incidents when they were at the Boardwalk, but they've pursued a steady music policy, playing progressive, Euro house even when it was ignored by the press.

Other places may be about dressing expensively or feeling smug, but like most nights run by DJs, 'Tangled' is centred very much on the music. According to Phil, 'Our strength has always been that around eleven-thirty, just when things are ready to move up a gear, we kick off the dancefloor with records the crowd get into, but probably don't know and can't get hold of. "Tangled records", we call them; records we break on the dancefloor.'

More than anything, you sense that Terry and Phil care about the music and the quality of the records, and, as a result, they get an audience that does the same. Phil has a theory: 'I always say that if a record isn't good enough to get people travelling from Liverpool or Preston all the way to Manchester to hear it, then it isn't worth playing.'

'Tangled', being weekly, has plenty of space in its calendar for guest DJs. Phil and Terry tend to go for people they know and trust, preferably not through agents, but on a personal basis. Phil is always falling out with agents: 'Agents for the so-called big names always treat us like they're doing us a massive favour, but I see it the other way round; we're giving the DJ the chance to have a great night and play to a great crowd.'

Phil and Terry use two other residents, Herbie Saccani and Steve Thorpe, in a second room, and book a lot of unknown guests from around Manchester. One of their regular guests a few years ago almost gave them some problems, though. He ran occasional nights locally and always got two or three hundred people to them, so they started booking him at 'Tangled' and he always turned up, worked well and brought a good crowd. But then they started to hear rumours that he was a policeman; someone knew someone who had seen him arrest somebody in a car park. This didn't bother them, but when they asked him he admitted he had been a policeman but claimed he'd given up the job. Then, one weekend, the DJ's picture was in the *News of the World* alongside a story not just confirming he was a policeman, but alleging that he was a drug dealer. He'd been seen and photographed by the newspaper at a party in a flat above the Dog and Partridge in Disley. A warrant was issued for his arrest. The 'Tangled' boys haven't seen him since.

'Tangled' have overcome hard times and the ups and downs of the Manchester vibe, but the only thing that seems to bother them is keeping ahead of the big commercial clubs and getting their music right. Through 2001, even after seven years of 'Tangled', they are still reinventing, moving ahead, having realised that the world is catching up with them: 'Records we used to play that were one year ahead of the game are just two weeks ahead now the scene has gone overground.'

The 'Electric Chair' has also survived trends, and is now one of Manchester's flagship nights. It was launched back in 1994 by Luke Cowdrey and Justin Crawford, both of whom were DJ-ing at Ten Bar in Tarif Street. 'We were a reflection of a feeling among our mates that Manchester was a bit boring, clubs had got aggressive and there was also a dominance of very commercial music everywhere,' says Luke when I meet him in the insalubrious, smokey surroundings of a bar in Manchester called the Blob Shop. 'The Haçienda was in a dull period, things were flat, apart from a few nights like "Headfunk". Justin and I just thought we'd put on some monthly parties for our friends at the Roadhouse, a haven for us and our mates who were bored.'

The Roadhouse was a dirty old rock venue, but it was the only place they could hire cheaply on a Saturday night. Even then, the club was only available to Luke and

Justin after ten o'clock, following a gig by the Mighty Wah. They promoted the first 'Electric Chair' by ringing up all their mates and encouraging them to come. 'It was rent-a-mob, I suppose,' Luke admits. 'We didn't promote it on a street level or anything like that. We did some flyers, just horrible bits of photocopied cardboard – we weren't being intentionally lo-fi, we just weren't skilled – and we gave them to our mates.'

They had no hopes of making their name as DJs: 'We wanted something unpretentious, easy, just based on a passion for music and nothing else. It was a case of getting up and doing it; most of our friends were very humorous about the whole DJ culture, anyway, and we would never have got away with being self-important about it.'

As well as reacting against some of the nights on offer at the time, the Unabombers were also inspired by clubs they'd been to in the past – Luke mentions 'Occasions' and 'Jive Turkey' in Sheffield – and determined to bring to the nights a wide variety of funk, soul and house. In the face of the regimentation of dance music, they wanted to recapture something of the eclecticism of clubland in the mid- and late-1980s.

In 1994 and 1995, just as the 'Electric Chair' was up and running in the grotty Roadhouse, the music magazines were full of talk about super clubs. Luke explains their attitude to clubs like Ministry of Sound and 'Cream': 'We honestly had no bad feelings towards that scene, but it was just that we were trying to provide a bit of extra choice, first for our friends, and then it became a wider thing. From the roots we had, and the music, we just felt we were being squeezed out.'

If somebody had looked at it with a business head, to try to find a formula for success in clubland, they would probably have done exactly the opposite of what Luke

and Justin did; they'd have built a big club and booked
Boy George and Jeremy Healy. Luke acknowledges this,
but also insists they weren't trying to be obscure: 'We
didn't want to have that "we're the most underground
club" attitude either, that horrible notion of what is in
and what is out. We will still play what someone might
regard as an obvious track or a pop track not because
we're being ironic but because we like them. Now we
might play an r&b track even on a night when, say, Carl
Craig is playing.'

They filled the Roadhouse with their friends for the
first two months, had a dodgy third month when Andy
Votel cleared not just the dancefloor but the whole club
when he played 'Jesus Christ Superstar', but the fourth
was sold out, with a queue outside. They extended out of
the back into the loading bay, which added a few dozen to
the capacity, and played downtempo stuff in there. 'We
were just very lucky, I suppose. It was all about timing.'

They brought in guest DJs like Fila Brasilia, Mark
Rae, Winston Hazel, Harvey, Ashley Beedle. 'British DJs,'
explains Luke. 'People that we loved, who had some
heritage. Also, there was no point for us in getting in
some moody DJ. We wanted people into the vibe who
would get drunk, get into it, and people who would do it
for a hundred quid – that was another factor!'

In 1998 'Electric Chair' moved to the Music Box, a
bigger club. They maintained the same booking policy,
but an increased capacity meant they could afford a few
more expensive DJs, and some Americans, like François
Kevorkian, Carl Craig and Joe Clausell: 'Our booking
policy hasn't changed. We've never booked anyone just
to pull in numbers; me and Justin said that the moment
we do that we'll stop doing it.'

Luke explains what it's like being a DJ and promoter:
'You're a control freak, but in a positive sense; you get

involved with the way the club looks, the flyers, the doormen. We care about no wankers in the club, no gangsters, and doing whatever to create the right environment. We have a hand in everything, right down to which slides get projected on which walls.'

It's not just Manchester which has some strong nights promoted by DJs. High profile nights run by DJs include 'Progress' in Derby, 'Out in the Sticks' in Todmorden, 'Ultimate Base' and John Digweed's 'Bedrock'. Recently I went to see Scott and Scooby at 'Shindig' in Newcastle at Foundation (a venue formerly known as the Riverside), who have been running their own nights for more than ten years.

Promoters soon realise that the key to success and longevity lies in getting the details right. It's not all good times and glamour; there's meetings with club owners, trying to deal with guest DJs and their agents, tracking down designers, making sure printers meet their deadlines, trekking round shops and bars handing out flyers. At first you can do jobs like flyer distribution yourself, handing them out outside clubs or leaving a pile in shops and hoping the staff don't bin them as soon as your back is turned, but once you get started, you can delegate some of the jobs to companies that service the club industry. Keith Patterson at Exposure in Manchester has a mini-empire; his team distributes flyers all over the North and Midlands. He's with me in Newcastle, as keen to see St James's Park as he is to get on the dancefloor at 'Shindig'.

All promoters develop theories, a rationale for every blip in the attendance. You might find that on the first sunny weekend of the year you get a surge of people, especially girls who've just bought new outfits for the summer, keen to show them off. Later in the summer, you might be hit by an exodus of clubbers to Ibiza. If you are in a university town or city, you benefit every October when there's a new influx of students. At 'Shindig' the attendance tends to be biggest on the first and last weekends of the month, when people have just got paid. 'Shindig' is well established, though, and rides some of the ups and downs of demand, but promoters can never quite take their eyes off the ball; it's an unpredictable, stressful and competitive industry.

'Shindig' is in a strong position because Scott and Scooby augment their DJ-ing with hand-picked guests. The Saturday Keith and I are in Newcastle, Lottie is playing; she's not the biggest name in clubland but she has begun to rise in the top fifty DJ lists, and she plays in all the right places in Ibiza – like Space and Pacha – and all the right clubs in Britain, like Fabric, 'Bugged Out' and 'Back to Basics'.

Early in the evening at the Fog & Firkin I meet up with Scott Bradford and one of the other resident DJs, Craig Dewson. Shouting to be heard above indie muzak, they give me some background to 'Shindig', the last ten years or more. Scott and Scooby started off at Rockshots doing their own Friday night called 'Rebellion', motivated by a dissatisfaction with what else was on offer, but then fell victim to something that bedevils young promoters: they built up a night in a previously empty, hired venue, only for the club owners to step in, move them on and announce that they're going to do the night in-house. As in most similar cases, the club's own attempts failed miserably.

After a spell doing nothing, Scott and Scooby moved to Club Afrika, a small club with a capacity of 200 people, and they began doing every Friday and Saturday night there; these were the first official 'Shindig' nights. After a quiet start the club began to sell out every weekend, but they only lasted seven months; the club was already in

financial trouble, barely keeping the receivers at bay
when 'Shindig' started, and Club Afrika couldn't afford to
stay open.

'Shindig' moved on to Thursdays at another club,
Bliss, and began to attract more students. It was there
that Scott and Scooby met Rob Cameron, a manager at
Bliss. Things took off there for a while, and then it was the
same old story: the club thought they could do it better
themselves and forced them out, although Rob moved on
with them, and remains a part of the team. 'He's pretty
much the backbone,' explains Scott. 'Rob sorts out the
deals with the club and keeps our feet on the ground.'

They linked up with Jim Maudsley who helped them
get into the Riverside. This was 1994, and 'Shindig' moved
from Thursday to Saturday, originally just on one floor,
although they expanded to two floors by the end of the
first year. The main floor was American house and
garage-oriented, while the second floor guests included
more underground DJs, like Andy Weatherall, Justin
Robertson and Gemini. They began associations, linking
up with like-minded promoters running other nights,
including 'Up Yer Ronson' in Leeds. Sasha played the first
year of 'Shindig' at the Riverside, and so did Brandon
Block. Craig had been DJ-ing with them off and on; he'd
moved to London for a while, but when he returned he
became the resident DJ in the second room.

Until they moved 'Shindig' there, the Riverside had
been a live venue which catered for indie bands, but had
become rundown and was rarely very busy. The 'Shindig'
boys transformed it – with a lot of effort. This is how committed to the cause they were: even before they opened
the doors for the first time, Scott and Scooby bought
some cans of paint and gave the venue a new colour
scheme themselves. Then they cleaned the toilets up.
From the outset they took in extra elements, and installed

them every Saturday: 'We used to take in the decor, lights – we bought a load of lights – and a sound system that we bought for the backroom where Craig was playing. We bought all our own decks and mixer, everything; we put everything in there and we had to do the whole place up every Saturday afternoon.'

Up until the last few months they've continued to be very hands-on: 'We've done most of it ourselves. Over the years we've had people come in and help us but we've found a lot of it to be unreliable – people come and go and get sick of doing it – so we've found the best policy is to do a lot of it ourselves. We just get in there and get it done, even if it's a pain in the arse sometimes, it's got to be done.'

They took on all the other responsibilities themselves too, including distributing flyers and most of the DJ-ing, but the era of the guest DJ had arrived, so they began booking guests almost every week; in 1995 'Shindig' highlights included a night with Masters at Work and a Junior Boy's Own party in February.

They'd come that far purely on the strength of their dedication. Scott admits they'd no formal game plan: 'To be honest, it wasn't until two or three years into the Riverside and it was starting to get really busy that we realised we had to do it sensibly and get accountants in and start doing it properly. Up until then we were just young lads doing what we really enjoyed: playing records and putting parties on.'

In 1996 John Digweed, Dave Seaman and Josh Wink all played at 'Shindig'. Using the club as a base, a network was developing around their activities. It was clear that Scott and Scooby knew what they were doing; they branched out and started 'Hullabulloo' at the university, with Danny Tenaglia guesting. At 'Shindig' they continued to refine the music policy, and also promoted a huge

Radio One show in conjunction with Sound City New-castle at the Telewest Arena, at that time the biggest dance event the North-East of England had ever seen.

'Shindig' hosted more nights – a Ministry tour date plus, in 1999, the End tour with Layo & Bushwacka and Mr C – but the venue closed for refurbishment in 1999 for six months. By this time the club had been sold to the company who own Po Na Na. Early in 2000 the venue reopened, renamed Foundation, and the Slam DJs played the relaunch party. They now have guests most weeks, but they're discreet about the costs of the DJs. I'm intrigued, so I badger Scott to give me some figures. I ask him to tell me the most he's ever paid a DJ.

'Um, I can't say really! A lot!'

Have you ever paid a DJ more than ten grand?

'No.'

Have you ever paid a DJ more than five?

'Yes. I think about eight thousand is the most we've paid. It's a lot of money, isn't it? We have a structure. If a DJ goes over a set price which we have in our budget we put the door price up a pound or two or three, but we try to put a limit on it so it doesn't go up too much.'

For a long established night like 'Shindig' booking good guests helps maintain press interest and also keeps the music fresh, but Scott and Scooby, as residents, have a closer knowledge of the crowd. Scott admits there have been occasions when they've booked a DJ, but as they've started playing they soon realise that the residents could have done it better themselves. At one time, he thinks that nearly half of all their guests maybe weren't really worth their fee: 'We're pretty careful now, but maybe at one time it was fifty per cent, but now we're a lot more open-minded, and even if maybe we don't personally like what a DJ is doing, we judge it by whether the people who paid the money to get in there are enjoying it, and if they're enjoying it, then fair enough; we can respect what that DJ's doing.'

Have you ever had to get a sub-standard DJ off the decks?

'We haven't, although we've come close to it! I can't really say who, but on a couple of occasions there's been people playing and we can see it's just not working and you're fishing around, thinking should we tell them to get off or should we just let it go, but the sort of people we are, we're pretty timid when it comes to things like that.'

So you let it go?

'Yes, and then apologised to all the regulars afterwards!'

What do you say to the DJ in that situation?

'We just drop hints, but it's usually blatantly obvious that it's not working. It's very rare that it happens, to be honest. It was different when we first started booking guests and you have to sample people, try them out, and it's trial and error a bit, but now we've been going for so long we know what we're looking for and we take it from there.'

The 'Shindig' boys have all got day jobs. Craig works in a trendy clothes shop and DJs at the Po Na Na bar on a Friday night. Scott and Scooby and Mark work in the Flying record shop. Scott has been working at Flying for ten years – it used to be called Trax Records and was bought by Pete Waterman who then sold it on – and values his job there because it's a chance to listen to music all day and meet clubgoers who give him feedback on 'Shindig'. Scott and Scooby, along with Mark Armstrong, Chris Scott (who made the Happy Clappers record 'I Believe') and Bill Brewster, also have a record label, Forensic. Rob works in the planning department at the City Council.

Later, Keith and I wander off to find the club. We

know it's up the hill because that's what Scott told me, but soon we're lost. Keith picks a soggy flyer off the road. He has a habit of doing that anyway, being in the business. It's advertising the regular Friday at Foundation, 'Promise', and gives us the club's address in Melbourne Street. We stop a cab at some traffic lights and the driver tells us to go left and left again, which turns out not to be strictly true but it gets us there. When we turn into the top end of Melbourne Street we can see the entrance of the club 200 yards away. We practically skip to the door, both buzzing with expectation. It's part of going out, the build-up, the feeling you get when you walk towards the entrance to a club.

It's 10.15 when we arrive and Scott is outside. He introduces us to Scooby. Scott is watching the road, keeping an eye on what's going on. Although it's still early – the club has only been open a quarter of an hour – there are taxis arriving constantly and the queue is nearly to the end of the building, with fifty or sixty people, maybe more, waiting to get in. 'There's always a queue at this time,' says Scott. 'When Erick Morillo plays here the queue goes round the corner and disappears out of sight.'

Foundation is an old warehouse. Like many cities around Britain, the buildings that rose and fell as Newcastle's industries developed and then went into decline have begun to be reborn. Warehouses and factories have become hotels, bars and nightclubs. Craig takes us on a tour of the club, trying to describe to us what the place was like when it was a mucky indie venue. The DJ booth dominates one wall; it's where the stage was, where the bands played. I like the symbolism of this, the change from live music to dance music, from indie rock to proper house. The DJ box looks set to stay, encased in metal, sturdy. According to Craig, the building is haunted: 'The assistant manager has seen lights going on and off, the sound of music coming from empty rooms, weird shit.'

There's 'Shindig' decor all round the club, orange and purple logos on the wall, and a large video screen. Before the refurbishment, the club had two separate floors, but there's now a balcony round three sides of the main room and steel pillars breaking up the dancefloor. Big silver cubes like the ones decorating the main room at Southport hang from the ceiling.

Upstairs at the back of the building there's the second room where Craig plays disco, Salsoul and funky house. As you walk in, the floor of the corridor is frosted glass; it used to be clear glass but people standing on the ground floor looking up could see up the girls' skirts. Craig's room holds about 200 people, but opens later than the rest of the club, so it's locked up now. I tell him that I'll make sure I hear him play later. He introduces me to Paul who used to work at Toko. Craig tells me about the Big Market, Newcastle's infamous drinking area, a place notorious for heady drunkenness on a Saturday night. He's a drinker himself, but he's keen to distance 'Shindig' from the activities at the Big Market: 'No-one with any sense goes there, even though Newcastle is famous for it.'

Craig's been a part of the 'Shindig' team for years and has watched Scott and Scooby through different eras, working hard, enjoying it: 'Scott and Scooby are the shyest kids I know. The interview tonight, Scott was shaking a bit, like. He doesn't want attention on himself, which is good, it's a good quality in a person.'

Just before 11pm, the club is something like three-quarters full, but there's no queue outside, which makes me a bit anxious about Scott's chances of a sell-out this week. He says there'll be another surge of customers around 11.30, the ones who've been drinking. A couple more taxis arrive. Scott's slightly bothered by the quality of the crowd; according to him, they had to turn a few people away earlier: 'More than usual, meatheads who wouldn't fit in with the crowd. It's a bit slow for girls, to tell you the truth. We always get a lot of girls in, but when someone like Alistair Whitehead or Erick Morillo plays we get loads of girls.'

We watch the newcomers queuing, but other people are already leaving the club, including a group of three girls in lilac, pink and purple, who get into a taxi and go. I ask Scott why people would be leaving before the night's barely begun. 'I've no idea, sometimes it's people who don't really know anything about us, but they hear it's the place to be so they come down and then they realise they'd rather be in some kind of Ritzy club. Also you get people club-hopping. They come here for half an hour and then move on.'

We stand there, enjoying the sight of the queue building up. The guest list queue to the left is also getting busy. A number of the people coming in exchange greetings with Scott. A girl in a wheelchair arrives in a cab with three friends. Scott leaves my side and checks that a doorman is going inside to open a side door, and then accompanies her to make sure she gets in safely. He deals with it very efficiently. It's a Saturday night and some star DJ names are probably lording it in a VIP bar before their set, gloating about their latest remix fee, but Scott's down to earth; this helpful, watchful person standing in the cold outside the club is going to leave the front door, take his jacket off, open a box of records and DJ to 900 people in just a few hours' time.

At least it's not raining, although it's cold, and we're stamping our feet to stay warm. Lottie arrives at 11.15, and gets out of the cab, smiling under her fringe, her trainers gleaming white. Jim gets her record bag out of the boot of the cab; he's been ribbed all night about looking like Eddie Yeats from *Coronation Street* but is insanely good humoured about it. I follow as he leads the way past the bar and down some stairs through the backstage area. Lottie has two people with her and she introduces them to me: Zoe – Caroline Prothero's niece (Caroline is a big cheese in clubland) – and Zoe's boyfriend Chris. Lottie tells me she used to go to the Haçienda in 1989 and 1990. She thinks she might have heard me DJ, but you never know. 'It's ancient history,' I say.

Mark Armstrong is about to finish his warm-up set. The DJ-ing equipment on the stage includes four decks and two vari-speed CD players, but he's only using a couple of the decks. He's keeping the music beaty. He puts on his last record – the 6400 Crew's 'Hustler's Revenge' – and then he unplugs his headphones, signalling that it's Lottie's moment now.

Five mad lads all wearing blue shirts are cheering and screaming down the front. They're having the time of their lives, dancing, gurning, sweating, waving their hands in the air. Jim takes our drinks orders; Lottie has a Jack Daniels and Coke. She tells me she was supposed to be doing a gig in Preston the night before but couldn't make it, and she ended up round a friend's house drinking until 7am. 'I'm worn out,' she says.

She takes off her coat, takes a quick look through her records, pulls a few out and puts them near the front of her record box. The dancefloor is full. She puts on a Ron Carroll record, 'The Sermon', that starts with a vocal singing the praises of house music – 'House music is a healer when you don't feel good inside; house music is a joy, it's a spiritual thing' – and then dissolves into lovely squelchy bleeps and a bouncing bassline.

Out in the audience, two glow sticks are being waved in the dark, both in the hands of the same guy, one red and one blue. The mad lads down the front are about to explode with excitement; two of them have their eyes closed and sway slowly to the music with their arms aloft; one of the others has befriended the lad with the glow sticks. On the podium, a girl wearing a black top and dancing like she's treading grapes starts making complicated hand manoeuvres. Suddenly she freezes, sweeps her hair back, then starts treading grapes again. The room is lit with orange and purple lights, and the smoke machine is on, filling the dancefloor.

Lottie gets straight into her set, working the crossfader gently, settling into a sound; she plays straight up, mostly instrumental house with funky basslines. She barely looks up; a lot of her bouncy enthusiasm is reined in now as she concentrates, blending smoothly, going for gentle, relaxed mixing without much quick cutting. After a while, as promised, I wander up to see if Craig has started his set, but Scooby is on the decks upstairs. Craig gets on the decks about 12.15 and moves the music away from the tough beats Scooby has been playing. As I walk over the frosted glass and into the room, a girl walking the other way strokes my face as we pass; she's about a foot shorter than me and appears and then disappears into the crowd. I'm not sure what it's about, but no-one seems to notice. Perhaps I imagined it.

Back in the main room Lottie is an hour into her set, playing something by Silicone Soul and a track by Peace Division (Peace Division are Lottie fans and their 'Dance Daze' EP included a song called 'Lottie's Vogue' inspired by her dancing at the Miami Music Conference), then she plays more Subliminal releases, the Kings of Tomorrow single 'In the Night', and tampers with the effects buttons. A couple of the mad boys have disappeared from the dancefloor. The others are clapping during the breakdowns. The grape treader on the podium is still doing semaphore.

The room is full, and even the people on the periphery

are dancing. There's one girl wearing a top that seems to
say OLLS on it who's probably the best dancer in the
room; boys sidle up to her so she keeps moving around
the dancefloor. Predictably enough, one of the mad boys
spies her and starts bending her ear, but you can tell she
doesn't want to stop to listen to whatever sweet nothings
he's shouting at her. Soon he gets the message and he
goes back to his mates and she goes back to wearing out
her trainers.

Keith likes hanging out in the DJ box at gigs because
you get a great view of the crowd, but also, I think,
because he hopes some of the attention might rub off on
him. And sometimes it does. A lad in a tight blue t-shirt
with slightly spiked up hair waves at him. He thinks Keith
is DJ-ing. 'Wicked!' he shouts at Keith, and Keith happily
accepts his praise. Then the guy catches my eye and calls
me over. He's shouting at me. He usually goes to a club in
Middlesbrough, he says, but this is better: 'It takes the
piss, I fucking love it.'

The smoke machine is on overload, and the dancefloor looks like it's been hit by the famous fog on the Tyne.
The podium disappears from view under the smoke. I
notice a bald lad in a silver t-shirt, in his thirties, near the
front. He's off his head having fun, dancing like he's
miming a cowboy lassoing a heifer. Then he cups his
hands in the air and jumps up and down, waving at Lottie.

Lottie isn't looking up. The stage is about four or five
feet high and between her and the edge is a bank of decks,
mixers and CD players, so there are a good few yards
between her and the audience. She's concentrating on
pulling the right records out of her bag, and on working
the effects. Toko Paul asks me what I think. 'I think it's
great,' I tell him. 'Not an ounce of cheese but a great
crowd. They're accepting of the music. It's a good crowd
for DJs.'

Zoe is still on the stage, just behind the speakers. She keeps sitting down, on the stairs, on beer crates, anywhere; she tells me she goes to the Empire in Middlesbrough, and stays with friends in Sheffield and Leeds and goes out there a lot. Mostly she comes to Foundation for 'Promise' rather than on a 'Shindig' Saturday; on Fridays it's progressive, featuring DJs like Matt Hardwick, Parks & Wilson and Nick Warren. She tells me she prefers the music on a Friday, and then she sits down again.

It's just gone one o'clock and Lottie orders another JD and Coke. She's been dancing a little, though not really letting go, and I wouldn't call it voguing exactly, just a hip wiggle. She turns to her records, but before she replaces the record she's just played she fans herself with it. I ask her if she's hot. She tells me she used to carry a little portable fan but one of her friends told her it looked ridiculous so now she fans herself with records.

Out on the dancefloor the crowd are still loving it. The sound system is good and clear and it's helping Lottie; she plays minimalist records, shuffling drum beats with funky basslines and wobbly bits of keyboard, and on this system you can hear every bit of the music. The crowd at 'Shindig' is strongly local, very loyal, with a smattering of new people every week. Everybody is having fun, there's no sense that they're too cool to enjoy themselves. 'Shindig' reminds me and Keith of 'Golden' in Stoke, not because of the music ('Golden' is harder, trancier) but because it's so down to earth, local and relaxed.

Newcastle is traditionally a drinking town, and like everywhere else in Britain on a Saturday night there's probably also plenty of ecstasy around, but wandering around Foundation I don't see any pissheads or drug casualties, no slumped bodies, no-one falling around. And there's no cocaine; Keith meets someone who's spent over half an hour trying to buy a gram (unsuccessfully). There are no bad attitudes; the boys are wearing smart shirts, the girls are dressed up, but there's no preening or posing. I spy a lad in shades on the dance-floor. Wearing shades in a club is a major fashion *faux pas*, of course, but I'm sure Lottie's not to blame; she has an immaculate collection of trainers and looks well groomed tonight. You can choose your friends but you can't choose your audience.

The crowd are going with it, punching the air when records reach their crescendo, dancing, doing all kinds of funny arm movements. A whole lot of them look like they're miming card dealing. The bald lad in the silver shirt is still occupying his few square metres near the front of the stage; through the night there's been a bit of coming and going on the dancefloor, but he's not moved.

It's getting near the end of Lottie's allotted two hours. Scott and Mark are going to take over next, playing one record after another. Usually, DJ-ing, you're improvising your choice of what to play when, reacting to the crowd, so it's not written in stone, but all the time you have to have some idea of where your set is going, like a chess player thinking several moves ahead; you're ready for anything but in your mind's eye you have the next few records mapped out. Going one on and one off with another DJ means you must know and trust each other very well if you don't want to lose the thread of the night.

At exactly 1.30 Lottie finishes. There's no microphone, so she doesn't get a big send off as she unplugs her head-phones, but the first hundred or so people in front of the stage can see she's packing her bags and they clap and she claps back, with her hands over her head like a foot-baller saluting fans at an away match. Scott and Mark play an even more stripped-down sound, pure drum tracks with gospel vocals over the top. Scott seems to be working from CD. They've decided to do three records on and three off. It goes well, for about forty minutes. You can tell they know the crowd well; there's a bond there, between the local heroes and their loyal crowd.

I'm standing a few feet away from Scott, talking to Lottie, and she keeps telling me she's going to get off back to the Malmaison soon and we can do an interview there, but she continues to accept more drinks. Suddenly the record jumps and the music stops, and we both turn to see what's happened. The needle is off the record, and Scott has taken a couple of steps back from the decks, looking shocked. Someone's thrown a glass and it's landed on the record. Mark, Jim and the others can't believe it. Scott is amazed. 'This has never happened before. What the fuck is going on?'

It could have been worse; at least the glass didn't break or hit anybody, but we glare out into the club trying to work out where the glass came from (it seems to have come from the left of where we are). Scott is still shaking his head. Someone goes off to check the CCTV and a clump of doormen appear on the edge of the dancefloor. Scott has put another record on and the crowd is dancing again. There's no long-term damage to the night but Scott is clearly saddened by it. When you have a lot of friends and regulars in the club, you have a close relationship with the crowd. You're all part of the night, building it, sustaining it. A club is like an oasis, an escape. You don't expect aggression, destructiveness; that's a part of the world you're leaving behind.

The lad in the silver shirt has gone, and I see him up near where the glass came from, obviously interrogating people about what happened; he knows what's gone on and doesn't like it. But the CCTV doesn't seem to have picked anything up. Scott just has to get on with it – it's just one of those things. He's apologetic, but I tell him not to worry.

Keith has already gone off to bed; he's accepted one too many drinks. Lottie decides it's finally our turn to leave, but first disappears in order to get paid. We say our goodbyes to the other DJs, and Lottie gives Mark and Scott a hug. Jim takes us to the front door. There are no cabs so I grab her record bag and we walk to the hotel. She's only brought one bag with her, which contains maybe seventy records in all. She tells me she never takes more records than she needs, just the records she wants to play; she hopes they'll be the same records the crowd want to hear. Walking down the hill, we give the night a thorough post-mortem. I'm still amused by some of the dancing. I'm trying to explain some of the moves to her; there's all that juggling and that one, dealing cards.

'I love that, and that one packing boxes!' she says. 'I knew that when I was at Quadrant Park and I used to wear leggings, a vest and Travel Fox trainers and do this quick little rave dance.'

We're not far from the hotel, but Lottie is concerned that the bag is heavy for me. It's an occupational hazard for DJs, carrying boxes (the other is deafness). Lottie has already injured herself once. I tell her about Erik Rug in Paris who had to take nearly six months off after tearing his back; the doctor told him he should have carried two bags, one either side of his body, and balanced the spine. She tells me Sasha missed a gig at 'Bugged Out' because he'd injured his back changing a tyre, which sounds unlikely.

It's just gone three in the morning when we get back to the hotel and there's only a few people in the Malmaison bar. Lottie decides to nip upstairs to change her top and I check my tape machine is working. After DJ-ing you stink of cigarette smoke, sweat and alcohol. I'm thinking about those tight shirts Judge Jules and Ferry Corsten wear; for me, it has to be a loose fit. When Lottie reappears we have a brief discussion on ideal DJ-ing wear. I'm trying to get my thoughts together. I'm tired and I've not even been working.

DJ-ing is like doing the night shift; it plays havoc with your body clock. Nevertheless, it's rare to be too tired to DJ; even if you're tired before you begin, once you get on the decks you don't feel it, you're swept away by the job and the atmosphere. The minute you start to pack your records away, though, and take that first post-set deep breath, then you feel tiredness sweeping all over you. You're physically wrecked, but at the same time adrenalin is still pumping and your mind is working. Sometimes when I get into bed an hour after a set I can still hear basslines in my head, and mentally I'm still putting one record on after another. With this mixture of physical tiredness and mental jumpiness, it's hard to wind down.

I set the tape running and start telling her what I've been thinking about. 'You're right,' says Lottie, 'I didn't feel tired when I was DJ-ing but my energy level just drained when I finished.'

You stayed on for an hour after you played, though, so you can't be that tired.

'I just feel sometimes like I just want to do my job and then go home, but then the adrenalin you use when you're DJ-ing goes gradually so I find I have to stay up just to wind down.'

That's your excuse for staying up late and drinking.

'I can't do that forever, I know.'

I laugh, and remind her she's got years of partying left in her. 'You're not even thirty.'

'No, but I can tell I'm slowing down.'

Lottie grew up in Chester and used to travel over to the Haçienda, and then became a regular at Liverpool's legendary Quadrant Park where the DJs included James Barton, John Kelly and Andy Carroll. Turned onto dance music in a big way, she started DJ-ing in Chester at High Society on a Thursday and also at Muswell's where she had been working behind the bar and then suggested to the owners that if they paid her a little bit more – all of twenty-five quid – she would take decks in and it would help pull a bigger crowd. Every Saturday Lottie and her brother used to haul her decks down there and she would DJ, and the plan worked: when she left, the night was so well established that Bottom Dollar's Matthew Roberts took over.

Eventually she was drawn towards London: 'I went down to London because everything had gone a bit stale. Manchester wasn't really happening any more, although Liverpool was really good. I was doing the gig at Muswell's and I was finishing at one in the morning and then me and my mates would get a lift down to London for about half past three when "Trade" opened and we would go to "Trade" and stay in London all day Sunday and go back to Chester on Monday morning.'

Phil Howells was her guide in London. He works at London Records, and went to Chester to sign K-Klass, didn't sign K-Klass – they signed to DeConstruction instead – but met and married Lottie's best friend Claire. Lottie was going out with Claire's brother Richard, and it was her and Richard and Claire who started going down to London every Saturday night to 'Trade' at Turnmills. Occasionally they'd travel to London midweek, to visit nights like 'The Fruit Machine'.

Lottie tells me how she eventually moved away from Chester, lived in Phil's flat in King's Cross for her first two months in London and took a job working at Agnes B. Through Phil she got a DJ slot at a London Records party in a hotel in Canary Wharf alongside Malcolm Duffy, Tall Paul and Pete Tong. This was in 1991, and the party was full of pop groups like the Communards and East 17 swanning around the hotel swimming pool. That was her first gig in London. Through Phil she also met Red Jerry and their visits to 'Trade' every Sunday continued: 'We were called "hetero hell", because about eight of us would walk in, all male and female couples. Mostly, for two years, I only went to gay clubs in London.'

The music at 'Trade' at that time was hard. Although she doesn't go there any more, she describes 'Trade' in that era as 'the most exciting club I've ever been to in my life'. Lottie's devotion to that mid-1990s 'Trade' sound intrigued me. I've always had these gender generalisa-tions: that hard, heavy techno – along with head-nodding hip hop and deep noodly house – appeals mostly to men, whereas girls like funkier records, more songs, more soul. Lottie knows I'm generalising wildly. 'I hear this all the time but I don't really think that,' she says. 'To be honest I like funky, soulful stuff but I think techno can have some funk in it – trance I don't think does at all, I find that really soulless – but funky techno and house is what I really love. I had three years just because of "Trade" where I loved really hard music.'

Wasn't that scene very druggy?

'Well, it was like that when I was seventeen, eighteen and listening to vocal stuff, Denise Lopez, Ce Ce Rogers, all sorts of stuff at the Haçienda. I think it was more the energy and the excitement of the hard music and the club itself, everything just seemed right. I could accept harder music which I hadn't done before because it wasn't tacky.'

I'd been thinking about my theory, and realise I've amassed some evidence that totally contradicts my argument; like the fact that although Lottie, Smokin Jo, Paulette, Jo Mills and Angel play house, most of the famous female DJs seem to specialise in harder music, like Lisa Lashes, Anne Savage, Lisa Pin Up, Alison Marks.

Lottie agrees: 'The most popular female DJs all seem to play really hard music. So, no, I don't think there's girls' music and boys' music. I really don't think that girls' music is garage and boys' music is hard. I think boys' music is underground.'

I think boys read magazines and hang around the record shops whereas girls go out on a Saturday night.

'Maybe that's part of the make-up of boys, to be a bit trainspotterish. Making models, collecting things, and there are some girls like that, but it's not very common.'

Lottie explains that her fondness for the harder sounds has waned: 'When I hear hard music now it's all drum rolls, peaks and troughs, and much of a muchness, it's different now to how it was. Then it was exciting and very underground but I didn't like what it progressed to.'

But then it's always more exciting at the beginning of something, isn't it?

'Yes, and I loved all those Dutch records around then, stuff I wouldn't play now. When I walked into "Trade" it felt amazing, like walking into Quadrant Park.'

Except you'd walk into Quadrant Park and hear some massive piano anthem!

'Yeah, like Catherine E, "I'm Alright". Yeah, we'd all dance to some right shit!'

In your Travel Fox trainers?

'Correct!'

Lottie and I are trading the titles of Italian piano anthems from 1990, 1991, records like 'Electric Choc' and 'JJ Tribute'. We know they're not the classic purist New York house records some DJs might feel the need to convince themselves they were brought up on, but we're laughing, a couple of excitable clubbers at 3.45 in the morning reminding each other of records we used to love, classic e-rush party tunes heard all over the North-West of England ten years ago. She namechecks De Melero

'Night Moves' and Jinny 'Keep Warm' (still Lottie's brother's favourite ever record).

When she's talking Lottie says 'really, really' a lot. She's doing what she's always wanted to do, she's DJ-ing, travelling, making records, and I guess she knows she's leading a really, really good life. Then she gets back to her 'Trade' years: 'I was working at Agnes B and living for the weekend. It was a really, really exciting time for me. I was in London and that was exciting, and it was going off at "Trade". The DJs got paid next to nothing but they were some of the best DJs I've ever heard.'

Red Jerry had started Hooj Toons and offered her a job there, so she left Agnes B. 'Tall' Paul Newman's father is the owner of Turnmills, and Paul had become a resident at 'Trade' in 1990 aged nineteen. Four years later, he launched 'The Gallery' at Turnmills on Fridays, and he asked Lottie to be a resident, playing an early set in a nine-hour night. When it first opened, 'The Gallery' was quiet for six months or more, until Paul managed to pull a big crowd in to celebrate his birthday. From that night on it never looked back. Lottie kept her residency there until she was too busy to commit to it every week. In the early days at 'The Gallery' she was also working at Ricky Tick's in Soho as well (playing for five hours for fifty pounds). It was her apprenticeship: 'I don't think you're a proper DJ if you've just been buying records for a year. I think you have to have a collection and you have to have gone out to certain clubs and collected certain records. When you're DJ-ing you have to be playing records for a reason, because you love them, not because you've just bought them.'

You're saying you've got to have some depth and some history, and you're not a proper DJ until you've got out of the bedroom?

'You've got to do your time.'

That's why those cheap gigs and first gigs are worth doing, the experience of working a crowd, any crowd, is so important.

'In some ways the best DJs are warm-up DJs because they know how to build a night, which is a difficult thing. When I started to do peak time slots I'd been doing warm-up gigs at "The Gallery" for so long that it took me a while to realise that you just bang straight in there. I'd always thought about building the night, and thought about what the next DJ would be playing, obviously, because if you play big records at eleven o'clock you ruin the flow of the night.'

Lottie has an agent, Becky, who works out of the same office as 7 magazine. Before that she'd occasionally ended up in the wrong kind of club, when a promoter booked her thinking she was going to play a certain style and got it completely wrong. She remembers 'Sweat' in Northampton when she was on the same bill as the hard house star Lisa Pin Up. Lottie had doubts about the gig before she'd even left the house. When she arrived, the music was 140bpm, verging on the happy hardcore. She felt physically sick, knowing the crowd just weren't going to want to listen to her after Lisa Pin Up. The promoter would hear none of it. 'No, it'll be brilliant,' he kept saying. It wasn't: 'I went on and I played three records – the three fastest, hardest records in my box – but then I had to get off and he was OK about it, and he paid me, and it was awful, it just wasn't the club for me. I'm not a bad DJ and that wasn't a bad club, but it just wasn't right.'

Do you do a lot of travelling on your own?

'I have done, a lot.'

Is that a bit lonely?

'Really lonely, yeah. But most of my stuff abroad now I have someone with me. When I went to Las Vegas and Chicago, Becky came with me, and she really looked after me and it was good to have a mate there and she got my money at the end of the night and things are much more fun when they're shared. You go somewhere good and you want to share it with somebody.'

DJ-ing abroad is an honour and a treat. You jet in somewhere, meet the promoter and the team at the club and a few hangers on. It's a great way into a city or town or culture; you don't have to spend ages seeking out like-minded people in record shops or dodgy bars like you might if you'd arrived as a tourist. You get instant mates.

'Yeah, yeah.'

Lottie waits for me to continue. I start telling her about this extreme, strange thing that sometimes happens to me when I'm travelling alone. If I've got a gig in two or three hours' time, I'm sitting in the hotel room and sometimes it begins to feel a bit unreal and I have this urge just to check out and go home. This isn't just a DJ thing, I guess. Maybe it's the same for other performers, entertainers in the public eye, actors, say, or musicians. It's to do with life on the road disorientating you.

It doesn't always come naturally to me, being sociable, but you seem to enjoy being out in a club crowd; it doesn't faze you, does it?

'I usually do party and I get on the dancefloor and I go back to somebody's flat and I stay up until the morning, but the trouble is when you do that all the time then you're expected to keep doing it, and if you don't for one reason or another people notice and they think you're being really rude, so there's pressure on you. Unless I'm just using it as an excuse to stay up all night!'

There are DJs who have built their reputation on staying up all night – the caners who get known for their endless partying, rather than their music. I'm not sure that's a reputation worth having.

'Yeah, and then there are DJs who don't go to awards and openings. I'd rather be like Andy Weatherall; I want to be known for my music and not for my antics. I have an image that I like partying and I'm sociable, so I know at the moment I'm somewhere in between.'

What makes a clubber become a DJ?

'Loving it so much and taking it that step further. You can dance away on the dancefloor but the DJ has to to find out what that record is and they have to get it on the Monday. I can be having a really good conversation with somebody, but if a great record comes on then it's like "I'm sorry, I don't want to be rude but I have to find out what that record is called." That's what differentiates people who aren't ever going to be DJs and people who are.'

Lottie strikes me as enthusiastic and not particularly ambitious, not in a pushy way anyway. She's playing in the clubs that she respects; she co-hosts a radio show with Caroline Prothero on Ministry of Sound's digital radio station. And then she does some production. Until the near end of 2000, she was reticent about studio work, but by October she was doing a track called 'Bushroot' which was released by Duty Free, and remixing Billie Piper's single 'Walk of Life'. Early in 2001, the M&S track 'Salsoul Nugget' was released, her most successful remix to date.

Despite the attention all DJs get, there have been few occasions when she's lost her temper, and she's never had a glass thrown at her:

I can't believe that happened. It was so out of order! I was somewhere, and there was this girl who was stood right near to me and I don't know what music she wanted but everybody else was enjoying themselves; that's the thing when you're DJ-ing, everybody can be enjoying themselves and it only takes one person to go 'You're shit' or 'Is it going to be like this all night?'

Anyway, every time I saw her this girl was pulling a face and huffing and puffing and gesticulating and it was doing my head in.

Even though everyone else was having a great time?

'Yes, because it knocks you for six if you think someone's not enjoying themselves, even if you know it doesn't really matter what one person thinks, but I just turned round and said, "Right, c'mon, what's wrong with you? What do you want to hear? What do you want?" And she was like "I just wanted it to be a bit more uplifting." I said, "Well, it's not," and I thought don't do that; don't make me feel crap when I'm doing my best.'

I'm thinking about some of my gigs. 'That's not a really bad experience,' I tell her.

'I know. Nothing really bad has happened. Touch wood.'

Lottie is playing with her cigarette packet, and I get the feeling she might want me to bring our conversation to a close. It's nearing that point in the night when the other hotel guests will soon be coming down to breakfast. Lottie begins to describe what DJ-ing is like when everything fits into place:

When it works you have this feeling that people really understand and people love it and people love the records as much as you do, and you put the records together and it flows and you don't even have to think about it, and it just goes on and on, and everybody is enjoying it as much as you are and no-one gives a damn about anything, they're just getting it. When you first hear a record you love I'll play it twenty times at home, over and over again. When you play records like that out and you can see people love it as much as you do, it's the best feeling.

You feel that whoosh of something from the audience, don't you? It can be unpredictable, too. I mean, at 'Back to Basics' you would hope for a good night, but you get to some pretty unlikely places and have a great night with a great crowd.

'Yeah. "Sugar" in Leamington Spa is another good one, they love their music, all that Masters at Work stuff, really good tunes, proper house. The crowd is open-minded and they know that there's no way the promoter's going to put anyone cheesy or tacky on.'

If you look up and the dancefloor has started thinning out a bit, or the card dealing and the packing boxes aren't quite happening, does that affect what you're going to play next?

'No, not really, not any more. I've learned that you must play what you really like, but I might play the records in a different order if I think that might help, something slightly tougher maybe, or something that I was going to play half an hour later I'll play earlier. When you first DJ you haven't got confidence and you start worrying about what records to play to get them going and what records to play to keep them there, but now I've got more confidence I think this is really good and I've got them in a groove; you have to get them in a groove.'

And then what do you do?

'You have to get the crowd where you want them to be and then they're listening, so you can get the best out of each record. If you have a really, really exciting record and you play it after a manic record then it might get lost and it won't be exciting. You get them in a groove and then you can go anywhere you want.'

We're talked out, but happy. It's now nearly five o'clock, and we call it a day. We've had a great night, and like every good night, the glow has lasted. Keith and I drive back to Manchester full of it.

Karl Marx – who, as well as wanting to change the world, enjoyed a good night out – said that in an ideal society there would be no division between labour and leisure. He would probably shudder at some aspects of DJ culture: the commercialisation of clubland, the relentless market manipulation and the exploitation of logos and brands, but I hope he would acknowledge the value of Scott and Scooby hands-on, painting the toilets, hanging the drapes, bringing some colour, life into a disused warehouse up a wet hill in Newcastle, their work melting into play. There's a Noël Coward quote Tom Rowlands from the Chemical Brothers likes to use: 'Work is more fun than fun.'

Music is a lifeline, but clubs bring people together. At worst, it's a tasteless cash-in, but at best a club night is a focus for a community, and a celebration. Phil Morse: 'The people who come to "Tangled", they feel it's their night, their music, that they can talk to us when they see us in the street, that they're a part of "Tangled", and they are, we all are; and that's what the word "club" means.'

Local, committed, undercapitalised promoters tend to do this better than the bigger clubs. The bigger clubs give off the same kind of impression as Manchester United; you can acknowledge that they do what they do well, but their overriding commercialism grates, always asking you to buy into the brand.

I'm reminded of words DJ Ian Levine has used in connection with Northern Soul, but which are perhaps more widely applicable: 'If you worked from Monday to Friday in a launderette or something, you spend your whole life living for the weekend. When the weekend comes you have your music, you feel part of something. Les Cockell was a road sweeper in Yorkshire, but at the weekend he was a DJ at the Twisted Wheel. He was *somebody*.'

Clubland is powered by those characters – Phil, Terry, Luke, Justin, Lottie – living for the weekend, people like Scott and Scooby, uncynical people doing what they love, being excited about it. I left Newcastle with an over-whelming desire to go back to 'Shindig' at the earliest opportunity, and seek out Lottie next time I got a chance. You can get addicted to all this.

The Biggest Buzz
Pete Tong, Graeme Park and 'Ain't Nobody'

During an average week DJs don't do much DJ-ing. The rest of the time some of them do day jobs, or wander around record shops. Mr Scruff can spend fifteen hours a day going through his record collection, listening to new records, or digging about for old records, LP tracks, unreleased bits and pieces. Then he gets on a train with his bulky boxes of vinyl and his favourite mixer wrapped up in a bin-liner. Paul van Dyk gives half a dozen interviews in the space of a couple of hours, and then has a month in the studio to finish his album. You could be a DMC turntablist falling asleep next to speaker stacks on a Sunday afternoon in Birmingham. Or you could spend your time away from the decks messing about in hotel rooms, eating at strange times, losing your diary, going to parties, sitting in the pub whingeing.

Networking, being out and about, meeting promoters or club owners, forging alliances with other DJs, hawking mix tapes round clubs, hanging out, being seen – all this helps get you gigs. It's a general rule about the music business that you have to do the hanging out; that to get on, it's to do with who you know, or who you do your drugs with. When I suggested this to Lottie that night at 'Shindig', I think she thought I was being overly cynical: 'I don't know, that would be a sad state of affairs. I think that if you're a really amazing DJ then hopefully it doesn't matter who you know or who you don't. Ultimately, I don't think anybody can have any success as a DJ unless they have a passion for music; your career will be very short-lived if you haven't.'

Time spent seeking out tunes, and trips to record shops, is never time wasted. Some records will come to find you, pre-release copies of records sent out by promotion companies hoping that play by a DJ will build demand. They target DJs who are high profile, or who do radio, or who happen to work close to chart return shops. Graeme Park gets a hundred records mailed to him every week. Even after nearly twenty years of DJ-ing, listening to them isn't a chore: 'I still get a kick out of opening up the mailers and seeing what's new and there'll be lots of crap in there but also probably three or four really good records, two of which could go on to get massive.'

Plenty of DJs use time away from the decks to make records or remix. Many do radio shows or run record labels, or, if you're Pete Tong, both. When I finally catch up with Pete Tong he's in his office at London Records, content, over forty, and enthusiastic. Pete Tong now presides over his radio show, does voiceovers for advertisements, releases mix CDs every year, writes magazine columns, plays in clubs and runs a major record label, although, unlike Jimmy Savile, he's not yet presented *Top of the Pops* wearing a suit made out of bananas.

He's survived when others have failed, gone mad, lost track of the music, or given up once they'd grown up. Tong is still doing it: 'My personal motivation is that I have to enjoy it and I have to feel that I'm doing something refreshing, getting off on the music, I always have to be taking a certain amount of risks, introducing new records.'

So you think a certain amount of reinvention is involved in sustaining a long career?

'Definitely, and I just think it's down to my enthusiasm for change. When we were soul boys we got into jazz
funk, when we were into jazz funk we got into hip hop,
when we got into hip hop and when we were into Def Jam
we got into house music. It was always the next thing.'

And now?

'Well, obviously, although house music has been a
consistent area to be in for twelve, thirteen years now,
you know yourself that the music we play now is radically
different to what we were playing in 1988, '89.'

A year or so ago Pete Tong appeared to make a conscious decision to take a step towards credible clubs like
'Bugged Out' and 'Bedrock', and he recorded a mix
CD for *Mixmag* entitled *Pete Tong's Deep Funk Theory*.
The CD and the gigs showcased a slower, deeper house
sound – no anthems, no trance, no big breakdowns –
and appeared to be an effort to reposition his career and
renew his credibility. He half agrees with this: 'Sometimes the content hasn't changed much, it's just the way
people perceive it, but I take opportunities to make a
point of showing that I'm doing different things, and of
course gigs at "Bugged Out" or "Back to Basics" encourage me to play something different, and I like playing the
occasional – dare I say it – showbusiness-type party
because you can maybe play hip hop or something.'

And in all those years, those twenty-odd years, have
you ever played a bad record?

'A bad record,' says Pete, repeating the phrase slowly
as if he can't quite believe what I've asked him.

I mean when you're playing out.

'No, not really. In retrospect I've probably played
records I wouldn't play any more, without question.'

He's laughing now but I still get the feeling he thinks
I'm trying to stitch him up. I rephrase the question. Have
you ever played a record you regretted playing?

He thinks not: 'No, no, I think I've played records that at the time I probably thought were quite good. An example would be "Zombie Nation" which I thought was genius, but because it went so huge it would have been cheesy to keep playing it; it's usually those records that are cool for four and a half seconds and then become unbelievably huge and everyone is pissed off with them.'

Somebody interrupts us. 'It's in the car,' Pete says, talking to his colleague now about some New Order tape Pete's left in his car.

So I ask him what crappy records he might have played when he was a mobile DJ.

'I've played "Dancing Queen" a few times,' he confesses.

Have you ever played 'Tiger Feet' by Mud?

He laughs. 'Only when I started, doing school discos. And "My Friend Stan" by Slade I remember playing.'

So you can remember a time when records like that filled the dancefloor?

'Absolutely!'

I tell Tong that I have a wedding to do later in the year, and that when I mentioned wedding DJs to Paul van Dyk he was at great pains to distance himself from them. I explain to Pete that I've only done two weddings before, four or five years earlier, as big, big favours. Pete Tong tells me that when he got married in 1989 Peter Young from Capital played jazz and soul and funk. Last year Tong himself played at a wedding in New York for his friend Lucas White. Twenty years ago when he was a mobile jock, Tong did plenty of weddings. 'When I started out I ruined quite a lot of people's weddings,' is how he puts it.

In his youth he remembers sitting in his parents' dining room listening to radio DJs like Roger Scott, Rosko, Greg Edwards, Robbie Vincent, absorbing all the sounds needed to complete a soul boy's apprenticeship. Although he started off as a mobile jock and then moved into clubs, he reckons he was fated to do radio: 'I was always fascinated by the art of radio and I remember even writing down the records they played and thinking about the sequence of the records and analysing it like that was a very early thing for me.'

The buzz of DJ-ing in a club is obvious. I've seen Graeme Park at the height of the Haçienda era, wet with sweat, joyous, with his hands in the air, accepting, celebrating the crowd's mad passion. I ask Graeme how radio work could match that. 'It's a different type of buzz,' he says. 'For example, the other Saturday I went into the studio at half past seven on a Saturday night, there was nobody else in the building, it was dark, I had to turn the lights on, turn the volume up, and there's me on my own in the building and if anything goes wrong I'm fucked, so there's a little bit of adrenalin there already and then you fire your first jingle and it's you on your own talking to the audience.'

The Galaxy network stretches across the North of England from Newcastle over to Manchester, then down to the West Midlands, and on to Bristol, the South-West and South Wales. In February 2000 Galaxy 102 was censured by the Radio Authority for playing mainstream chart music instead of the 'rhythmic' tracks it promised to play as a condition of being granted the licence. It's still commercial during the week but it's got a separate identity at the weekend, with DJs like Tim Lennox, Boy George, Paul Oakenfold, as well as Graeme. 'It's the only viable national alternative to Radio One,' he points out, 'and when you're there on your own playing records to thousands of people you really do get a buzz off it.'

Clubs and club DJs have played their most significant role in the history of music in Britain when they've been playing music you couldn't hear on the radio; like the Scene club which pre-dated Radio Caroline (well before the establishment of Radio One). In the 1990s we witnessed Radio One trying to catch up again, a few years after acid house, recruiting the likes of Pete Tong, Gilles Peterson, Fabio & Grooverider, the Dreem Teem and Danny Rampling, DJs who were big in the clubs and on pirate radio.

I can remember reading an interview with Alison Limerick when her brilliant 'Where Love Lives' was being played in every half-decent house club in the world, but was getting no radio play. It's exactly the kind of record that would now be played incessantly. The rush towards dance music on the radio is good in many ways, not least because it reflects and acknowledges an important scene, but it's also had the effect of putting clubland on the back foot. Clubland is less secret, less exciting.

Dozens of records – 'Pump Up The Volume', 'Don't You Want Me' by Felix and the Original's 'I Luv You Baby' – owed their success purely to their play in dance clubs prior to their release, and although there are still records that radio takes a few weeks to get hold of, especially in UK garage, generally the days of club-only hits have gone. Now, within a matter of hours, a dancefloor filler goes straight onto the daytime playlist. This change is part of the way our instant, global culture operates. The dance music infrastructure that now underpins clubland – big clubs, magazines, promoters, commercial radio, trade fairs – is as much about money-making opportunities as anything else. Once money moved in, dance culture became compromised.

Graeme agrees there's a downside to the successful invasion of the airwaves by dance music in the last five or six years, that it might have diminished the excitement of clubland. Clubs meet the demand to go out all night, to experiment with music, drugs, fashion, life. But clubs no longer have the monopoly on the music – if it's not on the radio, it will be on the Internet – and in many parts of the country, clubs no longer have a monopoly on late nights either. In the early 1990s licensing laws were relaxed, triggering a rise in late night bars. As Graeme says, 'Every bar has a more-or-less competent DJ whacking out the tunes everyone knows.'

In the best clubs you can play brand new records, and if you're programming the music with any skill, people will get into it, but with radio virtually setting the agenda in dance music, this has changed audience expectations. When Graeme explains this he sounds like Roger Eagle trying not to get swept away by Motown: 'I'm playing in clubs now and there's this whole culture of "Yeah, Parky, this is fantastic but when are you going to play something we know?" and you ask them like what and they request some record that's everywhere and you tell them you're not going to play it and they say, "Why not, everyone plays it," and you say, "Exactly!" and sometimes they just don't understand.'

Some DJs will be flexible in what they charge if they're keen to play the right kind of club. Graeme Park has a reputation for rarely lowering his fee. 'Arrangements can be made,' he says, 'but if you have a price you should stick to it. It's negotiable up to a point but people sometimes expect me to play at their club on a Saturday night for a third of what you normally get.'

How do they justify this to you?

'They try to justify it by saying, "Yeah, yeah, but it's going to be real," and phrases like that that they come out with. I just point out to them that I do real gigs. All my gigs are real.'

So you wouldn't do a cheap gig?

'I wouldn't say I never discount my rates, because if

it's a small club that only holds five hundred people and they traditionally charge a fiver they're not going to be able to afford me, but if I want to do the gig then something gets done.'

What if you doubled-up and did two gigs in one night?

'I've never really been a part of that philosophy of trying to cram as many gigs as you can into a night, although this week I'm doing two gigs on Saturday, and it's twice the money but it could be half the fun. When people do three gigs a night they're only playing for an hour each gig.'

That's shite, don't you think?

'Totally.'

As we know, DJ fees can sometimes be astronomical. Are they worth it, I wonder, and would Pete Tong be able to justify getting paid thousands of pounds for just a couple of hours' work? Tong's busy, and we are interrupted again. He picks up the phone. 'Hold on a second, I'll call you back,' he tells the caller.

Do you think DJs get paid too much?

'No, I think that for entertainment value DJ-ing was an under-rated art going way back, late 70s, early 80s, and the fact that DJs do get paid a considerable amount is testament to the success of what they do.'

You're talking about supply and demand. DJs get paid whatever the promoter thinks he or she is worth in terms of generating doortake.

'Yeah, that's the bottom line. I've always thought if you're not worth the money, you won't get booked. We're not holding the industry to ransom; people don't have to come, promoters don't have to have you.'

It's like performance-related pay: if your name, reputation and performance fill a club with 2,000 people paying £15 each, you'll get reward. If you empty a dance-floor, you'll get dumped. The market decides your fee.

'Correct. You can demand big money but if it's not working then it will only be a while before you're found out.'

Despite frequent complaints that DJs are overpaid, for every DJ reaping the benefits at the top of the profession there are literally hundreds still doing the twenty quid gigs. And not many make it; DJ-ing is a hazardous and insecure profession and only a very small minority make a decent living from it.

The DJ superstars can earn a lot, like film stars, lending their talents and their name to a project. Some film stars seem more choosy than others; some will do anything for a quick dollar, some will lose their way, some will always be Dennis Hopper. Many will be paid millions of pounds for a few hours' work – which they make look easy – and then the rest of the time they do interviews talking up their achievements and swan around getting their names in magazines. Just like DJs.

Even without financial rewards, DJs lead a charmed life. Andrew Ross has described how, in recent years, the cult of the DJ has achieved 'priestly proportions'. Whether a DJ is a priest or a prostitute, I don't know, but DJ-ing is certainly a great buzz. Jimmy Savile has enjoyed his life, but when I first asked him about his early days as a club DJ he was adamant: 'DJ-ing is the biggest buzz, the biggest buzz.'

Every DJ enjoys working a crowd, the music, the noise, the sense of creating something from nothing. Many DJs also enjoy the trappings of the job. On ninety per cent of occasions when I get a ride in a taxi and tell the driver I'm a DJ, the driver will say, 'I bet you get all the girls, don't you?'

DJs do take advantage of girls but girls take advantage of DJs, too. If there's a girl at a loose end in a club, a DJ is easy pickings, and if the DJ isn't willing there's always the promoter, or one of the doormen. I asked Lottie if any lads hit on her and she reminds me she goes out with Dan Kahuna, a DJ.

Between getting divorced and meeting Jenny, Graeme Park admits being tempted: 'I suddenly found myself thinking that I could fully abuse the situation and it was surprising how easy it was. If you want to take advantage then you can. The thing is, at the end of the day we just play records and our status has evolved thanks to the media. OK, we're popular, but there are all those people who want to know you for what you are rather than who you are.'

I tell Graeme about Tom Wolfe's report on his trip to Tiles, how he spotted even back then, in 1967, that the DJ was the centre of attention; it's as if the lads want to be the DJ and the girls want to be seen with him. 'That kind of throws my argument about the media,' says Graeme, 'but I can see that; my Grandad in the 1940s and 1950s was a big band leader and he's always told me he was very popular with the ladies!'

When you were single you didn't hold back?

'I did take advantage of the situation, because I thought why not? But since I met Jen and we got married, I'm not interested, but I think I'm still aware that it's out there if I wanted it, even with me being thirty-seven and slightly overweight! That's the whole thing; if I was in a club now, just a punter in a club, people wouldn't pay me a blind bit of interest, and if I did catch the eye of an attractive young lady, it would be like, "Yeah, right mate!" But on the decks, headphones on, you make eye contact and suddenly everything's changed.'

It's not surprising that the attention, the fun, cocaine, the extras, go to a DJ's head. Like pop stars, DJs get some fame and surround themselves with yes men, there's no-one holding them back, keeping their feet on the ground.

Ego takes over. If you're DJ-ing for a few pounds, a few pints and a taxi fare home, then of course you're doing it for the love, but the lifestyle of the superstar DJs has brought some mixed motivations into the equation. There'll be people into the money, people who just want to participate because they want the fame, not because they have anything to say, or any unique vision. The majority of DJs love their music, but young promoters like Phil Morse have noticed how things are changing: 'Four or five years ago all the DJs were music lovers first and foremost, but a business mentality has crept in. Now DJs can come across more business-minded than music-minded.'

Another change of emphasis is the tendency to venerate technical ability over originality or taste. For Luke Unabomber, not being the most technically adept DJ didn't threaten the longevity of his 'Electric Chair' night because he runs the club with flair. His lack of technical prowess is endearing but an exception: 'We'd been to clubs where the mixing has been incredible but the music was bland and insipid, with no soul or passion, so we just did our own thing.'

Phil Morse is exasperated by the business ethos, especially when it's often the lesser known names rather than the big names that rock 'Tangled': 'Most of the big names bore the crowd; the night is based around big records, rather than a DJ playing a clever twenty-minute mix going nowhere.'

Phil doesn't just fall out with agents, he sometimes has a problem with the more aloof DJs, and the ones who do more than one gig a night: 'DJs who just turn up and then go. We can't be bothered with them.'

Tony Wilson was a fan of Leonard Cohen, and first had his view of music turned upside down when he saw the Sex Pistols play in 1976. He remembers how acid house changed his view again, opened his eyes to the joys of the disco, and filled his club, the Haçienda. He puts it like this: 'Remember I fought against disco all my life, and this battle against disco had gone on and on, but the real moment for me was staring down from the DJ box one night when Mike Pickering was DJ-ing and suddenly going "Oh, fuck, now I get it"; the democracy of the art experience, it's everybody – it's the people who made the record, it's the DJ, it's everybody dancing – and it isn't four guys on a stage with white lights on and everyone else in the dark.'

He thought this communal, democratic impulse was refreshing. Now he thinks dance music has lost its way: 'What dance music has become is one guy with a white light on him and everyone in the fucking dark, which is precisely how it wasn't meant to be.'

But dance music is so big, surely there's unstoppable momentum behind it now?

'Absolutely unstoppable momentum for it all to end sooner rather than later. It will all be over in a year, I prophesy. It will just suddenly die.'

How do you reconcile that view with 15,000 people in a tent at a festival buzzing off Carl Cox, or the queues round the block for DJs outside clubs up and down the country every Saturday night?

'Dead culture, Dave, dead generation, all about to end. There were queues round the block for Rick Wakeman.'

Pete Tong starts chuckling when I report Wilson's comments to him. 'I can't see it all ending,' he replies. 'I think it ebbs and flows. I don't know what he's trying to get at, but I would like to think myself that there would be something else going on apart from DJs, new bands or whatever, but that doesn't mean it's going to replace DJs. I've been around it for so long that I've seen it go up and down a few times anyway.'

Wilson's point is that the acid house era seemed like a revolutionary moment, a world away from the hierarchies of rock music, but over time the culture has made the same mistakes as rock music; it's become bloated with self-important stars, the DJ superstars. It wasn't meant to be this way.

Tong accepts some of these criticisms: 'Sure, I can see people being guilty of taking themselves too seriously and the ego thing being more important than the music and also I can see other DJs trying to be so exclusive that they're in danger of missing the point of entertaining.'

Do you think the revolution created a new set of stars, a new elite hanging on to power?

'Maybe three years or so ago the same twenty DJs were going round the same ten clubs playing to the same twenty thousand people and that was starting to get unhealthy.'

One factor that has reduced that problem has been the way the music has gone global in the last couple of years. As they explore the world, getting to hear the likes of Paul Oakenfold, Pete Tong, Sasha or Carl Cox play is harder than it ever was. In addition, the DJ-ing stars of UK garage – EZ, Norris 'the Boss' Windross, Masterstepz – have risen to prominence as their music finally makes its mark in the mainstream. Joey Negro and Mark Rae, and other DJs who are having success as artists and remixers, attract increased attention. And then you get new names, like Lottie, Steve Lawler . . .

'Yes,' says Tong, 'and Lisa Lashes, Fergie. A whole new set of people starting to get recognised.'

As those DJs who came to prominence in the acid house era get older, are they hanging on beyond their sell-by dates?

'That's something I think about all the time, but there are no rules, no rules that you should get a red card after x amount of years. I haven't got the answer to it. I can't imagine being here when I'm sixty, that's for sure. To be honest, I didn't really envisage being here when I was forty.'

Ultimately the dancefloor will decide; it's unforgiving to a DJ if it doesn't want you. The top names will be toppled if the customers stay away, although it's unlikely this will happen now that so many vested interests are involved in dance music. As the DJ industry grows – radio stations and websites and magazines feeding off and feeding into it – even Pete Tong is moved to comment; he calls some of the media surrounding DJs 'self-perpetuating bollocks'.

It's probably no coincidence that DJs, like stand up comedians and celebrity chefs, are products of the 1980s, a decade which extolled the spirit of individualism. Value was placed on aggressive, independent success rather than the general condition of the community. DJ Hype remembers how the status of the guy with the records changed in the mid-1980s from being an anonymous player contributing to a collective effort to being a sovereign power. He recalls sound systems in the mid-1980s where DJs and rappers were working together, going out under a collective banner: '1987 was the end of an era because suddenly it was all about individual DJs. Before then it was sound systems.'

The 1980s witnessed other changes in our society besides the emergence of a new breed of superstar DJ. There was a rise in conspicuous materialism, and this too has seeped into DJ culture. Ashley Beedle started DJ-ing in the 1980s in the early days of the London acid party scene: 'There was a strong grassroots understanding among the clubbing crowd. People like Jay Strongman and Paul Murphy had a strong awareness about politics and dance music. People just don't give a shit any more. We've been sucked into a champagne lifestyle.'

If you read the right magazines you can't escape the way DJs have become celebrities; you'll know that Trevor Nelson has two Mercs, Lottie drives a vintage Triumph Stag, Fatboy Slim has a Saab 900 convertible, Tall Paul has a Lexus, Sister Bliss has a BMW, John 'OO' Fleming drives an Audi TT Roadster, John Digweed has a classic Alfa Romeo Spider and Carl Cox has four cars (the last time he counted). Dave Pearce doesn't drive, neither does Paul van Dyk, Armand van Helden or James Lavelle (neither does Sasha but he's still bought himself an Audi A8). You'll learn that Mikee B from the Dreem Teem loves to wear anything by Prada, Tall Paul only shops on Bond Street, Steve Sutherland has 200 pairs of shoes, Anne Savage has a lovely Dolce & Gabbana top but she's happy to shop at Top Shop too, and Dave Pearce always checks out Boxfresh. You might even know that Lisa Loud endorses Nivea. This is the press release: 'According to Lisa, DJ-ing is physically demanding and dehydrating. Yet looking good is crucial. Lisa's sun-kissed Balearic look is maintained with simple yet disciplined skin care.' Thanks, of course, to Nivea.

All DJs are different; for every one that dreams of hanging out poolside with Erick Morillo in Miami, there's another who would never want that (or claims not to). Most of the people I've chosen to talk to – Paul van Dyk, Norman Cook, Norman Jay, Lottie, Sasha, Pete Tong – are people who DJ because they love music, who got into it because they were music fans; the fame and the money seems like a bonus to them, a happy, lucky coincidence. But as in other professions, some of the people who get to the top deserve it, totally, and others are there because they make ruthless career decisions. Whatever their original motivations, the DJ superstars now live their lives in a showbiz bubble.

Another change that Graeme Park points out is how the bpms have increased; over the last fifteen years the average tempo of floor-filling dance music has accelerated from something like 120bpm to 132. Graeme has noticed this progression: 'I remember when house music came along in 1986, '87, JM Silk "Music is the Key", and I can remember thinking "Fuck me, how fast is that?!" but you play it now and it sounds like it plods.'

Yet when it was played at the first raves everybody went bananas.

'Absolutely ballistic, yeah.'

Is it the drugs as well?

'I don't know, maybe it is.'

The closure of Home after allegations of drug dealing was followed in May 2001 by a police raid at 'Gatecrasher' which led to thirteen arrests and the discovery of a 'substantial amount' of drugs. The connections between hard house, trance, drug use and the big commercial clubs were becoming increasingly conspicuous.

Dr Bob Jones presumably sees the commerciality of what goes on now as similar to the excesses of Caister in the 1980s, except the piss artists in the main room have been replaced by a load of biscuit munchers. 'It should be "Who are we going to see? What are they playing?" Too often it's just "Are we sorted?"' he says.

In the drug-addled world of clubland, you could be forgiven for thinking that some of the records out there only make sense if you've had some pills. Pete Tong doesn't agree: 'I've never really gone along with that thinking. I wouldn't deny the fact that you can have an enhanced atmosphere, if the crowd are all E-ed up or something.'

But the drugs and the music are so inextricably linked.

'Yeah, yeah, but weren't they always? Woodstock, Jimi Hendrix, the Doors.'

And the mods.

'The mods, reggae. I mean, there's something else going on.'

Despite his relaxed attitude to ecstasy, Tong himself is no caner. In fact, after a quick drink in the bar, he usually leaves the club as soon as he's finished his set. 'I've got friends who've gone missing for weeks, taken every drug known to mankind and then got divorced,' he says. 'I do my fair share of partying and socialising, but I don't feel the need to go out and get fucked-up every night.'

With increasing drug use in our society in general – in the army, in the City, in record company boardrooms, in pubs, on street corners, behind closed doors – you wouldn't predict that clubs will be drug free in future. You could predict, however, a growth in non-ecstasy-related nights. For every action there is a reaction, and for every club too big, too corporate, too bland, too full of E-heads, there will be two or three opening elsewhere, looking to capture a different kind of vibe.

Clubland is gratifyingly hard to predict because no-one controls it. Sometimes, listening to the elder statesmen of the UK's acid house scene, or the American garage DJs, you'd think that the key, and the secrets, belong to a small group of people, the originators. But the power of dance music is in its pluralism; it's no longer about the original scene. It's an impure, communal activity, and as it moves round the globe, it gets transformed. People might try to pin it down or claim credit, but popular culture is shape shifting. No-one owns it. Yet.

You'd also be safe to predict that the DJ superstars will continue to earn good money. And that people will moan about this. Some of the criticism that DJs are overpaid springs as much from bitterness as anything else; there's a lot of bitterness in the music industry – bands bitter about other bands, backstabbing. And the old complaint that the DJs aren't even the people making the records no longer holds true. The fact is, the DJs are making the records they play. And remixing them. DJs are now in a stronger position than ever before; no longer just hired hands entertaining a party. Like Fatboy Slim, they're one man brands.

Another prediction – or, rather, a hope – is that we'll see eclecticism in the way the major DJs play. In music it's always been those crossover moments that move things forward: Hendrix melting psychedelic rock into jazz, the punk/electronica of PIL or New Order, the gospel/soul/hip hop of Lauryn Hill and Jill Scott. DJs tend to play safe, play a one-dimensional sound, no changing tempo, nothing unexpected. Once Pete Tong would have played right across the board; at the Milk Bar in 1989 or 1990 you'd have heard him and Dave Dorell playing predominantly house music, but then they would suddenly be going into Depeche Mode, or St Etienne, or hip hop. Now things are focused, labelled. I'm looking for DJs who will loosen the boundaries, not close things down.

The predictability of it all is often as much to do with the expectations of the audience as the DJs. At 'Gatecrasher', once the trance sound had been established, the regular clubgoers soon became renowned for giving a DJ who deviated from that a hard time. A lot of DJs privately wish they could broaden their playlist, but feel boxed in. Some can have an over-optimistic view of what the crowd will get into. Like Tim Sheridan from the Dope Smugglaz: 'I was playing at "Cream" and I stopped the music, pulled out a copy of "Welcome Aboard" by the Love Unlimited Orchestra and bellowed at the top of my voice, "Behold, children, the World's Greatest Record." And they were like "Yeah, wicked! He's going to play the world's greatest record!" About twenty seconds into it half of them had fucked off.'

We'll always need someone to play the music. Super-stars may come and go, some may hang on, but dance music will go on, the clubs and the music, nights of sweaty madness. If for no other reason, people will be drawn to dance music by default, when there's nothing much happening in the world of rock guitars. Unless DJs can come to the rescue of live bands, that is. Who knows – perhaps the future lies in collaborations, like the way Morcheeba use a DJ and Andy Smith DJs with Portishead (the DJ as conductor, leader of the orchestra). If DJs are becoming more like musicians, as the turntablists claim, the way they have taken to using effects, flanging and dis-torting like the sound systems operators of old – taking out the treble, mashing up the bass – then perhaps there's more work to be done with non-DJ musicians. Like Peter Parker in Fingathing, playing breaks on the decks while Sneaky plays double bass; or DJ Pogo working with jazz saxophonist Courtney Pine.

DJs will continue to be employed to create a vibe, the right soundtrack, even, or especially, outside of a normal club or bar. Sometimes taking a DJ out of the controlled space works – like when Andrew Weatherall played a set to accompany a showing of *Nosferatu* at Manchester's Cornerhouse Cinema – but one of the non-club gigs that shook my desire to spread my wings was an Asda super-market party in a hired hall in Manchester, probably my most humiliating DJ-ing experience. I DJed for three hours that night, playing something like forty-five records, and people only danced to two of them. I'm not sure who was more tortured – the audience who clearly hated everything I was playing, or me.

I tried everything within reason: Motown, Daft Punk, Snoop Doggy Dogg. At one point they interrupted my set to make speeches and hand out prizes to their colleagues, and those few minutes were a merciful release. Someone

at the supermarket loved my clubs in town and had persuaded everyone else they should hire me for the night. It
was bad; she thought it was a coup having me play, but it
turned out to be a disaster. It was somebody's good idea
at the time, but within just a few moments, a record or
two, I realised that what the Asda party really needed was
an experienced mobile DJ. Someone with no fear of being
too obvious.

According to Bill Brewster, his tongue perhaps close
to his cheek, some aspects of the mobile DJ's craft – the
ability to pace a set all night, eclecticism – mean that
mobile DJs are closer to the spirit of pioneering New York
DJs like David Mancuso and Larry Levan than today's
superstars – who turn up and play a short peak-time burst
of beat-mixed hits: 'The mobile DJ may well play the most
predictable and tawdry array of pop staples, but the
mobile DJ knows how to take an evening from an empty
room to peak hour and back again. He knows how to
work a crowd. Even if he does this playing Bachman
Turner Overdrive records.'

Although I'd enjoyed the two weddings I'd done years
before, my Asda night was relatively recent, the experience still raw, and I felt the need to check out a mobile DJ
before my wedding engagement, to try to get a sense of
what 'something for everyone' really meant. I went to a
school disco where the DJ was using CDs and playing the
worst kind of ancient cheese, including 'You're the One
that I Want' from the *Grease* soundtrack. At someone's
50th birthday you could get away with songs like that, I
thought, or at some 'ironic' student disco, but these kids
weren't going for it at all. Nine- and ten-year-old girls
were in the corners of the room ignoring the music and
trying out their Spice Girls routines instead, while nine-
and ten-year-old boys ran round the room fighting, the
lot of them high on Coca Cola and cheap crisps. I knew

the DJ's music would be dodgy, but his microphone skills weren't too hot either; nobody could make out a word he was saying. When he realised this he started bellowing into the microphone, which made him louder, but more, not less intelligible. The parents at the back put their hands over their ears. The kids looked blankly at each other. His performance was a study in ineptitude which led me to conclude that Bill Brewster was being over-generous. The sixty quid or whatever the headmaster had paid him was a bigger waste of money than the three grand anyone's ever paid out for Sasha. Sasha costs more but is better value; there's a difference between price and value (the price is what you pay, value is what you get).

When the request to do a wedding came, I wasn't sure I wanted to do it, or that I could do it. After all the high profile, highly paid gigs I've done, DJ-ing at a wedding is a bit of a challenge for me. I can't hide behind a clever pro-moter, a swish club, a great warm-up DJ or a reputation. Those nights at the Haçienda, the Boardwalk, 'Cream', Ibiza and Home, my fifteen gigs in Paris, the trips to America and Germany, and the thousands of hours of experience I've gained aren't going to count for much when I'm faced with a wedding audience.

When Norman Cook married Zoe Ball he asked Stretch of Stretch & Vern to play, but Norman also took along his own box of classic wedding seven-inch singles. Unfortunately, he locked his box in the boot of his car, so during the speeches Zoe's father pleaded with the guests to help him break into it. As it turned out, there were records and DJs everywhere by the time the party started, and Norman had agreed some guidelines. I asked him what they were, hoping for some help. 'The idea was not to have moody DJs trying to be holier-than-thou, but for it to be a bit daft, and it half worked,' he says. 'Tom and

Ed were playing Abba, stuff like that; we didn't want anybody to play cool records, just ones our grannies would
dance to.'

The only record Norman played was Groove Armada's
'At the River'. Steve Coogan cut his nose open. In the end
the party got a bit messy and complicated, Norman
admits. 'There wasn't much dancing at one point, everybody was running around falling in lakes and doing tons
of drugs in the rooms. There was about twenty minutes
when nobody was dancing and all the grannies were
saying, "Where's everybody gone?"'

At weddings there are so many different people to
please. From the bride and groom, to the girls from the
office, to Great Uncle who wants some Glenn Miller and
Great Grandma who wants something with a tune. The
best man will be very, very drunk, and determined to hear
Divine Comedy. And there's the dreaded record choice
for the first dance: usually 'Wonderful Tonight' by Eric
Clapton or 'Everything I Do' by Bryan Adams. I comforted
myself with the thought that the bride and groom were
Rebecca and Neil, whom I'd met when they had worked
at Kiss 102 and Galaxy in Manchester. They weren't like
Ricky Martin fans or something. There would be roads,
I hoped, I wouldn't be expected to go down. The one
signposted 'Divine Comedy' for starters.

Neil called me three months before the wedding. He
told me that the two of them had their first dates at
'Yellow', that the records I played there formed the soundtrack for their love affair. They couldn't offer me any
financial reward, but they kept up this line of very effec-
tive emotional blackmail; I was being given the chance to
make someone happy. 'Rebecca would be made up if you
did it,' said Neil. How could I say no? Also I remembered a
newspaper article explaining that the population of Jersey
put away more drinks per head than anywhere else in the

world – the equivalent of thirty litres of vodka each a year.

But once I put down the phone I couldn't stop worrying about the wedding. Knowing a lot about superstar DJs would be of no help. Out of the context of the right club and the right audience, much of what they do wouldn't make sense; if I replicated Paul van Dyk's 'Time Flies' set or played everything Lottie played at 'Shindig' I'd bomb. I'd be Gilles Peterson at Space.

Would I have to play 'Hi Ho Silver Lining', 'Stayin' Alive', the Human League doing 'Don't You Want Me?', Take That singing 'Relight My Fire'? I didn't have any of those records; I don't even have any Robbie Williams. I've also got nothing by Bachman Turner Overdrive. I worried that I was going to be vulnerable to criticism from the guests. I began to imagine people coming up to me: 'No Robbie? No Madonna? What have you got then?'

Neil and Rebecca promised me there would be a real mobile DJ on first. They also asked David Dunne to play, so I had an ally. But at the back of my mind I still worried that maybe I should go and look for some bog standard party compilation. The Asda night still haunted me.

The wedding reception is set to take place at a beach-side hotel called L'Horizon. The party is being held in the Brasserie, basically a large bar with a dancefloor right next to the hotel swimming pool. The guy with the equipment, Ed, introduces himself. He tells me what clubs he's done in Jersey, and the name of somewhere he's on tomorrow night, but the music is already turned up loud and I can't hear what he's saying.

So is there a good scene in Jersey?

'It's bouncing, mate.'

I ask Ed if they ever put on rave parties down on the beach and he shakes his head: 'The younger kids, they'd love it, but you get nabbed for doing stuff like that.'

Do they do drugs on the island?

'There's a lot of smack here.'

My mouth drops open in disbelief but Ed is insistent: 'There is, the Portuguese bring it in.'

Blimey.

'Come down tomorrow, mate, there'll be tablets everywhere.'

I tell him I'd thought Jersey was crime free.

'You're joking me, aren't you?' he replies, fiddling with his mini-disc, pressing buttons, trying to find a track to get somebody on the dancefloor. It's all going a bit Asda for him.

I introduce myself to Alan, the camcorder operator making a video of the day's events for the bride and groom. Alan tells me he used to be a DJ: 'Weddings were the hardest thing in the world to do. The little ones might want some pop, and the older ones will want a waltz or a quick step.'

The world of DJ-ing has changed, I tell him, it's all about technique now, superstar DJs, mix CDs, four cars and hotel rooms the size of Jersey. He knows this: 'Yeah, it's different. They're into rave stuff aren't they, young DJs.'

I found myself wanting Alan's approval and encouragement and list some of the records I've planned to play – a bit of house, some Motown, and some disco. 'Disco,' he thinks. 'Yes, that's good, that's my era.' It's just the bit of encouragement I need.

I knew the first dance would set the tone for the evening, and when Neil and Rebecca get on the dancefloor to 'Spellbound' by Rae & Christian, I'm pleased with their choice and even more encouraged. Then Neil comes up to me and asks me to go on in half an hour. Five minutes later Ed is playing M-People's 'One Night in Heaven', which moves smartly into 'Movin' On Up', and I realise he is playing a pre-recorded medley of M-People hits. Neil returns: 'Dave, look, I said to him no M-People. Oh God, I don't want M-People. Listen to it.'

I try to calm Neil down. 'Don't worry, M-People will soon be over,' I tell him.

'I don't care,' Neil shouts. 'If he doesn't stop playing M-People, my marriage will soon be over too.' I realise how much all this means to him, and over the next few minutes my anxiety returns. Then Ed plays something by Duran Duran and I see Neil hastening across the room towards me. I have a canapé in my mouth. 'Dave, you're on,' he tells me.

I'm rooting in my boxes. The first record on is always important; I need something easy, I decide, something to break the ice. I dig out Dee Lite's 'Groove is in the Heart'.

Duran Duran fade away and I put on Dee Lite, and Neil and Rebecca start dancing, as do about twelve or thirteen other people, with one or two more getting on the dancefloor as the song goes on. Now I need to consolidate, keep these people on the dancefloor. I put on a version of 'Slow Train Running' by the Doobie Brothers; it's well known to anyone who went out in 1993 or 1994, a remix by Sure is Pure. Then I play 'We Are Family'.

The dancefloor is relatively small, and holds maybe fifty people, but now they're all up and dancing. They've been drinking all day, but have held themselves in check during the afternoon. I sense that all that might begin to change. Mark, who works at the Ministry of Sound, is whooping it up. During 'We Are Family', everyone joins in at the first chorus and Mark takes off his shirt, twirling it round his head.

I search in my box for some Michael Jackson remixes but accidentally start cueing up Moby's mix of 'Beat It' while I search for a Roger Sanchez mix of 'Don't Stop Til You Get Enough', which eventually I find. This could be corny, but I'm not on the microphone and I feel like I haven't quite crossed that line. Then I play Joey Negro's new single, then '900 Degrees' by Ian Pooley.

A few records later, I'm back to party favourites: 'He's the Greatest Dancer' and 'Sex Machine'. Mark is loving it. So is Neil's mum, who's not been feeling well all day but she's now dancing, happy. The music seems to be working.

The two bridesmaids, Caroline and Jenny, are sitting near the edge of the dancefloor. Jenny asks me for 'Sweet Sensation' by Shades of Rhythm. She remembers rave's glory days. It's a wonderful record which, fortunately, David has in his box, so I dig it out and play it. The brides-maids are having a good time, and there's five or six people with them, so for a few records I focus on them, reckoning that if they're enjoying it everyone else will be.

One of the bridesmaids is a lifeguard, which might be handy given the close proximity of the hotel swimming pool to a dancefloor full of heavy drinking partygoers. I ask Jenny who they think will be first in the pool. It's so inviting, clean, still. 'That guy with his shirt off,' she says, pointing at Mark.

'Yeah,' I say, 'the greatest dancer.'

Neil reminds me to play 'Somebody Else's Guy', which he's already told me is one of Rebecca's favourite records. With lyrics about a girl battling to win over an uninterested man, I'm a bit hesitant in case it sends out the wrong message on a wedding day, but Neil is insistent. 'It's one of the records she used to come to hear you play,' he tells me.

'Somebody Else's Guy' works a treat. There's a bit near the end when the music drops down and it seems as good a time as any to play another 1980s girlie anthem and my trump card: 'Ain't Nobody'.

It's only 10pm. Things will get a lot more messy before the night wears on. I play 'Love's Theme' by Love

Unlimited, and records I've heard, loved, dug up since I started my adventures on the wheels of steel: 'Harlem Shuffle', 'Rapper's Delight', 'Runaway', Fatboy Slim's bootleg version of '(I Can't Get No) Satisfaction', and Lottie's mix of 'Salsoul Nugget'.

I'm playing music for myself, for them, but ultimately for all of us. It's not 'Cream', the Haçienda or Home. There's no fridge full of beer, no-one to carry my boxes, and although Alan has suddenly come alive, swooping round the dancefloor with his video camera, the film isn't going to end up on Rapture or Channel Four. There's no VIP room, but that doesn't bother me. None of that bothers me; I'm playing some of my favourite records, loudly, and everyone is enjoying themselves. It's hundreds of miles away from deep funk theory, from ruthless career moves, hype, bandwagons and ancillary merchandising streams, but I'm smiling. It's already a night to remember. For my last record I decide to play Candi Staton singing 'You Got the Love'.

David Dunne is up next, and Candi Staton fades away. I've played my set, and it's worked. I'm relieved, tired, elated. Getting the ending right is as hard as knowing how to start. The record finishes, I slide it back into its sleeve, and then I hear a big splash behind me. I don't need to turn round to know Mark is in the pool.

CODA

FAC 401
the Last Night of the Haçienda

When the call came, I wasn't sure. I had various reasons for resisting the temptation to get involved with restaging a Haçienda night. The Haçienda had been an important part of my life – the scene, I suppose, of my glory days – but I was uneasy about being dragged back to it all. Those Haçienda years have sometimes seemed like a heavy weight for me to carry, just as Manchester's club scene has also stumbled after the acid house era and Madchester. We'd hit such heights; the years that followed seemed like an anti-climax.

But we've survived, and dance music has moved on. New clubs have had their moment, and the Haçienda has a living legacy: all the DJs and musicians who were first turned on to dance music there, including the Chemical Brothers, Justin Robertson (for Justin, 'the Haçienda is completely the reason for what I'm doing now'), Laurent Garnier and Sasha (for Sasha, 'the Haçienda opened my ears to the power of music'). I'd met Sasha there, that time he came into the DJ box with my friend Zeeba. I don't know when it was, I've lost all track of time.

Understanding how club culture has developed, its roots, the history – all that's good. But nostalgia isn't so appealing to me. Fifteen years ago, when I watched from the DJ box as a new generation of music fans embraced computer-generated music, rewrote the rules and threw themselves into dance music, I hoped that we'd continue to embrace change, and not live in the past like those previous generations forever banging on about Woodstock, Wigan Casino or the Sex Pistols at the Free Trade Hall. Nostalgia demands that you believe things were better back then and, by implication, that the new generation have lost out.

I worked at the Haçienda from 1986 to 1991, and at other times, too. I was sacked twice, reinstated twice, I resigned once, and I was DJ-ing there on the night it suddenly closed – Saturday 28 June 1997 – as a result of the club's debts, and with no last night, no final celebration. Stuck in the shadow of those good old days, the management had run out of money after years of failing to recapture the popularity the Haçienda had enjoyed in the late 1980s. In retrospect, there are still a few of us who think that the closure could have been avoided, that a future had slipped between our fingers.

It was over three years after the club had closed and thirteen years since acid house changed the club – changed *everything* – that the idea of restaging a Haçienda night was floated by a company looking to make *Twenty Four Hour Party People*, a film set in Manchester and featuring several scenes at the Haçienda during the acid house era. The timing was ironic: just a few months earlier the original site had been sold to property developers and the Haçienda had been demolished. After the demolition, bits of the club were auctioned off, bricks, the dancefloor, mirrors from the toilets, taps from the sinks. Interest was huge; camera crews from Channel Four and CNN were at the sale and the website attracted hits and bids from round the world. The demolition of the Haçienda had somehow boosted its legendary status.

In America, especially, the Haçienda is best known for

being the club owned by New Order; in the mid-1980s they were a stadium band in America and their earnings from records like 'Blue Monday' helped to subsidise the club during its lean years. But, as a result of the growth and globalisation of dance music in recent years, it's the club's role in the rave revolution which has contributed most to its prestige; the Haçienda provided a home for house music in an era before the scene went overground and commercial, pre-dating Ministry of Sound and 'Cream'. The Haçienda made mistakes – endearing, human, regrettable mistakes – but emerged to become the Studio 54 of our era. In 2001, and with talk of a film, the profile of the Haçienda was higher than when it was open.

Director Michael Winterbottom wanted to make a film about punk and acid house – the two great pop revolutions since the 1960s – centred on Factory Records, New Order and the Haçienda. He looked through archives at original footage and realised how poorly the acid house years were documented; at the time, no-one thought to film the Haçienda, the queues, the DJs. We knew we were on to a good thing, but jostling for a place in the history books just didn't come into it. Our only interest was finding the best records to play the next weekend, which is how it should be.

Stuck with a lack of footage, Michael Winterbottom decided to restage a Haçienda night. As the club had just been demolished, this required building a film set that looked just like the original Haçienda. When I talked to the film company in their temporary offices in Manchester, the scale of their ambition and commitment became clear: for one night only, the Haçienda would be recreated brick by brick, pillar by pillar, in an old iron works in Ancoats. They were prepared to spend £150,000 on the set and clearly wanted to get all the details right.

Sitting around a table listening to old tapes, Mark Tilsley, the set designer, sketched prospective layouts of the club for me. He wanted to be clear exactly where the cloakroom was, where the podiums had been, and when various changes were made to the club, including the resiting of the DJ box from an obscure bunker under the stage to the middle of the balcony overlooking and dominating the dancefloor. He promised me they would be looking at old photographs in order to work out what colour the lights were. Michael Winterbottom sat and watched, smiling; I think he knew this attention to detail would help persuade me to get involved, to help create one last party. They wanted me to market the night to attract the clubbers, and coordinate the security, the music policy, the ticketing. Mike Pickering – Factory A&R man, and the most important DJ at the club – agreed to play at the event; his view was that the chances of getting it right were improved if the original people were involved.

The clubbers who would be invited to the night were, in effect, unpaid extras. For the purposes of the film, and the authenticity, the average age of the audience needed to be early twenties, so we had to resist throwing it open to all the old regulars; nobody wanted the camera to pan across the crowd and see a bunch of grizzled old ravers. This younger generation of clubbers, with their faster bpms and different fashions, would have to be given some guidance on how to dress in baggy rave gear, but at the same time we told people we didn't just want a roomful of clichés. Rebecca Boulton in the New Order office laughed. 'But that's what it was like sometimes, wasn't it?'

It was an important event, with a lot riding on it. The footage had to be good; I'd watched films about Studio 54 – *54* and *The Last Days of Disco* – and never saw anything which would have made me want to be there. Watching clubs on films or TV is no substitute to a club experience that engulfs you. More importantly, we also wanted to be sure we would enhance the reputation of the Haçienda, not ruin it. Some of the letters we received, begging for tickets, were from people who never went to the Haçienda but wanted a chance to live the dream; we wanted those people to walk in and understand how good it was. Two teenage girls from Moston wrote to say that they wanted to be at the film shoot to see what all the fuss was about: 'Our mums are sisters and the Haçienda is all they ever talk about.'

A flyer inviting people to apply for tickets for the event was commissioned for distribution outside clubs like 'bed', the Music Box and 'Golden'. Pete Tong mentioned the event on the radio, and 'Cream' posted the news on their website. Soon we were inundated with applications for tickets, some with covering letters, or poems, photographs, photocopies, artwork. A guy wrote explaining that he needed to win over a girl in the office and he reckoned a date at the event would do the trick (he got two tickets), a couple sent a photograph of themselves lounging in their Haçienda-themed living room (two tickets). We sent out tickets to anyone who'd taken this kind of trouble, whatever age they were; we realised we needed to invite some of the original ravers who knew the tunes, who cared the most. A lad from Cheadle begged us to let him enjoy 'one more night of carnage' (yes). A girl sent a picture of herself opening a fur coat and showing off her breasts (yes, of course).

Word spread via websites and e-mails, another example of the way the world had moved on in the last dozen years, but also confirmation that digital technology hadn't just changed music-making but had also transformed the way we communicate. I left a message on someone's voice mail and they replied with a text message: I HAVE 2

B THERE!! Soon I was inundated with text messages, e-mails and smiley faces :)

We had a thousand tickets to give away, far too few. Darren Partington from 808 State asked for six. Andy Fisher, who has the only known complete collection of Haçienda birthday posters, got in touch. Bobby Langley, who paid £1,100 at the auction for the original DJ box, offered us the use of it, but the team at Twenty Four Hour Films wanted to rebuild it from scratch. About three weeks into the work I took a look around, astounded. Mark and his team had done a remarkable job. The architecture was spot on, the colour scheme a perfect match, although the floor was cleaner than it had ever been in the old days, when you'd get home from the club with your shoes caked in some unidentifiable black sludge.

After I'd walked across the unblemished dancefloor and up to the balcony, I couldn't resist a quick look out from the DJ box at that unforgettable view over the dancefloor. Just a few months previously I'd seen the club while it was being demolished, yet here it was again, as new. It felt familiar, and it felt just like the club, too: ghosts, memories and all.

There was one definitive version of the building, but so many differing personal versions of the history of what went on there. Tony Wilson phoned me to say he wanted to get involved with the organisation. He thought the recreation should reflect some of the violence that dogged the club in the 1990s. He expected to see trouble on the door and drug dealers in the club: 'There'll be riots outside, and fighting, and we'll film that as well.'

My version of that history, though, wanted to celebrate the spirit before the gangsters moved in; the riots on the door and troubles with security were among the contributing factors which led to the club's closure. I wanted it to be the best kind of night, to prove it could be done, keeping the wreckers at bay. As well as picking out some convincing letters, I was also being choosy about post-codes; not too many M14, M20 or M21, but some Wigan, Eccles, Bolton, West Yorkshire and Stockport. It began to feel like social engineering, my mission to find the ideal mix, to create a community of music lovers just like the Haçienda had been.

We mailed out the tickets, and had to let maybe 2,000 people down. I got another message from the film office: Darren Partington wants seven more tickets. I took the phone off the hook; I needed time to sort out my records and decide what to wear. On the afternoon of the event David Dunne sent me a text message from the train from London: KICKERS & A MAMBO SHIRT. Arthur Baker had checked into the Malmaison: I'M HERE. C U THERE. AB.

Back at the set, Mike Pickering and I attempted to soundcheck but our records were skating, jumping, drowned by feedback. A van was despatched to B&Q to collect four concrete slabs to calm the decks down. Then at 6pm the fire officers arrived and imposed a new set of conditions – more building work had to be done and bigger emergency signs displayed; there was talk of delay or even cancellation. By 9pm there was a massive queue outside, but only a few people were being allowed in. Once they'd seen the set, many of them laughed with joy. The likeness was amazing (when Tony Wilson had seen the set he'd cried). The queue outside continued to grow. Miranda sent me a text message: ITS FREEZIN LET UZ IN!

The doors finally opened properly at 9.30pm. Somebody came up to me and asked where the toilets were; 'Over there, where they've always been,' I said. I was talking like I was in the real Haçienda.

I had imagined that somehow we'd be playing the

part of DJs, and the crowd would be pretending to rave, but within five seconds of the doors opening no-one was faking it. I played Lisa Lisa & Cult Jam's 'Let the Beat Hit 'Em'. There were people on the dancefloor and I could feel it already; everyone had come with the right attitude, no-one was going to stand about and mock. There was a pact between us in the DJ box and the people of the dancefloor. DJ-ing is a communal effort, relying on an audience addicted to nights of sweaty madness, loud music, getting lost in smoke, standing too near the bass speaker, cheering a good tune, dancing all night, following a crowd to a party at a strange house in a different part of town, a few days later still feeling that glow.

At that point I knew the night was going to work. We'd already breached that magical moment when a DJ starts to lock into the crowd; together, they're up and away, powered by the music. The night unfolded, a great party, a celebration of what had been achieved, but also of our survival and the survival of that original, pure clubbing spirit. It was genuinely emotional; New Order's Peter Hook was saying 'This is too much' all night with tears in his eyes. The dancefloor remained packed, a sea of cheering people, their hands in the air. It wasn't just authentic, it was real. It wasn't nostalgic; it felt contemporary. Once again I was losing track of time.

Mike Pickering played 'I Need a Rhythm'. Graeme Park played 'Dreams of Santa Anna' and borrowed 'Can You Party' from my box. I hadn't heard half the records for years and they sounded so good. I played 'Voodoo Ray' and 'Rhythm is a Mystery'. Jon Da Silva played 'It's Alright'. Outside there was no trouble at the front gate. The fire officers had requested that the warehouse loading bay doors stay open, so a freezing wind blew through the building, but on the dancefloor it was warm.

In the end, Tony Wilson had decided to play a more

constructive role and gathered together some old faces, but he'd left at eight o'clock, like a parent leaving the kids alone in the house to party. Steve Coogan – playing Tony Wilson in the film – was on the dancefloor. That was one of the things that made the evening seem like the strangest, best kind of dream: this mix of real people and their acting equivalents scattered around the club. Bernard Sumner from New Order was on the dancefloor, as well as the actor playing him (John Simm), and Peter Hook and the fake Peter Hook (Ralf Little), the real Bez, the fake Bez, the fake Shaun Ryder and the real Rowetta. In the DJ box Mike Pickering met the actor who was playing him in the film: Darren Tighe.

They were all set to film the moment Tony Wilson came to understand the power and potential of DJ culture. I thought Darren would be dressed in a Numero Uno t-shirt, like Pickering used to be, dripping with sweat, practically falling out of the box with excitement, but he wasn't. We had to fake him receiving the crowd's cheers, but when the cameras rolled as he stepped up to the decks and looked out, he seemed bewildered by what he saw, the crowd response to the DJ, up there, playing the records, feeling that rush, that exploding emotion. I tried to gee him up, but he froze, shell-shocked.

In the DJ box we just about maintained control in the eye of the storm, surrounded by frenetic scenes. We only had one request for a record: 'Pacific State'. All the other requests were based on: 'Can we do some lines in here?' Pills were being passed round the dancefloor, and some-one close to a podium was doing coke off a credit card. Under the balcony, four lines were chopped out on a table and two guys were on their knees hoovering them up.

In the DJ box we were working well, almost uncon-sciously, on instinct. We knew what we were doing, we knew the Haçienda well, and although we knew the majority of the crowd were now regulars at places like 'Cream', 'Feel', 'bed', 'Out in the Sticks', Code and Miss Moneypenny's, it felt like our natural audience out there, our community. There was something about the context, the building, Manchester, a cold Friday night.

The cameras kept rolling. The success of the event was tantalising. You're always looking for the perfect night and you get glimpses of that utopia sporadically. I think I knew how the mad lad in his silver shirt at 'Shindig' felt, the 'Tangled' regulars, Lottie at Quadrant Park, the tired, happy clubbers hanging out with Paul van Dyk at the end of his Cardiff set, everyone crushed round Fatboy Slim's decks at the Bomb. Those best moments, big moments; you look everywhere every day of your life to feel that electricity. The Haçienda film shoot was a one-off, but when something tastes so good you want more. Graeme found it all too much and left before the end.

I was confident we'd delivered some great footage for the film, and we'd also not let our memories down. For weeks afterwards I wasn't sure what to do; real life, other gigs, seemed drab in comparison. In the hours immediately after the event my mobile was clogged up with more mad messages and smiley faces. Then a sentence from Mike Pickering: A STRANGE & WONDERFUL JOURNEY IN TIME.

Mike had turned to me twenty minutes before the end and asked me if I'd play the last few records. Twenty minutes later 'Unfinished Sympathy' was fading out and down on the dancefloor a thousand people were clapping and cheering. My hands trembling, I banged on an encore record: 'Last Rhythm' by Last Rhythm. Bernard Sumner arrived in the box. He didn't want the night to end. He was imploring me, 'One more record, Dave. One more.' He didn't want to let go.

Acknowledgements
and References

Acknowledgements

My thanks go to everyone who has contributed in various ways to the making of this book, particularly Catherine, Jack, Raili, Paul Cons, Mike Pickering, Keith Patterson, Darren Hughes, David Dunne, Ian Brown, Bernard Sumner, Paul Oakenfold, Garry Blackburn, Ginger Tim, Greg Wilson, Bob Dickinson, Jason Boardman, Elliot Eastwick, Rebecca and Neil Ginnis, Nick Darby, Stuart Barber, Sophie Rochester, Paul Lambert, Luke Bainbridge, Athena Caramitsos, Fritz, Phil Howells, the Dublin boys (Martin Thomas, Fergus Murphy, Jimmy Costello), the Chorlton girls (Joleene, the Planes, Lisa and Kelly), 'Golden', 'Cream', 'Shindig', Shelly Preston, 'Do This, Do That', Joe Akka, David Vincent, Sacha Lord, Mike McCormick, Anthony H Wilson, Michael Winterbottom, Andrew Eaton, Marc Rowlands, 'Tonto Bongo', 'Time Flies', Lemn Sissay, Mark Reeder, Rob Deacon, Ben Beecham, Colin Sinclair, Phil Jones, Rebecca Goodwin, Linda Cheater, Kris and Steve, Ursula and Philip, Carol and Cairo, Nathan McGough, Miranda Sawyer and Jane Bradish Ellames. Special thanks to Andy Miller at Fourth Estate.

I am especially grateful to my parents for encouraging me to get on with doing what I love without ever telling me to get a proper job. Thanks also to the clubbers, DJs, promoters and interviewees: Pete Tong, Norman Cook, Graeme Park, Charlotte Horne, Sasha, Paul van Dyk, Norman Jay, Scott Bradford, Leanne Pritchard, Dave McAleer,

Dr Bob Jones, Chad Jackson, Richard Searling, Soul Sam, Brian Rae, Alex Lowes, Luke Cowdrey, Phil Morse, Jimmy Savile, Dave Cotrill, Mr Scruff and Treva Whateva.

Key Texts

Lloyd Bradley, *Bass Culture* (Viking, 2000)

Bill Brewster and Frank Broughton, *Last Night a DJ Saved My Life* (Headline, 1999)

Jane Bussmann, *Once in a Lifetime* (Paradise, 1998)

Nik Cohn, *Awopbopaloobop Awopbamboom* (Paladin, 1970)

Sheryl Garratt, *Adventures in Wonderland* (Headline, 1998)

Hanif Kureishi and Jon Savage (eds), *The Faber Book of Pop* (Faber, 1995)

David Nowell, *Too Darn Soulful: the Story of Northern Soul* (Robson Books, 1999)

Ulf Poschardt, *DJ Culture* (Quartet, 1995)

Steve Redhead (ed), *Rave Off* (Avebury, 1993)

Mike Ritson and Stuart Russell, *The In Crowd* (Bee Cool Publishing, 1999)

Emperor Rosko, *Emperor Rosko's DJ Book* (Everest, 1976)

Andrew Ross and Tricia Rose, *Microphone Fiends* (Routledge, 1994)

Nicholas Saunders, *Ecstasy & the Dance Culture* (Nicholas Saunders, 1995)

Jimmy Savile, *Love is an Uphill Thing* (Coronet Books, 1976)

David Toop, *The Rap Attack* (Pluto Press, 1984)

Craig Werner, *A Change is Gonna Come* (Penguin, 1999)

References, Notes and Soundtrax

To accompany each chapter, some records for your listening pleasure
are suggested.

Intro

Unless otherwise stated, all quotes attributed to Sasha are from various
conversations with the author.

p.x   '. . . commercial profile and credibility'; the acid house era didn't
       bring instant stardom to the DJs, but it did trigger changes which
       accelerated the rise in the status of DJs. The sub-cultural
       mavericks, especially the pioneers in New York, were cool, but if
       the story had ended in the early 1980s, disc jockeys would still be
       sidelined, and worshipped only by a small sect. What accentuated
       the profile and rise of DJs was the commercial success of acid
       house in the 1990s, as DJs first became conspicuous throughout
       a booming clubland, and then reached a wider public.

p.xiii '. . . popular but marginalised'; of Liverpool in the 1960s the big
       story has always been the Beatles, but Steve Higginson was an
       eye-witness to a different side to the city. For him, the appeal of
       dance music in the lives of the urban working class throughout
       Britain – specifically, the appeal of black dance music – has been
       downplayed by historians and music critics: 'You only hear about
       the Beatles when people talk about Liverpool in the 1960s, but I
       was there, and for me the city was always about thousands of
       white kids dancing to Stax, to Motown, to black dance music in
       the clubs every weekend.'

p.xiv   'ancillary income streams . . .' Ron McCulloch quoted in the
       Independent on Sunday, 12.9.99.

p.xvi   'people that make places . . .'; Darren Hughes quoted in
       7 magazine #69.

p.xviii Matthew Collin quoted in the Channel Four programme *The*

Chemical Generation. See also Matthew Collin, *Altered State: the Story of Ecstasy and Acid House* (Serpent's Tail, 1997).

Recommended Soundtrax for the Intro

Jaydee – 'Plastic Dreams' (R&S)

Shades of Rhythm – 'The Sound of Eden' (ZTT)

Leftfield – 'Not Forgotten' (Outer Rhythm)

Jimi Polo – 'Better Days (Sasha mix)' (DMC)

Sasha – 'Higher Ground' (DeConstruction)

Future Sound of London – 'Papua New Guinea' (Jumpin & Pumpin)

Various Artists – *Renaissance* Sasha & Digweed mix CD (Netwerk, LP)

BT – 'Dreaming' (Headspace)

Sasha – 'Xpander' (DeConstruction)

Various Artists – *Global Underground San Francisco* Sasha mix CD (Boxed, LP)

Bedrock – 'Voices' (Bedrock)

Steve Lawler – 'Rise In' (Bedrock)

Schiller – 'Ruhe (Humate mix)' (Data)

Bedrock – 'Beautiful Strange' (Bedrock)

Chapter 1

Unless otherwise stated, all quotes attributed to Paul van Dyk and Mark Reeder are from interviews conducted with the author.

p.1   '. . . plate-spinning job'; Dave Seaman, *7* magazine #75.

p.2   'I killed it . . .'; Gilles Peterson, *7* magazine #23.

p.3   '. . . American DJs who dominated the circuit'; many of them were more widely known in Britain than they were in America, and thus able to earn far more money DJ-ing abroad than in the States. In Britain, music feeds through quickly into the wider culture, but acid house took longer to make a difference in other countries. DJs visiting Britain from America still profess amazement at the ubiquity of dance music in Britain, the use of dance tracks on TV, the way dance music has become the new pop.

p.4   Paul van Dyk website: www.paulvandyk.de

p.17 For more on Michael Alig, see James St James, *Disco Bloodbath* (Sceptre, 1999).

p.25 '. . . the British used to shit on'; Laurent Garnier quoted in *DJ* magazine #57 (January 2000).

p.25 '. . . the brow of the hill'; Simon Raine, *7* magazine #67.

p.33 My least favourite request is probably 'Can I leave my coat here?' I used to get that all the time at the Boardwalk. Some nights the coats piled up around me, burdening me with even more responsibility. People sometimes used to take the wrong coat, by accident, or not. Kelly lost her mobile phone from her coat pocket. Barry had his car stolen (his car was parked outside, and whoever took his coat took his car keys and his car as well).

Recommended Soundtrax for Chapter 1

Kraftwerk – 'Autobahn' (Vertigo)
Golden Girls – 'Kinetic' (R&S)
THK – 'France' (Warp)
Moby – 'Go' (Outer Rhythm)
Humate – 'Love Stimulation (Paul van Dyk Lovemix)' (MFS)
Visions of Shiva – 'How Much Can You Take?' (MFS)
Various Artists – *XMix-1 The MFS Trip* Paul van Dyk mix CD (MFS, LP)
Spooky – 'Little Bullet' (Guerilla)
Way Out West – 'The Gift' (DeConstruction)
BT – 'Flaming June' (Perfecto)
Paul van Dyk – 'For an Angel' (Deviant)
Paul van Dyk – *Out There and Back* (Deviant, LP)
Laurent Garnier – 'Man with a Red Face' (F Communication)

Chapter 2

Unless otherwise stated, all quotes attributed to Sir Jimmy Savile are taken from interviews with the author, but see also his autobiography: Jimmy Savile, *Love Is An Uphill Thing* (Coronet Books, 1976).

p.38   '. . . the real way to play a jukebox'; Jack Kerouac, *On the Road*, p. 270 (Penguin, 1972).

p.40   Malcolm X quoted in Kureishi & Savage (eds), *The Faber Book of Pop*, p. 8 (Faber, 1995).

p.41   For more on the early days of DJ-ing see Brewster and Broughton, *Last Night a DJ Saved My Life* (Headline, 1999).

p.42   '. . . successful recording careers'; Sly Stone, incidentally, also started out as a radio DJ, in Oakland, California.

p.42   After becoming a disc jockey, Sam Phillips became an influential music producer (working for the likes of Chess and recording with Howlin' Wolf and BB King, among others) with a trademark sound, encouraging the guitars to let rip, giving the songs a heavy backbeat, and featuring raw tenor saxophone solos. His successes spurred him on to set up Sun Records in February 1953.

p.43   '. . . the original rappers'; Berry Gordy quoted in Ulf Poschardt, *DJ Culture*, p. 86 (Quartet, 1995).

p.45   'Rock & roll began . . .' Poschardt, p. 63.

p.45   '. . . culture makers'; Tom Wolfe in *The Kandy-Kolored Tangerine-Flake Streamline Baby*, p. 17 (Picador, 1981).

p.47   For more on Jimmy Savile in Manchester see Dave Haslam, *Manchester, England – the Story of the Pop Cult City* (Fourth Estate, 1999).

p.50   '. . . he was unconventional'; Savile's famous haircuts were sometimes the result of happy accidents. On one occasion, some juniors from Muriel Smith's (a ladies hair salon in Leeds) – regulars at Savile's nights at the Mecca – offered to do his hair for free. Their inexperience showed, however, and an attempt to bleach his hair blond failed and left it streaked and multi-coloured.

Jimmy decided to go with the flow, and kept it colourful, returning every fortnight for a different colour, eventually settling for a tartan design which he maintained for several months. This was the cut that made his name; his photograph was printed in the national press.

p.54 '. . . a decline commercially'; Jimmy Savile in the *Top of the Pops* Annual, 1975.

p.56 For George Melly, Rosko was ' a near genius . . . his wild alliterative freewheeling punning ego creates before our very ears an extraordinary pop monster. What's more he plays good records' (quoted in Poschardt, p. 96).

p.56 '. . . he took his radio personality onstage'; in the *Boyfriend* Annual of 1971 there's a feature asking various stars what their idea of Paradise is. The Emperor Rosko has obviously had some great adventures on the wheels of steel: 'Just a pile of spinning discs and a handful of groovy dancing people. Man, that's Paradiseville to me.'

p.57 '. . .a frustrated TV comedian'; Noel Edmonds in the *Top of the Pops* Annual, 1975.

p.57 '. . . dedicated all-round entertainer'; Dave Lee Travis in the *Top of the Pops* Annual, 1975.

p.58 '. . . you're in Dave Lee Travis territory'; Norman Cook in conversation with the author.

Recommended Soundtrax for Chapter 2

Wynonie Harris – 'Good Rockin' Tonight' (King)
Little Walter – 'Juke' (Chess)
Rufus Thomas – 'Bear Cat' (Sun)
Joe Turner – 'Shake, Rattle and Roll' (Atlantic)
Elvis Presley – 'That's All Right' (Sun)
Buddy Holly – 'Peggy Sue' (Coral)
The Shadows – 'Apache' (Columbia)
The Marvelettes – 'Please Mr Postman' (Tamla)
The Beatles – 'I Wanna Hold Your Hand' (Parlophone)

The Beatles – 'Daytripper' (Parlophone)
Freda Payne – 'Band of Gold' (Invictus)
The O'Jays – 'Love Train' (CBS)

Chapter 3

Material in this chapter draws on an interview with Dave McAleer
      conducted by the author, and from three written sources in
      particular: an interview with Guy Stevens by Charles Shaar Murray
      first published in 1979 and included in the collection Charles
      Shaar Murray, *Shots from the Hip* (Penguin Books, 1991);
      various pieces collected in Paulo Hewitt (ed.), *The Sharper Word*
      – A Mod Anthology (Helter Skelter, 1999); and an article in *Mojo*
      magazine #9.

p.62   'manic intensity . . .'; Guy Stevens quoted in Charles Shaar
      Murray, p. 321.

p.63   '. . . no-water flat'; Guy Stevens quoted in Charles Shaar Murray,
      p. 310.

p.64   '. . . a good radio set'; some Gary Brooker quotes are from the
      Whiter Shades of R&B LP liner notes; others are from an
      interview given to Angus MacKinnon published in *Street Life*,
      15.5.76.

p.64   The Beatles covered three Motown songs on their second LP:
      'Money (That's What I Want)' by Barrett Strong, 'You've Really
      Got a Hold on Me' by the Miracles, and 'Please Mr Postman' by
      the Marvelettes. British groups did well selling black American
      music to white America. The Rolling Stones had success in
      America with songs they first heard played by Guy Stevens; in
      October 1964 they had their first US chart hit with 'Time is on My
      Side', first recorded by Irma Thomas.

p.65   'I offered him Monday nights'; Ronan O'Rahilly quoted in *Mojo*
      magazine #9.

p.65   '. . . drug-crazed beboppers'; at Marlborough magistrates court
      the next day the Chief Inspector was called to present his
      evidence to the court. 'The Club is a bebop club run by musicians

who recently moved from other premises,' he began. The presiding magistrate interrupted. 'What is bebop?' he asked solemnly. The Chief Inspector's explanation didn't detail the niceties of jazz history: 'It's a queer form of modern dancing; a Negro jive.'

p.70   '. . . the golden seal of authenticity'; Pete Meaden quoted in Dave Marsh, *Before I Get Old – the Story of the Who*, p. 92 (St Martin's Press, 1983).

p.72   '. . . where it was at'; Pete Townshend quoted in Geoffrey Giuliano, *A Life of Pete Townshend*, p. 50 (Hodder & Stoughton, 1996).

p.72   For more information and background on drugs in mod clubs see Harry Shapiro, *Waiting For the Man: the Story of Drugs & Popular Music* (Quartet, 1988).

p.73   '. . . same way they take ecstasy now'; Johnny Moke quoted in Brewster and Broughton, p. 60.

p.73   '. . . you lose all guilt'; Pete Meaden quoted during an interview with Steve Turner reproduced in *The Sharper Word*, p. 166.

p.74   '. . . the ideal mod'; Richard Barnes reproduced in *The Sharper Word*, p. 83.

p.74   '. . . it was that good'; Ronan O'Rahilly quoted in *Mojo* magazine #9.

p.74   '. . . they could turn on the world'; Pete Meaden quoted in Giuliano, p. 50.

p.80   '. . . the idol of the boys'; Tom Wolfe reproduced in *The Sharper Word*, p. 64.

p.81   '. . . build up'; Guy Stevens quoted in Charles Shaar Murray, p. 314.

p.82   He also worked on one of Stevie Winwood's solo LP projects, although the LP was never released (it included covers of Dylan's 'Visions of Johanna', and, almost inevitably, 'Great Balls of Fire'), but two of the tracks Stevens had done with Winwood showed up on the Traffic LP *John Barleycorn Must Die*: 'Stranger to Himself' and 'Every Mother's Son'.

p.83   Patrick-Campbell Lyons quotes from *The Indiscreet Harlequin* on www.proculharum.com

p.84   '. . . carrying a joint'; Betteridge quoted by Mike Atherton in *Record Collector* (July 1999).

p.85   '. . . getting the most out of people'; Mick Ralphs quoted in *Mojo* magazine #9.

p.86   '. . . mixed-up period'; Guy Stevens quoted in Charles Shaar Murray, p. 315.

p.86   Guy Stevens had in fact worked with the Clash very early in their career, during the time they were putting down demos for their first LP. He had also met Mick Jones. In fact, Mick Jones was a teenage Mott the Hoople fan, and played in a glam rock band called the Delinquents in 1974, but was sacked on the advice of Guy Stevens.

p.87   '. . . don't take any drugs whatsoever'; Pete Meaden quoted during an interview with Steve Turner reproduced in *The Sharper Word*, p. 167.

p.89   '. . . a more pluralist audience'; Truman Capote was moved to give this eulogy: 'Disco is the best floor show in town. It's very democratic, boys with boys, girls with girls, girls with boys, blacks and whites, capitalists and Marxists, Chinese and everything else, all in one big mix.' Truman Capote quoted in Alan Jones and Jussi Kantonen, *Saturday Night Forever*, p. 140 (Mainstream, 1999).

p.91   '. . . it was like a religion to him'; Ronan O'Rahilly quoted in *Mojo* magazine #9.

Recommended Soundtrax for Chapter 3

Traffic – 'Mr Fantasy' (Island)
Chuck Berry – 'Maybellene' (Chess)
Ray Charles – 'What'd I Say' (Atlantic)
Barrett Strong – 'Money' (Gordy)
Bob & Earl – 'Harlem Shuffle' (Sue)
Martha & the Vandellas – 'Dancing in the Street' (Gordy)
Prince Buster – 'Al Capone' (Blue Beat)
Bob Dylan – *Blonde on Blonde* (Columbia, LP)

The Clash – *London Calling* (CBS, LP)
Cream – 'I Feel Free' (Reaction)
Procul Harum – 'A Whiter Shade of Pale' (Deram)
The Delfonics – 'La La Means I Love You' (Philly Groove)
Stevie Wonder – 'Superstition' (Tamla Motown)
Sly & the Family Stone – 'Dance to the Music' (Direction)

Chapter 4

Unless otherwise indicated all quotes from Norman Cook are from an
    interview with the author.
p.103 '. . . thank God it changed'; Chad Jackson quote from an interview
    with the author.
p.104 '. . . as close as any record'; David Toop, *The Rap Attack*, p. 107
    (Pluto Press, 1984).
p.105 '. . . everything is a cycle'; Bob Sinclar quoted in *Muzik* magazine
    (August 2000).
p.106 '. . . new sonic territories'; a phrase used by Kodwo Eshun in
    More Brilliant Than the Sun: Adventures in Sonic Fiction (Quartet,
    1998).
p.107 For more on Larry Levan and the New York scene, see Brewster
    and Broughton.

Recommended Soundtrax for Chapter 4

The JBs – 'Gimme Some More' (Polydor)
Chic – 'Good Times' (Atlantic)
The Salsoul Orchestra – *Anthology* (Capitol, LP)
Musique – 'In the Bush' (CBS)
T-Connection – 'Saturday Night' (CBS)
Eric B & Rakim – 'Paid in Full (the Cold Cut mix)' (4th & Broadway)
Chemical Brothers – *Dig Your Own Hole* (Junior Boy's Own, LP)
Underworld – 'Rez' (Junior Boy's Own)
Hardfloor – 'Hardfloor Acperience' (Harthouse)
Pizzaman – 'Sex on the Streets' (Loaded)

Fatboy Slim – 'Right Here Right Now' (Skint)

Fatboy Slim – 'Sunset (Bird of Prey)' (Skint)

Wildchild – 'Renegade Master (Fatboy Slim mix)' (Hi-Life)

Chapter 5

Thanks to Dave Cotrill for his time and the interview.

p.134 '. . . the utter loathing'; Morrissey quoted in David Bret, *Morrissey: Landscapes of the Mind*, p. 124 (Robson Books, 1994).

p.136 '. . . une France swing'; *Jazz Music* (December 1943).

p.137 Bruce Mitchell on Bud Powell, in conversation with the author.

p.139 '. . . a plot to undermine the morals'; quoted in Linda Martin and Kerry Segrave, *Anti-Rock: the Opposition to Rock & Roll*, p. 16 (DaCapo Press, 1993).

p.139 '. . . smash the records'; quoted in Martin and Segrave, p. 16.

p.139 '. . . acoustical pollution'; quoted in Martin and Segrave, p. 51.

p.139 '. . . as bad for kids as dope'; quoted in Martin and Segrave, p. 16.

p.140 'Elvis Presley is morally insane'; quoted in Cohn, p. 25.

p.140 '. . . exciting tempos'; quoted in Martin and Segrave, p. 29.

p.140 '. . . a menace to life'; quoted in Martin and Segrave, p. 29.

p.140 Frankie Vaughan quoted in the *Manchester Evening News*, 1.4.58.

p.141 '. . . monstrous threat'; quoted in Martin and Segrave, p. 53.

p.141 '. . . large quantities of soul records'; quoted in Sarah Thornton, *Club Cultures*, p. 60 (Polity Press, 1995).

p.142 '. . . a synthetic rock star'; quoted in Thornton, p. 62.

p.143 '. . . DJs and DJ f**kin' culture'; *Melody Maker* (21 August 2000).

p.144 '. . . black-worshipping soul boys'; quoted in Paul Gilroy, *There Ain't No Black in the Union Jack* (Hutchinson, 1987).

p.146 '. . . deranged throb'; William Leith quoted in Redhead, p. 19.

p.147 '. . . playing real instruments'; Morrissey quoted in Bret, p. 24.

p.148 'political'; Morrissey quoted in Bret, p. 62.

p.149 '. . . civilised raving'; Mark Rodol, *The Chemical Generation* (Channel Four, May 2000).

p.150 '. . . a new strategy of resistance'; Poschardt, p. 22.

p.150 '. . . twenty-first century begins'; Eshun, p. 2.

p.150 '. . . from the mainstream'; Poschardt, p. 19.

p.150 '. . . a marketing scam'; Armand van Helden, *DJ* magazine (June 2000).

Recommended Soundtrax for Chapter 5

Danny & the Juniors – 'At the Hop' (ABC/Paramount)

Link Wray – 'Rumble' (Cadence)

The Shangri-Las – 'Leader of the Pack' (Red Bird)

The Trammps – 'Sixty Minute Man' (Buddah)

Sam Cooke – 'A Change is Gonna Come' (RCA)

James Brown – 'Say It Loud, I'm Black & I'm Proud' (King)

Freda Payne – 'Bring the Boys Home' (Invictus)

Staple Singers – 'Respect Yourself' (Stax)

MFSB – 'Love is the Message' (Philadelphia International)

Curtis Mayfield – 'Move on Up' (Buddah)

Various Artists – *Stand Up & Be Counted* (Harmless, CD)

The Children – 'Freedom' (DJ International)

The Isley Brothers – 'Fight the Power' (T-Neck)

Public Enemy – 'Fight the Power' (Def Jam)

Chapter 6

All quotes attributed to Richard Searling, Soul Sam and Brian Rae are from interviews with the author. Two outstanding books provided some background material for this chapter: David Nowell, *Too Darn Soulful – the Story of Northern Soul* (Robson Books, 1999), and Mike Ritson and Stuart Russell, *The In Crowd* (Bee Cool Publishing, 1999). See also Ian Levine's video documentary *The Strange World of Northern Soul*. Among the websites worth checking are www.nightowlclub.com and www.soul-a-go-go.demon.co.uk

p.153 '. . . first rave culture'; Brewster and Broughton, p.77.

p.166 'Brian Rae presents . . .'; these gigs didn't always run smoothly. On one occasion the Temptations were advertised, but they'd played New Century Hall in Manchester the night before and the *News of the World* had rumbled them as a fake outfit; the real Temptations were in Chicago. Brian decided the gig in Warrington should go ahead anyway: 'We'd sold a thousand tickets in a hall that held five hundred.'

p.168 '. . . wild animals'; Brian Phillips quoted in Nowell, p. 42.

p.169 '. . . come home from the pub'; Brian Rae quoted in Nowell, p. 42.

p.170 '. . . all the negative stuff'; Colin Curtis quoted in Nowell, p. 85.

p.177 '. . . even more contemporary space'; Colin Curtis would be playing jazz funk and Ian Levine disco. Colin Curtis looks back on their partnership: 'We had a good rapport. I liked him as a character. I liked the fact that sometimes he could be a bull in a china shop. I could believe in what he was believing', quoted in Nowell, p. 112.

p.180 '. . .camera crews from Granada TV'; coverage in the media can be detrimental. In 1993 the Basement Jaxx started a club night in Brixton, but decided to finish it at the beginning of 1999. Felix Burton: 'When it was just a word-of-mouth thing, it was great, and completely unpretentious, but when we had all these fashion victims trying to get on the guest list, and then stood there waiting to be impressed, it all got horribly spoiled', quoted in *Q* magazine (April 2000).

p.180 '. . . Northern Soul went into decline'; Brian Rae still got out and about. He recalls going to Stringfellow's new club, Cinderella Rockefellers in Leeds: 'A brilliant place that; full of all your archetypal club people; like air hostesses. He always got the right clientele in.'

Recommended Soundtrax for Chapter 6

Darrell Banks – 'Open the Door to Your Heart' (Revilot)
Wilson Pickett – 'In the Midnight Hour' (Atlantic)
Junior Walker & the All Stars – 'Shotgun' (Motown)
Len Barry – '1-2-3' (Brunswick)

Dobie Gray – 'Out on the Floor' (Charger)
Sandi Sheldon – 'You're Gonna Make Me Love You' (OKeh)
Jimmy Radcliffe – 'Long After Tonight is Over' (Stateside)
The Supremes – 'Stoned Love' (Tamla Motown)
R Dean Taylor – 'There's a Ghost in my House' (Motown)
The Mohawks – 'Champ' (Pama)
Rose Batiste – 'Hit and Run' (Revilot)
Carstairs – 'It Really Hurts Me Girl' (Red Coach)
Vicki Sue Robinson – 'Turn the Beat Around' (RCA)

Chapter 7

Unless otherwise indicated, all quotes from Norman Jay, Dr Bob Jones
and Alex Lowes are from interviews with the author. The LP
Various Artists, *Good Times with Joey & Norman Jay* (Nuphonic)
is recommended.

p.190 '. . . totally on the button'; Norman Jay quoted in sleevenotes for
Good Times with Joey & Norman Jay.
p.190 '. . . like a sexy job'; Pete Tong quoted in *XFade* magazine (June
1999).
p.194 'I used to buy reggae . . .'; Norman Jay quoted in sleevenotes for
Good Times with Joey & Norman Jay.
p.198 '. . . at the right place'; Judge Jules quoted in *DJ* magazine #114
(May 1994).
p.204 'House music broke the scene up . . .'; Trevor Nelson quoted in
Touch magazine #113 (February 2001).

Recommended Soundtrax for Chapter 7

Lyn Collins – 'Think (About It)' (Polydor)
Martine Girault – 'Revival' (Opaz)
The SOS Band – 'Just Be Good To Me' (CBS)
The Whispers – 'And the Beat Goes On' (MCA)
Fatback Band – 'I Found Lovin'' (Important)
Soul II Soul – 'Fairplay' (10)

Alyson Williams – 'Sleep Talk' (Def Jam)
Public Enemy – 'Rebel Without a Pause' (Def Jam)
Blaze – 'So Special' (Motown)
DJ Clue – 'Back-2-Life' (Roc-A-Fella)
Blackout – 'Mr DJ' (Independiente)
Jill Scott – 'A Long Walk' (Epic)
Sticky feat. MC Dynamite – 'Boo' (Social Circles)
Various Artists – *Good Times with Joey & Norman Jay* (Nuphonic)
Various Artists – *Real Garage* Masterstepz mix CD (Ministry of Sound)

Chapter 8

Thanks to Leanne Pritchard (DJ As-If), Stuart Barber and Chad Jackson
for the interviews, and to DMC for access to the events.

p.219 '. . . definition of a turntablist'; Babu interview with Christo Macias
from www.turntablism.com

p.220 '. . . the roots of turntablism'; for more see David Toop, *The Rap
Attack* (Pluto Press, 1984).

p.220 '. . . I felt myself moving the record'; Grand Wizard Theodore
quoted in Alex Ogg & David Upshal, *The Hip Hop Years*, p. 28
(Channel 4 Books,1999).

p.235 '. . . things aren't as good now'; Nikki is speaking before Code had
opened.

p.247 '. . . this isn't hip hop'; Mr Scruff quotes are from an interview
with the author.

p.247 '. . . it's technical and it's emotional'; Treva Whateva quote from
an interview with the author.

p.248 'You win a battle . . .'; Rob Swift quote from
www.turntablism.com

Recommended Soundtrax for Chapter 8

Kurtis Blow – 'The Breaks' (Mercury)
Afrika Bambaataa & the Soul Sonic Force – 'Looking for the Perfect Beat'
(Tommy Boy)

Grandmaster Flash – 'Adventures of Grandmaster Flash on the Wheels of
    Steel' (Sugarhill)
West Street Mob – 'Break Dancin' – Electric Boogie' (Sugarhill)
Various Artists – *Smokin Beats* (Tuff City, LP)
Boogie Down Productions – 'You Must Learn' (Zomba)
EPMD – *Strictly Business* (Fresh, LP)
DJ Shadow – *Endtroducing* (Mo Wax, LP)
DJ Vadim – *USSR Repertoire* (Ninja Tune, LP)
DJ Rectangle – *Ultimate Battle Weapon* (Ground Control, LP)
Various Artists – *Hee-Haw Brayks* (Dirtstyle Records, LP)
Various Artists – *DJ Pogo presents Block Party Breaks* (Strut, LP)

Chapter 9

Unless otherwise indicated, all quotes from Scott Bradford, Luke
    Cowdrey, Phil Morse and Lottie are from interviews with the
    author.
p.258 'Shindig' website: shindig.org.uk
p.284 '. . . you feel part of something'; Ian Levine quoted in Nowell,
    p. 292.

Recommended Soundtrax for Chapter 9

Ralph Falcon – 'The Sound' (Miami Soul)
Deep Dish – 'Stay Gold' (DeConstruction)
Sessomato – 'Moody (King Unique Dark Dub)' (Junior)
Dan Robins – 'Chanting in the Dark (Pete Heller mix)' (Junior)
Kings of Tomorrow – 'Finally' (Distance)
Richard F – 'The Way' (Subliminal)
Various Artists – *Singles Collection 3* (NRK, LP)
Various Artists – *Must Be The Music* DJ Paulette mix CD (Nervous Record)
Various Artists – *7 Live #2* Lottie mix CD (DMC)
Ron Carroll presents The RC Groove Project – 'The Sermon' (Riviera)
M&S – 'Salsoul Nugget (Lottie mix)' (FFRR)
Little Green Men – 'Need' (Forensic)

Outro

Unless otherwise indicated, all quotes from Pete Tong, Norman Cook, Luke Cowdrey, Phil Morse, Anthony H. Wilson and Graeme Park are from interviews with the author.

p.298 The top end of the market has boomed – more expensive DJs, bigger advertising budgets, conspicuous corporate sponsorship, and the endless pursuit of ancillary income strands – but for every action there is a reaction, and the DIY set up is still thriving, DJs and their mates doing it for the love, the buzz. The big clubs go commercial and keep it safe to fill their halls and recoup their investments in trendy decor and foreign furniture and full page ads, so other club lovers look for something more intimate, less compromised.

p.301 '. . . are we sorted?'; Dr Bob Jones in an interview with the author.

p.303 '. . . the World's Greatest Record'; Tim Sheridan in *Muzik* magazine (November 1999).

p.305 '. . . the mobile DJ'; Bill Brewster in *Jockey Slut* (March 2000).

Recommended Soundtrax for the Outro

St Germain – 'Rose Rouge' (Blue Note)
Portishead – *Dummy* (Go Beat, LP)
Romanthony – 'Hold On' (Roule)
MJ Cole – 'Sincere' (Talkin Loud)
Ian Pooley – '900 Degrees' (V2)
Photek feat. Robert Owens – 'Mine to Give' (Science)
Sueno Latino – 'Sueno Latino (Bushwacka mix)' (Expanded)
Moloko – 'The Time is Now' (Echo)
Rabbit in the Moon – 'Phases of an Out of Body Experience' (Hardkiss)
Furry Phreaks – 'Gonna Find A Way' (Love From San Francisco)
The Source feat. Candi Staton – 'You Got the Love' (Truelove)

Coda

p.313 Justin Robertson: 'The Haçienda is completely the reason for what I'm doing now. I can't stress how important that place was. You only have to look at the people who went through the door and went on to make contemporary music. Much more important than any other club in the country.' Quoted by Ben Arnold on www.burnitblue.com (March 2001).

p.314 '. . . continue to embrace change'; when there was talk of the Haçienda being turned into a museum, there was a general feeling that the last thing Manchester needed was to go the way of Liverpool, the way that despite everything that's happened there since the 1960s, Liverpool is still suffering a hangover from the Beatles, with nonstop nostalgia, streets full of souvenir shops and, indeed, a rebuilt version of the Cavern.

p.321 '. . . coke off a credit card'; Andrew Eaton, the film's producer, had been in Manchester for a couple of months filming: 'I can't believe the availability of drugs in this city.'

p.322 'Last Rhythm'; most of the Haçienda classics and the other records released in the last fifteen years can be tracked down at www.htfr.com; the best from the 1970s and 1980s at www.busstop-records.co.uk; for the Northern sounds follow the links from sites recommended on p.239

Recommended Soundtrax for the Coda

Peech Boys – 'Don't Make Me Wait' (West End)
Lisa Lisa & Cult Jam – 'Let the Beat Hit 'Em (Part Two)' (Columbia)
Todd Terry – 'Just Make That Move' (West End)
Laurent X – 'Machines' (Trax)
Mr Fingers – 'Can You Feel It?' (Trax)
Ce Ce Rogers – 'All Join Hands' (Atlantic)
Royal House – 'Can You Party' (Champion)
Inner City – 'Good Life' (10)
Orange Lemon – 'Dreams of Santa Anna' (Bad Boy)
A Guy Called Gerald – 'Voodoo Ray' (Rham)

K-Klass – 'Rhythm is a Mystery' (DeConstruction)
Sterling Void – 'It's All Right' (DJ International)
The Turntable Orchestra – 'You're Gonna Miss Me When I'm Gone'
(Republic)
Massive Attack – 'Unfinished Sympathy' (Circa)
Last Rhythm – 'Last Rhythm' (American)

Credits

CPSIA information can be obtained
at www.ICGtesting.com
Printed in the USA
LVHW040716310821
696510LV00007B/41